WINNING RIGHT

CAMPAIGN POLITICS AND CONSERVATIVE POLICIES

EDWARD GILLESPIE

THRESHOLD
EDITIONS

New York   London   Toronto   Sydney

THRESHOLD EDITIONS
Rockefeller Center
1230 Avenue of the Americas
New York, NY 10020

Copyright © 2006 by Edward Gillespie

All rights reserved,
including the right of reproduction
in whole or in part in any form.

Threshold Editions and colophon are trademarks
of Simon & Schuster, Inc.

Designed by William Ruoto

Library of Congress Cataloging-in-Publication Data

Gillespie, Edward.
Winning right : campaign politics and conservative policies / Edward Gillespie.
p.   cm.
Includes index.
ISBN: 978-1-4165-2563-9

1. Political campaigns—United States.   2. Conservatism—United States.
3. United States—Politics and government.   I. Title.

JK2281.G55 2006
324.70973—dc22
2006045500

Visit us on the World Wide Web:
http://www.SimonSays.com

To Cathy Gillespie,
the smartest political operative I know,
and the love of my life

Contents

PREFACE

The lessons in this book are derived from nearly twenty-five years in government and campaigns, from my time as a Senate parking lot attendant and a phoner in the basement of the Republican National Committee (RNC) through my tenure as RNC chairman.

In keeping with one of the maxims in the book—"In politics, nothing is ever as good or as bad as it seems"—I began writing it shortly after the 2004 election when it seemed President Bush and Republicans in Congress were on the verge of a long run of political dominance. As it was going to press, the president's approval rating was at 34 percent. ("That's because 34 percent of the voters actually know what's going on," according to my daughter Carrie.)

But the lessons here apply whether you're up or down. This book is organized by lessons learned for a couple of reasons: First, I hope it will help encourage people to go into politics and will help them if they do, and second, a chronological ordering would end up being a memoir, which I'm not vain enough to write.

While mixing lessons learned with campaign and other stories, I have tried throughout to distill some principles that can be applied to future campaigns and effective governing. The chronology of events given below, however, will help put the anecdotes in these pages in proper perspective.

But before providing a timeline of events, it's also worth putting my personal history into perspective, because in politics it's impossible to separate your personal perspective from your professional one.

I grew up in a traditional Irish Catholic household, one of six children. My father, John Patrick "Jack" Gillespie, is an Irish immigrant who became a small businessman, ultimately achieving every

Irishman's dream of owning his own bar. He is a bona fide war hero, having won two Purple Hearts, a Bronze Star, and a Silver Star in World War II's Battle of the Hurtgen Forest. I named my only son after him.

My mother, "Conny," was a political trailblazer of sorts, becoming the first woman ever to be elected to our township's school board. They both had an easy way with people, which I like to think I inherited.

Neither of my parents went to college, and I've never met anyone smarter than either one of them. My mother could have taught a college English course. She corrected our grammar until the day she lost her fight with cancer.

My family is clannish, perhaps to a fault. When my daughter Mollie was two years old, Cathy and I had a little girl over for a "play date," but Mollie wouldn't play with her.

"Why don't you want to play with Caitlin?" I asked Mollie.

"I only play with brothers that are my brother and sisters that are my sister!" was her defiant answer.

"It's in her genes," I said to her exasperated mother.

My view of America is shaped by my time growing up in a racially diverse community. Pemberton Township High School was 55 percent white, 45 percent minority when I was graduated in 1979. It was not only racially mixed, but racially harmonious.

My brothers and sisters and I all worked in our family's grocery store, the J.C. Market (J for Jack, C for Conny), a true "mom and pop" operation. We'd stock the shelves, sweep the floors, cut the lunchmeat, and work the register. Everything I know about politics I learned at the J.C. Market: Respect the customers, honor the competition, don't put your thumb on the scale, and hard work never killed anyone.

The Catholic University of America, from which I was graduated in 1983, was an institution where many of the graduates were, like me, the first generation of their family to attend college. It gave and continues to give many families their first shot at real upward mobility in a country where education is the doorway to opportunity.

Even with student loans and support from my parents (and my grandmother), I had to work three jobs while at CUA. I worked in the dining hall refilling the milk and juice and soda dispensers, I was a short order cook at the American Café on Capitol Hill, and I was a Senate parking lot attendant, "stacking" the cars of Senate staffers in the morning or "breaking the lot" at night.

While parking cars, one of my fellow attendants told me of an internship that was available on the House side. That internship led to my first job, which led to every other job. I've listed them here (along with significant moments) to help readers have a sense of where different anecdotes occur.

January–May 1983: Intern for U.S. Representative Andy Ireland (D-FL).

August 1983: Hired by Representative Ireland to work in his district office in Bradenton, Florida.

March 1984: Representative Ireland announces that he will seek re-election as a Republican, switching parties. I switch with him.

November 1984: Ireland is re-elected and promotes me to legislative assistant in his Washington, D.C., office. To help pay for moving and for the security deposit on a room in a Capitol Hill townhouse, I work part-time in the evening as a phoner, dialing for dollars at the Republican National Committee.

February 1985: Hired as press secretary by newly elected U.S. Representative Dick Armey (R-TX).

February 1986: Move to Lewisville, Texas, to manage Armey's first re-election campaign, fending off two Republican primary challengers.

July 1987: Armey passes the Base Closure and Realignment

Act as only a second-term member of the House, serving in the minority.

March 1991: Armey is named ranking Republican on the Joint Economic Committee and names me minority staff director.

January 1993: Bill Clinton is inaugurated president. Not coincidentally, Dick Armey is elected chairman of the House Republican Conference, ousting the more moderate Representative Jerry Lewis (R-CA). He names me policy and communications director for the House Republican Conference.

Fall 1993: Armey plays a key role in defeating First Lady Hillary Clinton's health care proposal with an October 13 op-ed in the *Wall Street Journal* charting its complicated structure.

September 27, 1994: House Republicans unveil their Contract with America, in which I named the ten pieces of legislation.

November 8, 1994: Republicans gain fifty-two seats to regain control of the House for the first time in forty years.

Fall 1995: Republicans in Congress and President Clinton clash over budget priorities, resulting in major parts of the U.S. government shutting down.

January 1996: Republican National Committee Chairman Haley Barbour hires me as director of communications and congressional affairs at the RNC to help hold the House and defeat Clinton in November.

February 1997: Upon leaving the RNC, I become president and chief operating officer of Policy Impact Communications, a public relations firm formed with Haley Barbour. It is designed to bolster lobbying efforts for clients of his government relations firm Barbour Griffith and Rogers.

July 1997: The Senate Government Affairs Committee holds public hearings on financing of the 1996 elections, with

Barbour the focus of Democrats who want to offset coverage of the Clinton White House's campaign fundraising practices. I help my friend and mentor prepare for the hearings and serve as his spokesman throughout the investigation. That same month, the House Republican Conference is rocked by a failed effort to remove Newt Gingrich from the Speaker's chair.

January 1999: U.S. Representative John Kasich (R-OH) forms a Presidential Exploratory Committee and asks me to help him with communications and messaging strategy. I travel the country with him, making repeated trips to Iowa and New Hampshire.

July 14, 1999: Kasich announces he is leaving Congress and abandoning his presidential ambitions. He appears at a press conference in Washington, D.C., with then-governor George W. Bush and endorses him for the GOP nomination.

January 2000: I leave Policy Impact Communications to form Quinn Gillespie and Associates, a bipartisan lobbying and public relations firm, with Jack Quinn, President Clinton's former White House counsel.

April 2000: Bush advisor Karl Rove asks me to participate in the "Gang of Six," a group of party insiders who serve as a link between the Austin campaign team and the Republican establishment in Washington.

June 2000: At the request of Karen Hughes, I go to Philadelphia to serve as program chairman for the Republican Convention, becoming right-hand man to Convention Chairman Andy Card.

September 2000: I move to Austin to help the Bush-Cheney 2000 communications team while Hughes travels the country with then-governor Bush.

November 10, 2000: I go to Miami to handle media surrounding the filing of *Bush* v. *Gore*.

November 13, 2000: I return to Miami to handle media and serve as a spokesman for the recount effort for two weeks before returning home to my family and Quinn Gillespie.

February–March 2001: My partner Jack Quinn appears before House and Senate Government Affairs Committees to explain his role as lawyer for Marc Rich, whose pardon by President Clinton as he left office created an uproar.

December 2001: Elizabeth Dole asks me to serve as general strategist for her 2002 North Carolina Senate campaign.

Spring–Fall 2002: In the wake of the collapse of Enron Corporation, which had been a Quinn Gillespie client, the Senate Government Affairs Committee under then-chairman Joe Lieberman (D-CT) scrutinizes all my firm's documents relating to energy policy.

June 2003: President Bush asks me to chair the Republican National Committee through the end of the 2004 election.

July 2003: Members of the Republican National Committee elect me chairman.

November 2004: President Bush is re-elected and Republicans gain seats in both the House and the Senate, marking the first time in seventy-eight years a Republican retained the White House while gaining seats in both chambers of Congress.

January 2005: President Bush is inaugurated for his second term, and Bush-Cheney '04 campaign manager Ken Mehlman succeeds me as RNC chairman. In February, I return to Quinn Gillespie (QGA).

June–November 2005: I take a leave from QGA to work in the West Wing overseeing the confirmation efforts of Chief Justice John G. Roberts and White House Counsel Harriet Miers.

November–January 2005: "Sherpa" for Justice Samuel Alito, advising him throughout his confirmation process.

INTRODUCTION

I was despondent over the loss.

"That first debate really killed us," I said to Jim Dyke, the communications director at the Republican National Committee (RNC), and Tim Griffin, his deputy and the RNC's research director.

"We had him on the ropes, and we let him back in."

It was a little before three in the afternoon on November 2, 2004, and we had been absorbing the 2:00 PM Election Day exit polls, which had John Kerry whipping President Bush in Pennsylvania and ahead in Florida and Ohio, all of which spelled doom. For nearly two years the three of us had worked nonstop to re-elect the president. Somehow, we had come up short.

"We blew Dean up too early," Griffin said. As research director, he'd compiled a thick binder on Howard Dean the year before. When we, like so many others, assumed Dean would be the Democratic nominee, Tim had fed some of it to the media. He'd been second-guessing himself ever since Dean's campaign collapsed in Iowa, since we all thought Dean would have been much easier to defeat than Kerry.

"Naw, he blew himself up," I said.

"Yeah. *We* didn't give that stupid scream speech," Dyke said, laughing.

We were in a small dining room on the third floor of the Eisenhower Building, the big white building next to the Republican National Committee headquarters on Capitol Hill. We were there because cigars were allowed, and I needed the release of a stogie and the consolation of two guys who didn't just work for me but had become my friends and confidants.

"You guys have nothing to be ashamed of," I said. "You were both fantastic. Just great. Stalwarts."

They said nice things about me. We cussed a lot. We invoked a few highlights from the past year, and then started shifting from our personal disappointment to our professional responsibilities.

As Jim and I kicked around ideas for talking points, Griffin took a call on his cell phone. When he hung up, he said, "You might want to hold off on those talking points."

He'd been on with one of the networks, and—once again—the exit polls were screwed up. We were back in the game!

I went back to my office on the top floor of the RNC. It was my third stint in the building. I had been there in 1996 under then-chairman Haley Barbour during the Clinton-Dole presidential year and the first election to defend the House majority after the '94 landslide.

In 1985, I had worked nights in the basement as a phoner. I always got a laugh in my speeches by saying, "I started my career at the RNC as a phoner. I'd sit in the basement, in a little cubicle, calling people at home and bothering them for money for the Republican Party. Now, twenty years later, I'm on the top floor, sitting in a big office—calling people at home and bothering them for money for the Republican Party!"

As soon as I got back to my office I got a call from Ken Mehlman, the Bush-Cheney campaign manager and one of my best friends. Over the past year and a half, he and I had been constantly on the phone to each other. I would tell people, "Cathy Gillespie is the first person I talk to in the morning and the last person I talk to at night, and Ken Mehlman is the second person I talk to in the morning and the next-to-last person I talk to at night."

"The numbers are screwed up," he said. "The sample's 60 percent women. They have us winning Catholics by ten and losing Wisconsin! That can't be. There's no way we're down nineteen in Pennsylvania. We can't be winning Hamilton County and losing Ohio."

Ken clicks off numbers in rapid-fire succession like that all the time. He has so much information in his head he can hardly get it out fast enough. Throughout the course of the campaign it would get me jumpy, but on this day I began to relax as his data washed over me.

By the 6:00 PM exits, things had righted themselves. It was becoming clear that Bush could win as I headed to the Ronald Reagan Building on Pennsylvania Avenue where the official Election Night Watch Party was being held. As RNC chairman, I was the host and master of ceremonies.

I did a round of stand-ups for the evening news shows, showing confidence to make sure our voters on the West Coast didn't pick up any sign of discouragement.

On CNN, I crossed paths with my Democratic counterpart and regular sparring partner Terry McAuliffe. McAuliffe and I had become like the sheep dog and the coyote in the cartoons. We'd beat the hell out of each other when we were on the clock, but got along fine after we punched out.

Each of us predicted with confidence that our respective candidates had won the election. Immediately after we were off the air, Larry King turned to Wolf Blitzer and said, "One of these guys is wrong."

It would end up taking all night to find out which one it was.

By 3:00 AM, Fox and NBC had called Ohio for Bush, but not Nevada, and ABC, CBS, and CNN had called Nevada but not Ohio. With the history of 2000 and the recount fresh in their minds, none of the networks wanted to be the first to call them both and confer victory upon the president.

I was back and forth with presidential counselor Karl Rove all night as he sat with President Bush two blocks away in the White House. We talked about the possibility of the president coming over to address the crowd, much of which was still assembled, but decided it would be best to wait. Our numbers were piling up in Ohio, and while it wasn't easy to be patient, it was pretty apparent we weren't looking at another recount scenario.

I was dozing on a sofa in the hallway behind the stage area when Karl called around 4:30 AM.

"Andy's coming over," he said, referring to White House Chief of Staff Andy Card. "He'll tell 'em [the crowd] that we expect to claim victory later today so everybody can go home and come back fresh."

My wife, Cathy, and I got to the Willard Hotel a little after 6:00 AM and asked for a 10:00 AM wake-up call. Shortly after getting it, Ken called (see what I mean?) to say that the Kerry campaign had been in touch and that Kerry and Edwards would hold an event around lunchtime to concede.

Utter relief. Thank God, no recount. I didn't think the country could stand another recount, and having been in the middle of the last one, I knew I couldn't.

Cathy and I had something to eat, watched Kerry and Edwards graciously concede on our hotel room television, then headed back to the Reagan Building for the president's victory speech.

Many political types remember that in his remarks that day, Bush dubbed Karl Rove "the architect," but if your name is Gillespie you remember that the president said, "I want to thank Ed Gillespie for leading our party so well."

For someone who'd spent twenty years in the vineyards of politics, being thanked by the president of the United States for helping him get re-elected is like winning the Oscar, the Super Bowl, and the Pulitzer all rolled into one.

No field is a greater meritocracy than politics. Karl Rove is still a few credits shy of his Bachelor of Arts, after leaving college early to work on a campaign (though he has taught college courses). James Carville, who helped lead the last Democrat elected president to victory, rose through the ranks from the Louisiana bayou. I was raised in the modest surroundings of New Jersey's Pine Barrens,

the son of an Irish immigrant whose children were the first generation of Gillespies ever to attend college, yet I was asked by President
George W. Bush to chair the Republican National Committee in
the midst of his re-election effort.

Our stories are not unique, but they defy much of the conventional wisdom about the world of politics: that political operatives
are slick, shady (or worse, crooked), mercenary, and unprincipled.
That you get ahead by shafting friends and colleagues. That people
get jobs only through patronage, and that competence is less important than connections.

The truth is that anyone can rise to the top of the political
profession if he or she is reasonably intelligent, willing to work hard
for long hours, puts himself on the line for people and principles he
believes in, and acts in an ethical manner. This is true regardless of
"connections," prestigious degrees, or financial means. In contrast,
people who play fast and loose with the facts, stab coworkers in the
back, or work both sides of the fence wash out, usually pretty
quickly.

In politics, all you have is your name. There are no parents to
market, no wells to drill, no cars to sell, no homes to insure. You are
worth what you are willing to provide in physical labor, what you
are able to offer in creative thought, and what the market estimates
is the value of your word as your bond.

Nearly twenty years ago, in his book *Hardball,* Chris Matthews offered a primer on this subject that I found invaluable, but
nine election cycles is like infinity in politics, and there is now a
need for something that reflects the realities of today's political environment.

I am fortunate to have been involved in nearly every major
political development of the past twenty years, from the Reagan realignment in the 1980s to the first Republican takeover of the U.S.
House in forty years, helping to draft 1994's Contract with America; from Bob Dole's losing presidential campaign in 1996 to Elizabeth Dole's winning Senate campaign in 2002, in which she became

the first woman senator from North Carolina in a year that Republicans recaptured the Senate in defiance of historical norms; and from George W. Bush's election and the historic recount of 2000 to heading the GOP when he was re-elected in 2004, with Republicans retaining control of the White House, House, and Senate for the first time in nearly eighty years.

The July 2001 issue of *The New Republic* quoted a White House aide saying, "Go look from 1994 to today, and if you step back and look at the big-picture direction of the country, the major political events, Eddie hasn't been on the fringes, he's been in the center."

Along the way I have witnessed some of our nation's biggest controversies and scandals, including Speaker Newt Gingrich's ethics woes and the controversial coup attempt on his speakership, the campaign finance scandals of the '90s, President Clinton's controversial pardon of Marc Rich, and the implosion of Enron Corporation.

I have learned from some of the greatest political leaders of our time what it takes to play for and win the highest stakes imaginable, and that these lessons are valuable not only in politics but in other areas as well.

The most effective people in politics understand that campaigns and elections are a means to an end, not ends in and of themselves. They are the way we choose people to govern, and how they govern is more important than how they get there.

President Bush's historic re-election will prove seminal in our nation's history, in terms of both domestic policy and national security. History will judge his firm sense of direction in what it takes to win the War on Terror as insightful and resolute. His economic policies are fostering growth and creating jobs. At the same time, his innate sense of decency and compassion will prove important as our country comes to terms with significant moral and ethical issues like stem cell research, same-sex marriage, and the general coarsening of our culture.

Winning Right is not a kiss-and-tell book. If anything, it's a "kiss-and-kiss" book. My first Cardinal Rule of Politics is loyalty, and I'm not going to violate it in my book. More important, my experiences in politics have been, with few exceptions, positive and inspirational. I'm not going to manufacture drama or "dirt" in hopes of boosting sales.

Lastly, American politics and our political process have been hurt by cynicism over the past thirty years, when in fact we live in the greatest democracy the world has ever known. In the hope of encouraging greater participation in our political process, I would rather try to drain some of the cynicism from the well than pump more poison into it.

PART I

LESSONS LEARNED

CHAPTER ONE

A Good Plan Beats a
Bad Plan, Any Plan
Beats No Plan

Winning campaigns are based on a coherent strategy and executed against a plan. A good plan will beat a bad plan, but any plan will beat no plan. A campaign that doesn't have an idea where its candidate is going to be scheduled two weeks from now, doesn't know what message it intends to be on next week, doesn't know what ads are going to be up in three weeks, doesn't know what its 51 percent of the electorate is composed of, or doesn't have a cash-flow projection is a campaign that is likely to lose on Election Day.

The Bush-Cheney '04 presidential campaign will be remembered as one of the best-conceived and -executed in history.

Our overarching plan for the 2004 campaign was, from the outset, to reinforce President Bush's greatest strength: the certainty of his leadership. You could argue with the hard decisions he had made, but you couldn't argue that he had been willing to make the hard decisions.

We felt that in a period of uncertainty, in both a national security environment fundamentally changed by the events of September 11, 2001, and an economic environment fundamentally changed by globalization, Americans wanted a sense of certainty in their executive.

In February 2004 we settled on "Steady Leadership in Times

of Change" as a "placeholder" slogan, but ended the campaign on it nine months later. With steady leadership as the central rationale for candidacy, we developed the messages and tactics necessary to reinforce it and made strategic assumptions that guided our actions throughout the course of the year.

We assumed a close race.

We assumed high turnout.

We assumed that security would be the most vote-determinative factor, and that would be to the president's benefit. All these assumptions turned out to be true.

The Bush-Cheney strategy table was in Karl Rove's dining room. Literally.

Every weekend of 2004 beginning in February, the Bush-Cheney high command would gather at Karl's house in northwest Washington for an hour and a half of strategic planning. The regulars at the table were BC04 Campaign Manager Ken Mehlman; White House Communications Director Dan Bartlett; BC04 Campaign Strategist Matthew Dowd and his deputy, Sara Taylor; Mark McKinnon, director of the ad team; BC04 Communications Director Nicole Wallace (who was at the time Nicole Devenish) and press secretary Steve Schmidt (a barrel-chested guy with a shaved head whom Karl nicknamed "Bullet"); Lewis "Scooter" Libby, Vice President Cheney's chief of staff; and longtime Republican strategist Mary Matalin, who was the vice president's former communications director.

With the exception of Wallace, who had come to the White House from Florida Governor Jeb Bush's office, and Schmidt, who'd been communications director at the National Republican Congressional Committee, every single one of the people at that table had been centrally involved in the 2000 campaign. The Bush campaign nucleus was a coherent unit of people who were loyal not only to the president, but to one another.

This group became known internally as "the Breakfast Club" because we would meet on a Saturday or Sunday at around 10:00 AM, and for breakfast Karl would whip up his patented "eggies," a very tasty, cholesterol-laden dish, served with mounds of thick slabs of bacon. The meetings remained a well-kept secret for more than five months before a July *New York Times* feature on the campaign revealed their existence, complete with photos of the participants and disclosure of the "eggies."

The focal point of the Breakfast Club was long-range planning, specifically a month-long calendar filled in with message, scheduling, ads, and outside events. Dan Bartlett would lay out what the official White House schedule dictated. We would take into account anticipated releases of official jobs numbers, foreign presidential travel, visits to the United States from foreign heads of state, congressional actions, and other items. Such things were beyond our control and had to be factored into our planning.

Once those days were Xed out we would fill in the days with things we wanted to be talking about and then try like hell to stay on our chosen messages. The resulting calendar might seem to be a jumble of colors and blocks, but to us it was our roadmap, and we guarded it like a nuclear code. I never left a meeting with one in my possession, always ceremoniously tossing it back on the table before I left so if one ever showed up in a news report I couldn't be blamed!

None ever did.

In contrast, one of the great things about running against the Kerry campaign was there was no guesswork involved. His staff loved to tell the *New York Times* and the *Washington Post* what they would be doing next week and the week after.

The frustrating thing about running against the Kerry campaign was their seeming inability to stick to their leaked plans.

For example, they had decided, smartly I believed, to close out the election on jobs, the economy, and health care. These were the issues on which Kerry most dominated Bush in the polls, and Kerry campaign strategist Mike McCurry called them their "closing argument." But when the *New York Times* ran a front-page story they'd been teaming up with CBS News' *60 Minutes* to break late in the campaign reporting that 377 tons of munitions were missing from a depot in Iraq, the Kerry campaign jumped on the story for days, abandoning their plan to hammer on the economy in the home stretch.

As Stuart Stevens, one of the Bush campaign's advertising team, might say in his singsong cadence, "If the question is Iraq, can the answer really be John Kerry?" I hated the munitions story, but everyone around the Bush-Cheney strategy table agreed with Matthew Dowd who said he'd rather be dealing with a bad national security story dominating the campaign in its closing days than a bad economic story.

Campaigns are shaped more by what you're debating than by how you're debating it. If Medicare is front and center in a campaign, it's not likely the Republican candidate is going to win. If tax cuts are the central issue of a campaign, the Democrat is probably in trouble. One of the challenges of any campaign is agenda setting, and at the end of the '04 presidential campaign, the Kerry team could not resist the temptation to fight on terms historically favorable to Republicans.

"THE ARCHITECT"

In his victory speech on November 4, President Bush referred to Karl Rove as "the architect" of the campaign. It's an apt description. It's also fair to extend the metaphor and say he's a hard-working builder, a skillful painter, and a tasteful interior decorator.

When I first went to the RNC as chairman, I asked Rove what he thought my top priorities should be. "Narrow the gap between the number of registered Republicans and registered Democrats," he said without missing a beat. I focused like a laser on voter registration, even leasing a fifty-four-foot, eighteen-wheel semi-tractor trailer we dubbed "Reggie the Registration Rig," which rolled across the country from target state to target state, hitting college football games, NASCAR races, Cinco de Mayo celebrations, and tulip festivals.

In my maiden speech at the RNC's Winter Meeting in New York in July 2003, I unveiled "the Chairman's Cup," modeled on the National Hockey League's Stanley Cup. There is only one, and it resides with the state party that registers the highest percentage of its voting-age population in a year. The competition for the Chairman's Cup was added incentive for our state parties to bring new people into the GOP.

In the 2004 cycle, the Republican National Committee, working with the state parties, registered 3.4 million new voters. The president's margin of victory was 3.5 million votes. Karl was dead on in his assessment of the national party's principal objective.

The first time I met Karl in person was on a trip to Austin in the fall of 1999. I traveled there with then House Budget Committee chairman John Kasich (R-OH), who was considering running for president the following year, as everyone assumed then-governor Bush was, as well.

Kasich spent the night in the Governor's Mansion, and I stayed at a nearby hotel. We met back at the mansion in the morning, where Governor Bush hosted us for breakfast, joined by Rove.

The conversation was light and free-flowing, and Bush was very straightforward. He talked about the prospect of running for president, the pluses and minuses. He had an insight no one else in the field shared, having seen his father run for president three times (counting his '80 primary bid) and vice president twice. His was not a romanticized view of the process or the presidency.

He told Kasich that if both were to run, "I'm not going to attack you. That's not what the race should be about." He playfully called him "Johnny Boy" a couple of times, which Kasich told me afterward he found condescending. (This was before Bush's penchant for nicknames became commonly known.)

I interjected once or twice in the course of the hour-long

breakfast, but Karl said virtually nothing, only responding to a question from the governor here or there. It was the first time I'd seen their interaction, and it sure didn't seem to fit the "Bush's Brain" nickname that had been applied to him by Bush's political opponents.

After breakfast, Bush gave us both a brief tour of the Governor's Mansion, and we left for the airport. I had no idea at that moment that I would end up working for George W. Bush little more than six months later.

In the interim, Kasich and I had a blast traveling the country, introducing him to Republican groups in key early primary states. John Kasich can crank up a crowd like few people I've seen in politics. When he's on, he can lift a crowd on his back and soar with them. And he's usually on. I got to know John when I was communications director for the House Republican Conference, and I would argue for him to close out debate on just about every major floor vote, which took a little courage since that was usually the prerogative of the House majority leader (my boss) or the Speaker.

I was leaving Des Moines on the same day Bush made his first campaign visit to Iowa. His chartered plane (which he'd glibly dubbed "Great Expectations") landed just as mine sat on the runway waiting to take off. I was dozing against the window when the pilot came on the speaker. "If you look out the right side of the plane, you'll see George Bush Junior's plane on the tarmac," he said, using the appellation that was common before everyone came to learn that the governor wasn't a "junior" and was distinguished from his father by the initial "W" (before they would be distinguished from each other by "41" and "43").

I raised the blind and saw the 737 sitting there, three chartered buses lined up on the tarmac to accommodate the traveling press corps, who were unloading TV camera after TV camera from the belly of the parked plane. A row of dignitaries lined up to meet him. It was a far cry from the two reporters who had ridden with Kasich in the back of the rented Ford Expedition the day before, and it wasn't too long after that that we came to the conclusion that John Kasich's Presidential Exploratory Committee would never convert its funds to a John Kasich for President Committee.

Kasich exited in style. It's possible to run for something and lose, but still come out ahead, and I always say of the Kasich presidential effort, "We got out better than we got in."

John decided not only to abandon his presidential effort, but to abandon his House seat. He and his wife, Karen, were having twins, and he decided that after nearly two decades in Congress this was a turning point. He didn't want to simply end with the negative announcement of his decision not to seek the Republican Party's presidential nomination, but to make a positive statement as well: He was becoming a George W. Bush supporter.

Talk about real news: "I'm not running for re-election to my House seat, I'm not seeking the presidency, I'm announcing my support for Governor Bush, and Karen and I are going to have twins!"

On July 14, 1999, the media were buzzing about Kasich's announcement, and Bush was happy to come to Washington to personally tip over the first domino to fall on his way to nomination.

From the hotel in Columbus where John made his announcement I called Karen Hughes on her cell phone. She was traveling with the governor and they were sitting on the tarmac in Iowa. I suggested that they bring two "Bush for President" baseball caps to put on at the press conference and John would announce that he was now on the Bush team. It was a little hokey, but I thought it would make a good photo-op that reinforced youth and vigor. Not every politician can wear a baseball cap. The ability to do so without looking goofy reflects an everyman quality that's appealing, and both Kasich and Bush could pull it off (in contrast to, say, Steve Forbes or Al Gore).

Bush came through a back entrance to the Ronald Reagan Building on Pennsylvania Avenue accompanied by Maria Cino, my old friend from our House days. She had run the National Republican Congressional Committee under Representative Bill Paxon (R-NY) when I was working for Armey and Haley. Maria's a lot of fun (she would later serve as deputy chairman at the RNC when I was chairman), but on this day she was all business.

Kasich greeted Bush, who said, "I really appreciate you doing this, John." He was almost somber, not as back-slapping as when we had been in Austin.

"I'm glad to, George," Kasich said, and by that time he really meant it. John's a fierce competitor and he wasn't happy to be quitting the race before it even really began. He and I were the last ones to accept the inevitability of his withdrawal, and I argued for him to stay at least through the first multicandidate debate on the grounds that the exposure would be helpful and he would excel in such a forum, but our strategist Don Fierce was adamant that if we hung on any longer we would start to look silly. Up in New Hampshire, a guest at one of Kasich's meet-and-greets backed over the hostess's dog, and John very graciously buried the old cocker spaniel in her backyard (after the event was over, of course!). The media had picked up on the quirky story, and the dead dog had somehow become a symbol of our nascent campaign.

Kasich introduced me to Bush, but as we shook hands the governor said, "We met before." I was surprised he remembered the breakfast of months ago, as was Kasich, who said, "I wasn't sure you'd remember."

"I served him bacon in my home," Bush said.

A couple of things about that. It struck me that he said the much more specific "bacon," not just "breakfast," and that it was in "my home," not "the governor's mansion." Second, he sounded mildly insulted by the notion that he wouldn't have remembered it—insulted not by an implication that he had a bad memory, but by an implication that he had bad manners.

For all I knew, this was in a briefing book he read on the plane on the way to Washington. *("Kasich will be joined by Ed Gillespie, who was with him in Austin at the breakfast. You served bacon.")* Either way, it was incredibly good form.

After Kasich endorsed Bush, I stayed out of the presidential contest, not working for any of the candidates in the field (Bush, John McCain, Elizabeth Dole, Steve Forbes, Gary Bauer, et al.), and did frequent guest appearances on cable news shows as one of the few Republican strategists out there not aligned with a campaign. The fact is, I was partial to Bush, but figured they didn't need any more help anyway.

That changed in January 2000, when John McCain shook up everything by trouncing Bush in the New Hampshire primary. The next day, I called the Bush campaign in Austin and told the press shop to start sending me talking points, as I no longer considered myself unaligned and would tell television bookers to identify me as supporting George W. Bush for president.

I didn't have anything against John McCain. I just believed Bush's brand of compassionate conservatism was the future of our party. I think Karl and others appreciated the fact that I called not when everyone thought Bush was the inevitable nominee, but on the day many people thought he wouldn't be.

Months later, after Bush had locked down the nomination, Karl asked me to be part of a group that served as a bridge between Austin and the Washington Republican crowd. Besides me there was former RNC chairman Haley Barbour, Bill Paxon, longtime operative Charlie Black, former Minnesota congressman Vin We-

ber, and Mary Matalin. We were dubbed "the Gang of Six," and
we'd meet every few weeks to share ideas with the so-called "Iron
Triangle," Karl, Karen Hughes, and campaign manager Joe Allbaugh.

Figuring out how to best use talent is an important part of any
campaign, and as Bush was running as a Washington outsider (if
not running an anti-Washington campaign), there was some angst
among establishment Republicans in the nation's capital. Karl
wanted a bridge to this group, a way they could funnel ideas into
the campaign and a way for him to funnel messages out. He didn't
want to change the outsider nature of the campaign, but at the same
time wanted to mitigate the carping in the press that would be inevitable without some form of structured contact with the Washington establishment.

One of my tasks was to think about Gore, and how best to approach him from an opposition perspective. Toward that end, Karl
gave me a thick polling report and asked me to dig into it.

Before this exercise, I had my own view of what people didn't
like about Al Gore. I thought he came across as a know-it-all, a condescending prima donna. What struck me in the polling report was
the consistency of responses to the "open-ended" question, "What
is it you like least about Vice President Gore?"

Instead of adjectives like "arrogant," "snobby," and "elitist"
dominating the sentiment, it was shot through with words like
"wishy-washy," "indecisive," and "weak." One respondent said, "I
think his wife wears the pants in that family."

I went through and quantified all the responses that fell under
the "wishy-washy" category versus the "arrogant" category, and the
vast lion's share were under wishy-washy. I told Haley, "They don't
think Gore's a jerk, they think he's a sissy."

One person said, "He told on his teammates." This prompted
me to do some research. It turns out that Gore was on his high
school football team and one night there was a keg party. Most of
the team went, but Gore didn't. The next day the football coach

was frustrated by the lack of energy in practice, and Al helpfully explained to him why so many of the players were dragging!

I shared my analysis with Karl, and it's one of the reasons we were so prepared to capitalize on Gore's pattern of flip-flopping in the 2000 campaign. We saw it early and laid the predicate down in the media, and he ended up playing right into it. Voters are smart, and they know what they see. This is another example of the need to be willing to let the data inform your conclusions, rather than letting your conclusions inform the data. I could just as easily have gone through and pulled out all the examples of responses that supported my own view that Gore's principal weakness lay in his perceived arrogance, but the preponderance of the data did not support my predisposition.

About a month after joining the Gang of Six, Karen asked me if I'd be willing to help handle the convention in Philadelphia. She said Andy Card was going to be the campaign's convention chairman, and they wanted someone to manage the program. I told her I'd be honored, and in May Andy and I took our first trip to Philadelphia on the Acela train from Washington's Union Station.

I had heard of Andy Card long before I met him. He was, and is, a strong Bush family loyalist. He'd been secretary of transportation for former president Bush, and was his deputy chief of staff before that. He'd been our party's nominee for governor of Massachussets in 1982. For the next two months, we'd be joined at the hip in Philadelphia.

The first meeting I went to, there was a discussion of the program. Someone said, "We think Colin Powell would make a great keynote speaker." I agreed, and asked where things stood with the speakers. I was surprised to learn that not a single one had yet been invited. It was June 9. The first day of the convention was July 30, less than six weeks away, and not a single singer, not a single speaker, not a single person to recite the Pledge of Allegiance had been lined up yet. We had our work cut out for us.

Someone kept saying that Gloria Estefan was going to sing on the first night of the convention, but I couldn't nail down whether this was true. It was one of those somebody knows somebody who knows her kind of deals, but I couldn't get a firm answer from the people who had been charged with working on the program to that point.

My old friend (and now business partner) Marc Lampkin, who was responsible for floor operations at the convention, would laugh every time someone mentioned Gloria Estefan, which was a little disconcerting to me.

"Why are you laughing every time we talk about Gloria Estefan?"

"Let me tell you something," Marc said in his raspy voice. "I'm more likely to sing on opening night than Gloria Estefan. Those guys are full of it."

Finally, I called a friend at the Recording Industry Association of America and asked him if he knew of Gloria Estefan's schedule for the summer, because we were counting on her playing Monday night of the convention.

He called me back an hour later.

"Gloria Estefan has a concert in Japan on July 28."

Strategy should define tactics, not the other way around.

The Kerry camp allowed their tactics to define their strategy, while we maintained the discipline necessary to have our strategy define our tactics. The best example of such discipline may have come in summer 2004, as we faced growing pressure for the president to unveil a new policy agenda.

Throughout most of the election year, the Bush-Cheney campaign had been almost constantly on defense, beginning in early January with the release of Ron Suskind's book, *The Price of Loyalty,* claiming that President Bush had planned to invade Iraq from the very beginning of his administration. Former treasury secretary Paul O'Neill appeared on January 11 on *60 Minutes* in his first interview since leaving the cabinet to air some of the damaging claims he made to Suskind in the book.

The month ended with David Kay, the former head of the U.S. weapons inspection teams in Iraq, informing a Senate committee that no weapons of mass destruction had been found in Iraq and that prewar intelligence was "almost all wrong."

And in between those two bookends, John Kerry cemented his reputation as a "strong closer" by coming back from the politically dead to win both the Iowa caucuses and the New Hampshire primary.

In the first week of February, the president went on *Meet the Press* and pledged to release all of his National Guard records, which he did later that month only to be criticized by the media for not doing so in a more timely and complete manner.

On February 10, the White House Council of Economic Advisors released *The Economic Report of the President 2004*, in which they suggested that the outsourcing of jobs overseas is a benefit to the economy.

Many of us on the campaign pointed out to our friends in the White House that, whatever the economic theory, outsourcing didn't feel like a benefit to a lot of unemployed workers in Ohio.

Meanwhile, John Kerry was winning the Maine caucuses, and the Virginia and Tennessee primaries.

March began with the release of February's monthly jobs numbers, which came in at a dismal twenty-one thousand jobs. A week later, the White House announced it was pulling the nominee for the newly created position of assistant secretary of commerce for manufacturing (the "manufacturing czar") after it was learned that his company had laid off U.S. workers and outsourced their jobs to China.

I joked to Dan Bartlett that I didn't mind so much the bullets we were taking in the chest from the Kerry campaign and the DNC, but the bullets in our back were starting to hurt!

On March 21, former national security staffer Richard Clarke appeared on *60 Minutes* to attack the Bush administration for failing to prevent 9/11, and for its prosecution of the war in Iraq, as a preview to his book *Against All Enemies,* which was published the next day.

After Clarke testified before the 9/11 Commission later in the week, the White House reversed its opposition to having National Security Advisor Condoleezza Rice go before the commission. By the end of March, the president and vice president had both agreed to testify before the commission as well.

The lowest point in the campaign may have come in April, when the report on abuse at the Abu Ghraib prison aired on *60 Minutes,* showing the despicable photos that all Americans found shameful. In the following week, over fourteen hundred stories ran on the prison abuse scandal, and our numbers began to sink.

The month ended as the deadliest one for U.S. troops in Iraq since the beginning of the war, with more deaths than in January, February, and March combined.

May was dominated by Defense Secretary Rumsfeld, Joint Chiefs of Staff Chairman Richard Myers, and other DoD officials testifying before Senate and House Armed Services Committees on Abu Ghraib prison abuses, and the murder in Iraq of American contractor Nicholas Berg in the first of a series of grisly beheadings that shocked the public.

On May 23, retired general Anthony Zinni appeared on—you guessed it!—CBS's *60 Minutes* to discuss his new book, *Battle Ready,* in which he lambasted the administration's plan for and conduct of the Iraq war.

June began with reports of President Bush consulting with his attorney over the investigation of the leak of the identity of CIA agent Valerie Plame, Vice President Cheney testifying in that probe, and CIA Director George Tenet announcing his resignation.

And June ended with Michael Moore's incendiary documentary *Fahrenheit 9/11,* about the war in Iraq and the Bush White House, which opened nationwide in 860 theaters and raked in $22 million in its first weekend, smashing the previous record for a documentary.

By July, when Senator Kerry announced John Edwards as his running mate and they were heading into the Democratic National Convention with the cover of *Newsweek* touting them as "The Sunshine Boys," I wasn't surprised to see the blind quotations from "Republican sources" and "sources close to the White House" urging the unveiling of a new policy agenda to try to change the storyline and get us back on offense.

It was a tempting thought, but our strategy was to hold off announcing new policies until the president's convention acceptance speech, using it to frame the debate in the election's homestretch on our own policy terms when it would matter most. Despite being down in the polls and weathering some negative press, we decided to stick to our plan.

It's at times like these that you have to trust your instincts and hope your strategic assumptions are correct. Despite all the technological advances of the past decade—the internet ads, the flash polls, the focus groups, and the like—politics at its core is still a gut check. Data can be read a number of ways. Little pictures can be construed to compose different big pictures. A sense of timing matters immensely. This is the critical and often determinative realm of politics that is more art than science, and the fact is, usually both sides tend to see the same thing. Their instincts are pretty much in sync.

David Espo, who covers congress for the Associated Press and is one of the finest political writers of this generation, says that political people aren't just Democrats and Republicans, they're either on this planet or they're not. One little-known fact about national politics is that in off-the-record conversations, Democratic and Republican operatives tend to reinforce one another.

Both sides essentially acknowledge the same swing states, concede the same issue sets, acknowledge the same strengths and weaknesses. Very rarely do you have professionals on the different sides actually disagreeing on the fundamentals of a race.

This is why I was confused in July. In April and May, I felt that we were winning, but I never felt that we had it won. In July, I felt that we were losing, but I never felt that we had it lost. In fact, while I always understood we *could* lose, I never once felt we *would* lose.

One of the great things about the Bush-Cheney '04 campaign is that we kept our bearings whether we were eight points down or eight points up. We never crossed the boundaries of either dejectedness or giddiness, but stuck to our strategy.

"Nothing in politics is ever as good or as bad as it seems."

My political mentor Haley Barbour, one of my predecessors as RNC chairman and now governor of Mississippi, has a saying: "In politics, nothing is ever as good or as bad as it seems." Those of us on the Bush-Cheney team understood this and believed it all the way through. We always believed the fundamentals of this race pointed to a close election in the end, and consistently said so. When we were up by thirteen points and said it would be close in the end, the press assumed we were trying to "lower the bar," and when we were down by ten points and said the same thing, the press assumed we were trying to spin things positively to keep our troops energized.

While we understood it could go either way, we felt that it would end up our way. The Kerry campaign, on the other hand, seemed to have come to the conclusion by the beginning of July that the race was all but over, and that the American people had made a decision to fire George W. Bush. It made me nervous that both sides, essentially looking at the same data, could come to such fundamentally different conclusions about the overall shape of the race. I didn't understand how they could be operating on such a different strategic framework.

I shot Karl a note to this effect, seeking some insight that would clear everything up and make me feel better. He replied, "If they're right and we're wrong, it's over."

Not the most consoling note ever, but certainly accurate.

In politics, as in any other profession, it's easy to believe what you see. What professionals have to guard against is seeing what they believe. The Kerry campaign's belief that the country had already decided to fire Bush was wrong, and it led to one of the most significant mistakes of the 2004 election cycle. They used their national convention in Boston simply to position John Kerry as an acceptable alternative to Bush without providing a substantive policy agenda for the American people to factor into their vote determination.

So their convention put a heavy emphasis on biography, with a focus on the senator's Vietnam service that bordered on self-parody by the time he came to the podium for his acceptance speech and opened with a snappy salute and, "I'm John Kerry, and I'm reporting for duty."

I was two blocks away from where Senator Kerry was standing at the time, in our opposition party war room. I glanced over at *Time* magazine's Matt Cooper, who was covering our efforts in Boston, and noticed even he could barely suppress a chuckle.

Kerry's lack of policy detail in his own acceptance speech made our decision to hold new policy for our convention even more effective. One of my worst fears was that Kerry would call for tax reform in his speech. I had sent Ken and Dan Bartlett an email in July pointing out all the times over the past two months that Kerry had talked about the tax code being too complicated, and suggested that we needed to be prepared to respond to a convention speech that called for scrapping our current tax code in favor of a flat tax or national sales tax. Happily, no such bold idea emerged.

The Breakfast Club crew, joined by Karen Hughes, held a conference call before Kerry's speech was even over to talk about what we needed to emphasize in our talking points, which was reinforcing the notion that Kerry was a negative pessimist and that he failed to lay out a positive agenda.

I hung up the phone and raced to our in-house studio for an interview with CNN. Analyst Jeff Greenfield asked me, "Ed, the Bush campaign has been trying to portray John Kerry as a dour pessimist. It seemed to me they went out of their way here to strike a theme as optimistic as you could possibly imagine, even using a Ronald Reagan line at the end, 'Our best days are ahead of us.' Can you really paint John Kerry, whatever you think of his policies, as a pessimist after tonight?"

"Well, he is pretty negative in terms of his view of the economy and of America's prospects, and I do think he's fairly pessimistic. But I do think that our highlighting that and pointing it out has caused him to try to change his rhetoric here. And this speech largely was, in many ways, a rehash of his standard stump speech that we've heard.

"Many people, though, probably heard it for the first time this evening, and the fact is he didn't lay out much new policy. He's not very forward-looking at all in this speech—very backward-looking, it seemed to me."

I stayed on the theme the following morning, telling the *Washington Post*'s David Broder, dean of the Washington press corps, about the mistake the Kerry camp had just made. "This is a huge opening," I said. "We're going to jump on it."

In keeping with our strategy, our convention in New York a month later revolved around the president's leadership. When the media saw our roster of key speakers—John McCain, Rudy Giuliani, Arnold Schwarzenegger—they assumed we were trying to reposition the president as a moderate, given that these three men often held positions on social issues at odds with the president's.

"If the Administration's hard line on Iraq is turning off some voters, Republican Party leaders are hoping to restore a more moderate face when it counts the most—at the party's national convention in New York City at the end of August," reported *Time* magazine in its July 5 issue, reflecting the broader media's take on the speaker selection.

They missed the point. These men are all seen as strong leaders in their own right, and they were attesting to George W. Bush as a strong leader among strong leaders. When Bush gave his acceptance speech, it was more like a State of the Union Address than a political rally speech. The policies he laid out in it served as the basis of our talking points for the last eight weeks of the campaign.

Throughout the speech, the president referred to "a new term," as opposed to "a second term." Kerry's lack of substance allowed the incumbent to be "new" and to be the reformer, while Kerry increasingly seemed old and status quo. Had we not resisted the tactical urge earlier in the summer to begin unveiling new policies, this opportunity could not have been exploited the way it had

I had suggested "new term" as a way of acknowledging a need for change without conceding that there was anything wrong in the first place. Talking about a "second term," I worried, would sound like a simple continuation of current policies, and while the public had doubts about Kerry, there was a desire out there for something new. If voters could get the steadiness and stability of Bush and a sense that things might be a little different in a second term, we'd have the best of both worlds.

One of the things I worried about in 2004 was "Bush Fatigue." Far different from the outright hatred those on the radical left held toward the president, I sensed a more subtle feeling among voters in the middle that while they valued the president's unwavering commitment to winning the War on Terror, he was taxing them (not literally, obviously, but figuratively). "New term" was a subtle way of addressing that fatigue.

It was incredibly hectic trying to pull it all together, but in the end the 2000 convention turned out to be one of the most successful ever. Conventions are the most important opportunity a presidential candidate has to convey an image, and in Philadelphia in 2000 the image of George W. Bush as a compassionate conservative and a "different kind of Republican" was hammered home in style.

Democrats mix and mingle with Hollywood celebrities as a matter of course, but conventions are just about the only time Republicans do. Our celebrities tend not to be the box office draws the Democrats have, as Hollywood is dominated by liberals. It was fun, though, to meet actor Rick Schroeder in 2000 and become friends in 2004 with Ron Silver, a serious student of elections.

About two weeks before the 2004 Election Day I crossed paths with Ron in the Fox News Green Room in New York City as I was about to appear on *Hannity and Colmes*.

"How are things going out there?" he asked.

"Good," I said. "I was just in Iowa, and I think it's gonna flip. I think we're going to carry it."

"That's great!" Ron said. "That's seven Electoral College votes, isn't it?"

It is. We may not have as many stars, but ours are smarter than the left's!

One time, I was standing in line at the McDonald's near our 2000 convention offices in Philadelphia and had just placed my order when my cell phone buzzed. It was the unmistakable voice of Arnold Schwarzenegger, whom we'd been trying to get to emcee a portion of the evening paying tribute to former Republican presidents. "Hello, Arnold," I said (this was five years before he became a governor), "thanks for calling back."

While I was talking to Schwarzenegger, the woman behind the counter was trying to get me to tell her if I wanted to super-size my fries. I put my hand over the mouthpiece and whispered to her, "I'm talking to Arnold Schwarzenegger!"

"Uh-huh. Do you want your fries super-sized or not?"

Schwarzenegger, by the way, was trying to drive a hard bargain: If he did the appearance, would Governor Bush give his wife, Maria Shriver, an exclusive interview after he delivered his acceptance speech? It was an offer we couldn't accept, and Schwarzenegger never made it to Philadelphia. (He was fantastic four years later at the convention in New York, though!)

The 2000 convention in Philadelphia was a huge success, perhaps the most effective ever in terms of branding. We worked hard to recruit African-American, Hispanic, Asian-American, and women speakers and entertainers. At one point we did a remote feed featuring the Reverend Herb Lusk, a former Philadelphia Eagles running back, from his church in North Philly with his gospel choir in the background, and then cut back to the First Union Center, where we had a gospel choir on stage. It was one of the highlights of the convention.

The media were cynical. My friend Kevin Merida of the *Washington Post* said he couldn't help notice the abundance of blacks on stage but the dearth of them on the convention floor where the delegates were seated.

"If you're accusing us of reaching out to minority voters, guilty as charged," I said. "If black voters come away from this convention with the sense they are welcome in the Republican Party, we will have been successful."

Bush emerged from Philly as "a different kind of Republican," and had strong momentum going into the fall homestretch.

The 2000 Democratic Convention, however, was more successful than I, and many other Republicans, realized. I thought "the kiss,"

when Gore planted one on Tipper before going onstage to deliver his acceptance speech, was one of the hokiest things I'd ever seen in politics. Somehow, though, it took.

The convention, and the reality that Gore was the incumbent vice president running in a period of peace and prosperity, eventually caught up with the Bush campaign, and by September there was a sense in Austin that things were slipping.

Labor Day is the traditional start of a campaign homestretch, and as it came the Bush campaign was in a period that advertising team member Stuart Stevens dubbed "rats and moles and falling polls."

"Rats" was a reference to a media sensation story about a Bush-Cheney ad attacking Gore's health care policies. Words describing his government-heavy approach scrolled from right to left across the screen, and one of them was "bureaucrats."

If you froze one frame, or one hundredth of a second, only the last four letters were visible—"rats."

Chris Lehane, the dark arts prince of the Gore campaign, pitched this to Rick Berke of the *New York Times* as a subliminal attack, insisting that ". . . rats" in the ad frame was like some death mask in the ice cubes of a liquor ad.

Amazingly, Berke bought it, and the *Times* played it on the front page. The 24/7 cable outlets played it over and over again, scrutinizing and analyzing and psychoanalyzing the spot for days. The Austin team found itself fending off charges that it was engaged in nefarious advertising tactics rather than debating the issue in the ad itself.

"Moles" was a reference to a strange incident involving one of Governor Bush's debate briefing books' being sent anonymously to the Gore campaign. Former New York congressman Tom Downey, a friend of Gore's who was helping him prepare for the fall debates, received the Bush-Cheney binder in the mail and immediately turned it over to the FBI.

There followed a media frenzy, with speculation that it wasn't a real briefing book but a decoy actually sent by Karl Rove to the Gore-Lieberman campaign in hopes they would use it to prepare wrongly for the debates. In Austin, there was concern that the briefing book was a real one, and that there was a "mole" in the campaign surreptitiously sending sensitive material to the Gore camp.

The idea that any presidential campaign would, A, be devious enough to work up a false briefing book to send to the opponent's campaign or, B, have the time to do so is ridiculous, but the notion consumed a great deal of space and time in the news media.

The more disturbing possibility was that there was a mole in the headquarters. Since there was a federal investigation into the matter, the few people who knew whether it was the actual briefing book were not free to tell everyone else on the staff what was going on.

It turned out that it was a real debate briefing book, and it had been stolen not from the headquarters but from the offices of Maverick Media, the advertising team headed by Mark McKinnon. One of McKinnon's employees had, for reasons known only to her, obtained the book and sent it off.

The "falling polls" in the "rats and moles and falling polls" trilogy need no further explanation.

Karl Rove began thinking about what was needed to help get things back on track and decided that with Karen Hughes now constantly on the campaign plane criss-crossing the country with Governor Bush, there needed to be someone in the headquarters to help punch up the speeches and think ahead of the news curve.

Rove's right-hand man Chris Henick called me one day to ask if I had any thoughts about who might be able to fill that role.

I thought about it for a while but couldn't come up with a suggestion. I popped into Haley's office (at the time he and I were partners in a communications firm we'd founded) to see if he had any ideas.

"Henick called," I said. Chris had worked at Haley's lobbying firm before taking a leave to move to Austin to help on the campaign. "They're looking for someone who can come up with some quotable lines for the governor's speeches, and help think ahead on messaging and events. Can you think of anybody?"

"Hell, Gillespie, he's talking about you!"

"Me? I can't move to Austin for sixty days!"

"Anybody can do anything for sixty days."

That night Cathy and I sat on our deck and discussed whether I should respond to Chris's question by recommending myself.

"You'd be like Cheney," Cathy joked, referring to the famous case of Dick Cheney heading up the running mate selection committee and ending up on the ticket himself.

Cathy Gillespie is a well-respected political operative in her own right. It was actually through Cathy that I came to know Karl Rove. In 1983, Cathy went to work for Joe Barton, one of the candidates running in the Republican primary to replace Phil Gramm in the U.S. House after he'd been elected to the United States Senate.

As chairman of the House Energy and Commerce Committee, Joe Barton is today one of the most powerful people in Washington, but back then he was an unknown engineer running in the first campaign of his life. Joe is a proud graduate of Texas A&M, which was in the heart of Texas's Sixth Congressional District, and Cathy was active in A&M's Political Forum student group.

When she agreed to head up Aggies for Barton, she became Joe's first paid campaign staffer and came into regular contact with Joe's political consultant, one Karl C. Rove of Austin, Texas. Karl recognized in Cathy early what many others came to know later—she'll get it done. As a senior in college, she became someone he considered a "go-to" person on a campaign in which Joe won the Republican Party's nomination in a recount by two votes, after losing on primary night by ten.

In 1986, she managed Barton's re-election campaign, in which his challenger spent more money than any other Democratic challenger in the cycle. In 2004, Bush Campaign Manager Ken

Mehlman asked Cathy to head up "W Stands for Women" at Bush-Cheney, one of the most successful coalition efforts in the campaign.

So on that evening in September 2000, I was talking not only to my wife about the prospect of moving away from home, but to a political peer.

"I don't want to go to Austin," I said. "I've already been gone too much for the convention. It's not fair to the kids."

While in Philadelphia for the convention, I had stayed close to John, Carrie, and Mollie by reading ten pages of a Harry Potter book to them every night. They'd sit around a speaker phone while I read from my office in Philadelphia. It made the separation a little easier, but it was still hard.

"Honey, they need you more than the kids do right now. We'll be fine. We can make it for two months. You need to go. The most important thing for our kids is that Bush get elected president."

She meant it, and I believed the same thing.

The next day I called Chris Henick back.

"I think maybe I'm the right person for the job you described," I said.

"Really? You'd be willing to come to Austin?"

"If you think I could help."

"That's great. Let me talk to Karl and call you back."

About a half-hour later, Henick called back.

"Karl wants to know if you can come tomorrow."

Two days later, I landed in Austin. I went straight to the headquarters from the airport and ran into campaign press secretary Mindy Tucker as I was waved through security. I dropped my bags in her office, and she walked me down to the main conference room, where a big meeting was taking place.

She pushed the door open, and as I walked in behind her she said, "Look who I found in the hallway."

Karl sat at the head of a conference table. He looked up and broke stride only long enough to say, "'Bout time you got here.

Grab a chair." That was the extent of my formal introduction to "the Austin crowd."

I crowded in between two advance people at the other end of the table and listened in as they went over the plan for the governor's message and schedule over the next five days.

After the meeting broke up, Karl told me I needed to catch up with Mark McKinnon and sit in on his communications planning meeting. Mark pulled me back to a smaller conference room across the hallway where we met with a few others to do a little forward planning.

As the meeting was winding down, I thought this might be a good place to ask something that I'd been wondering about before I left Washington.

"I don't know if this is the right place to ask this, or if it's even appropriate for me to ask," I began. "But where's Laura Bush?"

I have to say, in this regard, I was country before country was cool. I had wanted Mrs. Bush to be the first prime-time speaker at our convention because I just thought she was dynamite—attractive, forceful yet feminine, articulate, and the best character witness someone running for national office for the first time could have.

But since the convention, she'd been almost invisible, and especially near the end of August.

Mark McKinnon smiled as if he appreciated the question, and as if he liked the answer he was about to give. "The girls just started college. She's been getting them ready and settled. She's traveling with the governor again next week."

"Good," I said. "I think she's a huge asset to the governor." It wasn't like everyone in the room wasn't already aware of that, but at least they knew the new guy from Washington wasn't an idiot.

When I went down to Austin, it was arranged for me to stay at a Days Inn a short hop across the Brazos River from the campaign headquarters on Congress Avenue, but before I left for the night, Karl told me he had arranged a place for me to stay. "Call this number," he said. "Pat Oles is a friend of mine, and he has a pool house he can put you up in."

"Great. Thanks," I said. I took the slip of paper with the Austin phone number on it and headed back to my new desk, trying to figure out how I was going to get out of this. I'm not crazy about hotel rooms, but the thought of staying in some dumpy pool house with no phone or television for the next two months was even worse. But Karl Rove had graciously tapped a friend to put me up, and I wasn't going to start my time in Austin by insulting both him and his friend by rejecting their kindness and generosity.

Pat Oles could not have been nicer as he gave me directions to his house. I figured I'd just stay out there for a couple days and after they got tired of me staying there, I'd head to a hotel.

I got out of there around 9:30, pretty tired from a long day (it was 10:30 PM Eastern Time). As I drove through the neighborhood, I noticed that it was one of those suburban areas where old small houses on big lots were steadily giving way to new big houses. I lugged my bags out of the car and to the front door and rang the doorbell. Pat and Julie Oles both met me there, each picking up a bag and carrying it into the kitchen, where we sat to make our acquaintance.

I could tell right away that this was not an inconvenience to them, that they saw my staying in their home as a way to help elect their friend and governor the next president of the United States. At the same time, I wanted to convey to them as soon as I could that I was not some young campaign guy who was going to be coming in at all hours, that I had a family of my own and I was very appreciative of their kindness and would not in any way interrupt their own family life.

It was an easy, friendly relationship from the moment I sat at their kitchen table. After about half an hour, Pat said, "You're tired. Let's get you to your new home." We relieved Julie of bellhop duty, the two of us carrying my three bags out the back door and past the pool to a two-story pool house. When we climbed the stairs and Pat flipped on the lights, I saw a place that could grace the inside pages of *Town & Country* magazine. It was beautifully decorated. There was a thirty-six-inch television hooked up to a six-hundred-station cable system in the sitting room, top-of-the-line appliances in the kitchen, a small dining room table, and a bedroom with a queen-sized bed with ruffles and duvets and throw pillows galore. There was a walk-in closet, and a full bath and shower.

"Pat," I said, "as far as everyone in Washington is going to know, I'm living in a dingy little pool house with no hot water for the next two months. I'm like Kato Kaelin. I want them to think this is a huge sacrifice, not that I'm in one of the nicest places I've ever seen."

Pat Oles is one of Karl's oldest friends, having worked with him in the 1980 campaign of Bill Clements, the first Republican elected governor of Texas since Reconstruction. They go quail hunting together with their sons, and Pat knows what often goes missing from the seemingly endless stream of profiles of and stories about Karl: He is a good friend, and a devoted husband and father. When he and Darby moved to Washington, they bought their house based on what school would be best for their son Andrew, a decision Karl studied like it was a policy recommendation to the president.

Democrats tend to see Karl's hand everywhere in the Bush administration, and he is clearly one of the most influential aides in the White House, but as Education Secretary Margaret Spellings once said, "For Karl to be able to do all the things Democrats accuse him of doing, we'd have to change our policy on cloning."

The bottom line is this: Karl is incredibly efficient at converting ideas to action. A million good ideas get kicked around in campaigns and government meetings that are never acted on. Karl is the one to say, "Okay, but who in the political office is going to call the governor of that state to ask him to issue a statement? Who in the press shop is going to draft the statement for him? Who in the policy shop is going to vet the statement?"

Every organization needs that kind of driving force, and Karl is the hardest driving force I have ever seen.

///

Is time our enemy or our friend?

///

In Elizabeth Dole's 2002 North Carolina senatorial campaign, we knew that she was going to end up facing former Clinton White House chief of staff Erskine Bowles, but he first had to win in a three-way primary, which was being held late because of challenges to redistricting. Originally planned for May, it ended up being held in September.

The media wanted the general election campaign to begin before the primaries were over, and kept pushing Dole to engage Bowles sooner. Bowles would attack Dole, and the press would call for a response, but we would take a pass, noting that Elizabeth had her own primary to get through (a field of seven, none of whom posed a serious challenge) and so did Bowles.

"When do we get to hit this guy back?" asked a frustrated Marybrown Brewer, the Dole for Senate communications director. We were in a bar in Raleigh, and she had spent the day not hitting Bowles back for his latest attack.

"Don't worry, your handcuffs are going to come off soon," I said, assuring her that when the time came we weren't going to be shy about pointing out Mr. Bowles's shortcomings as a candidate.

One of the questions you have to answer in any campaign is, "Is time our enemy or our friend?" My strategic assumption was that time was our enemy. A longer general election campaign helped Bowles, a shorter campaign, Elizabeth.

This was not because Elizabeth Dole was a weak candidate. To the contrary, she proved to be one of the strongest candidates I've ever seen. It was simply a function of name identification and resources. Elizabeth Dole began the '02 North Carolina Senate race with 90 percent name identification and a seven-to-one favorable-unfavorable ratio. Her name ID could not go up much higher, and her fav-unfav could only come down.

"Name identification" is the percentage of people in a poll who recognize your name. "Hard name identification" is the percentage of people who not only recognize a name, but know generally what the person does (that is, people who are not only familiar with "George Pataki," but know he is the governor).

The percentage of those people who have a favorable opinion of you versus an unfavorable one is your "fav-unfav ratio." Dole's seven-to-one ratio was phenomenal, like nothing I'd ever seen before. Generally, if you have a two-to-one fav-unfav you're in great shape. But I knew it could only come down because a large number of those favorable voters were Democrats who would get an unfavorable opinion of her once a campaign was fully under way and she began taking positions on issues on which they disagreed with her.

With such universal name recognition, Dole was essentially the proxy incumbent in the race to succeed Jesse Helms. She enjoyed the benefit of a more unified party and stronger financial support (though we assumed the very wealthy Bowles would commit his own money to the race to ensure he would not be outspent).

Our plan called for Elizabeth to begin outlining her policies over the summer, and we mapped out a different policy to put forward each week between June and September.

The night of the primary, we went on the offensive immediately, putting out an invitation to Bowles to join us in not running campaign ads and instead putting up $2 million each to buy television time statewide to air debates. It was essentially the same proposal that John Edwards had made to Senator Lauch Faircloth in his winning campaign four years earlier.

It was completely unexpected, put us immediately on offense in the general election, and presented Bowles with a "damned if you do, damned if you don't" ultimatum. If he accepted, he would have relinquished the negative ads he'd need to overcome Elizabeth's dominant early lead. If he rejected, as we suspected he would, she would be on the side of the angels, having tried to stop all this negative campaigning before it began.

We gave reporters a copy of a letter that had been sent to Bowles as soon as he'd been declared the victor, and they hit him with it right away on primary night. His people were scrambling to figure out how to respond as we watched them on television from our campaign headquarters in her hometown of Salisbury.

Welcome to the race, Erskine.

A majority mentality.

Newt Gingrich had an almost obsessive devotion to planning.

The most remarkable thing about Newt Gingrich as a leader was his ability to foster a mentality of teamwork, of instilling a sense that the better the House Republicans did as a whole, the better each would do individually.

This was a complete reversal of the mentality that had prevailed for years among House Republicans, who by 1992 had been in the minority for nearly forty years. It had gotten to the point that most Republican members of the House never even harbored a hope that they would someday be in the majority.

Gingrich almost single-handedly forced a change from what we described as "the minority mentality" to a "majority mentality."

In the annals of Republican history, no single vote has had a greater impact than the single vote that elected Newt Gingrich House Republican whip over Ed Madigan after Dick Cheney left the spot in March 1989 to become secretary of defense. (Gingrich won by two votes, but if one vote had gone the other way the race would have been a tie and you could bet that then–minority leader Bob Michel would have figured out a way to break the tie in favor of his best friend Madigan.)

Before the outcome of that leadership contest, House Republican leaders were content to settle for "scraps from the table," helping Democrats pass massive spending bills in exchange for inclusion of a post office here, a demo project there. It's no surprise that GOP leaders traditionally hailed from the House Appropriations Committee—the committee responsible for spending our money. (Even today there remains widespread sentiment that there are actually three parties in Congress: Republicans, Democrats, and Appropriators.)

Whether Newt Gingrich precipitated polarization in American politics or was among the first to reflect it is a debate for the ages, but there is no doubt that his rise to leadership was a function of increased polarization.

Dick Armey was a strong Gingrich ally, and two years after Gingrich was elected whip Armey ran for chairman of the House Republican Conference against the sitting chairman, Jerry Lewis of California.

Armey's run was the natural outgrowth of a major fight in the summer of 1990 when Democratic congressional leaders and George H. W. Bush's White House met for a "budget summit" at Andrews Air Force base and agreed to "revenue enhancement measures," tax increases that broke the former president's famous pledge: "Read my lips: No New Taxes!"

Most everyone agreed it was a mistake, but there was a split among Republicans in Congress between those who agreed with the pundits in Washington that the mistake Bush made was making the pledge in the first place and the more renegade faction who felt the mistake was in breaking it.

Dick Armey was a leader of the renegades, and he drafted a "no new taxes" resolution to be adopted by the House Republican Conference. Getting a vote on a conference resolution—essentially a statement of policy—without the support of the leadership required getting fifty signatures.

Armey worked it hard, but Bob Michel didn't want members

to sign it, as he didn't want the conference to have to vote on a resolution that, if passed, would make it harder for them to vote on the House floor for a budget agreement supported by a Republican president.

Many thought Armey was breaking from the president in a very public and serious way. He was, but in his mind he was trying to save the president from breaking his promise, which Armey believed would prove damaging not only to the economy, but to the party.

There was little doubt how the voters felt—support for GOP Senate candidates, who were in a pretty strong position at that point, collapsed under their feet. Strong candidates like U.S. Representatives Lynn Martin of Illinois and Bill Schuette of Michigan dropped like rocks as Republican voters stayed home in droves that Election Day.

Dick Darman was the father of the backroom deal, and he came to personify the "pragmatic" wing of the Republican Party that the more conservative activists increasingly came to see as banishing the GOP to permanent minority status.

Armey's election as chairman of the House Republican Conference by four votes (two votes the other way would have resulted in the incumbent chairman remaining in his position—double Newt's winning margin!) in December 1992 was in indirect response to his having led the effort to pass a "no new taxes" resolution in the House Republican Conference during the "budget summit" of the previous cycle and in direct response to the election of Bill Clinton over former president Bush (also an indirect response to the new taxes enacted in violation of his pledge).

At President Bush's last White House Christmas party for members of Congress later that month, Dick Darman congratulated Dick Armey on being elected conference chairman.

"Thanks, Dick," Armey said. "I couldn't have done it without you. In fact, Bill Clinton and I are the only two guys in this town who owe our new jobs to you."

Clinton's victory in 1992 was unique in that a Democrat was elected president but Republicans picked up seats in the U.S. House. Armey's margin of victory as conference chairman had come by winning more than thirty of the forty-five new House Republicans elected that year. They had been impressed by a manual Armey prepared and distributed to each of them with specific guidance about how to set up their new offices, anticipate problems that plague every first-term member, and work effectively in the minority. (In contrast, Lewis sent each of them a booklet containing every current House Republican's Christmas card from 1992.)

Many members of the Class of '92 were reform-minded politicians who'd felt as much kinship to Ross Perot as to then-president Bush. This reflected the fact that the lion's share of Perot's 19 percent of the vote had come out of Bush's hide.

They were for term limits and balanced budgets, and against pork-barrel spending and U.N. command of American forces, a blend of modern conservatism and anti-Washington populism. They were the tip of the spear that would penetrate the Capitol two years later, when Republicans would gain fifty-two House seats in the historic election of 1994.

Every year, the members of the House Democratic Caucus and the House Republican Conference go on a "retreat" before the beginning of a new Congress to map out their respective strategies for the next two years. In 1991, the House Republicans had gathered at "Xerox University," the corporate conference center outside Princeton, New Jersey. (Peter Davidson of Dick Armey's conference staff joked that the motto of Xerox University was, "Where it's okay to copy!") In 1993 we opted instead for the much more spartan environs of Salisbury State University on Maryland's Eastern Shore.

One of the goals of the "Just Us Chickens" Group was to craft an appeal to the Perot voters of '92, to woo them (mostly back) into Republican ranks. (The "Just Us Chickens" Group was the name we gave to the rump group of the House leadership Gingrich and

Armey had started to subtly wrest control from House Minority Leader Bob Michel. The joke was that if somebody from Michel's office knocked on the door while we were secretly meeting to plot strategy and said, "Who's in there," our answer would be, "Just us chickens.") I had read a style section piece in the *Washington Times* about Frank Luntz, who had done polling for Ross Perot. Not long afterward, I was introduced to him at a holiday reception hosted by *National Review* magazine at the Willard Hotel. I asked him if he would be willing to share some of his data from the Perot campaign with the House Republican Conference, and he said he would.

I didn't know it then, but I was helping to create a media monster.

Luntz came to Salisbury and he stole the show. He began his presentation to the assembled Republican members of the United States House of Representatives by saying, "You don't know this, but people hate you." Some of the more senior members were completely offended by his remarks, but the more junior, and especially the newly elected members, were smitten.

Frank would later conduct one of the focus groups testing the Contract with America. He used that single task to essentially claim credit for its creation, and made a fortune selling politicians across the globe on the idea (thus was born the "Contract with Italy" and the "Contract with Mongolia").

It's unfortunate. A lot of people did a lot more work and had a lot more to do with its conception and development than Frank did, especially the members of the House Republican leadership and the candidates who signed the pledge. Frank is one of those consultants who believe that it's all about him, not the ideas or the candidates.

One of the reasons he was working for Perot in the first place was that Perot didn't have a stable of political professionals to call on. Frank was willing to abandon the party to help Perot hurt Bush 41. He was chastised in 1995 by the American Association of Public Opinion Research, for refusing to release the data behind his claim that every component of the Contract enjoyed the support of more than 60 percent of the public.

Focus groups are Frank's lifeblood. He loves them. He loves to probe people and dig out phrases from them. It is a legitimate skill, and he is very good at coming up with catchphrases. He is responsible for redubbing the estate tax the "death tax" (a fact everyone in Washington knows, because he made sure he was credited for it, instead of the members of Congress who actually repealed that egregious aspect of our tax code).

After the '92 presidential race, he didn't end up taking on many U.S. campaigns. By 1997, his clientele consisted largely of companies and interest groups that appreciated the fact that Luntz would provide their data and suggested wording that had "tested well in focus groups" to members of Congress.

With much fanfare, he announced in 1997 that he would no longer poll for political campaigns, citing disillusionment with politics, which elicited chuckles from pollsters who actually made their livings working on political campaigns.

One of those is Dave Sackett, a true professional who has guided many governors, senators, and congressmen to electoral victory. Upon hearing Frank's announcement, Dave announced that he was "giving up synchronized swimming."

At Salisbury State, the members and the staff stayed in dorm rooms with pressed-wood desks and cinder-block walls covered in thick white latex paint. The members broke into various issue working groups—budget, national security, crime, health care.

The seminal moment at the 1993 retreat was a heated debate over whether Republicans should put forward a budget of their own or just oppose Clinton's first budget. John Kasich, the energetic congressman from outside Columbus, Ohio, who was the top Republican on the House Budget Committee, wanted to put forward a detailed alternative to whatever Clinton proposed.

"I didn't come here to be against something," he'd say. "I came here to be for something."

It was a sentiment shared by most of his colleagues, but not all.

"It's their turn," Kansas Representative Pat Roberts responded to Kasich's call for a detailed alternative budget. "They won. They get to take responsibility. Let them explain how they're going to meet all his promises, without us distracting attention from it."

In the end, we put forward an alternative budget and Pat Roberts, as the ranking Republican on the House Agriculture Committee, supported it. With the whole House Republican Conference now invested in the idea that we had to have a positive agenda, the seeds for what would become the Contract with America had been sown.

In contrast to the 1994 congressional campaign and both Bush-Cheney campaigns, Senator Bob Dole's run for president in 1996 did not have a plan. It was plagued by "paralysis by analysis." They had enough data to choke a horse, but it ended up choking the campaign.

To be fair, Senator Dole's campaign was an uphill struggle to begin with, running as he was against an incumbent president in the midst of a booming economy and a peaceful environment (albeit one that masked the plotting that was going on in terrorist camps at the time).

But if the Dole team had a plan, I didn't know it, and if I didn't know it a lot of other people didn't know it, since I was the communications director for the Republican National Committee at the time.

When there's no plan, people substitute their own judgment, jockey for position, work against each other to promote their own, individual points of view. This was the case in both the Dole and Kerry presidential campaigns.

You not only need a plan, you need to get buy-in. The people responsible for executing the plan have to understand and accept it, and then the campaign's leaders have to impose it on everyone.

Timing is everything in politics.

Timing is everything in politics, and if you don't have a sense of when something is going to have the optimum impact, you won't end up maximizing it. The same policies Bush laid out in his September 2 convention speech could have been laid out in June and July, but they would not have had the same impact. Attacking Bowles before the primaries were over would not have had the same effect as it did after the primaries. Same policies, same attacks, different effects. Without a plan, your timing is not your own.

As a senator, Bob Dole had an impeccable sense of timing, as he demonstrated when the Clinton health care plan was working its way through Congress, and GOP House and Senate leaders were working to defeat it. Senator Helms had introduced a resolution rejecting the bill's linchpin policy of a federal mandate on all employers to provide health insurance.

In a meeting with Dole and other Senate GOP leaders, Gingrich and Armey and others from the House side were pushing for consideration of the Helms resolution. They were disappointed into silence when Dole cut them off, saying, "We can't pass the

Helms bill." But they smiled when, after about two beats, he added, "Now, if we give it another week . . ."

The elements of a strategic plan are fairly straightforward. You have to make some strategic assumptions. (Is time our friend or our enemy? Will we have more resources than our opponent, or less? Is intensity on our side, or theirs?) You have to honestly identify your strengths and your weaknesses, so you can emphasize the former and steer clear of the latter. You have to honestly identify your opponent's strengths and weaknesses. You have to identify your winning coalition. You have to sequence your steps and plot them out on the calendar and estimate a budget.

Doing these things enables you to execute a campaign on your own terms. Of course, one critical and often uncontrollable variable in all campaign plans is the candidate.

Nothing scared me more in the summer of 2004 than the constant pressing of the question, "If Kerry knew then what he knows now, how would he have voted on the war?"

"We don't know the answer to this question," I said at the Breakfast Club one morning. "What if he says, 'I'd have voted no'?"

My fear was that most Americans would agree that knowing what we know now, we wouldn't have invaded Iraq, and if Kerry said as much he'd be on the same side as a majority of Americans.

The flip side was that if he said "no," then his view was that Saddam should still be in power, and a majority of Americans remained firm in their belief that we were better off with Saddam out of power than in power. Perhaps more important, as Communications Director Nicole Wallace—a proponent of the tactic—pointed out, "We'd remind voters that the commander in chief doesn't get 'do overs.' "

But my concerns were irrelevant. This was Bush.

And this was his gut.

This was the box the president was in. He had concluded that, despite the Iraqi Survey Group's conclusion that there had not been stockpiles of weapons of mass destruction, invading Iraq and removing Saddam Hussein was still the right thing to do. As president, he didn't have the luxury of being for the war and against it at the same time.

But that's what Senator Kerry was getting away with, and President Bush had had enough of it. The media weren't pressing Kerry on the inherent contradiction of his positions, so the president figured he was going to have to do it himself.

He pressed over and over again until he smoked Kerry out.

As Kerry emerged from a photo-op in the Grand Canyon for his first press availability in five days, reporters repeated the president's insistent question and asked him what his answer was.

"Knowing what you know now, how would you have voted on the Iraq War Resolution?"

"Yes," Kerry said.

One word.

There it was. Despite all his criticism of the past month, he was still for the war.

In later accounts of this seminal give and take, Kerry campaign officials said that he had been out of cell phone and Black-Berry range during his time in the Grand Canyon, and there had not been an opportunity to prepare a more customary, nuanced answer to the yes or no question the president had been posing repeatedly for a week.

And that's the beauty of campaigns. All planning and polling aside, every once in a while the real nature of the candidates comes shining through. In this instance, the president's own instincts led him to pound away on one of the central issues of the campaign, violating one of the fundamental rules of politics—don't ask a question you don't already know the answer to.

And Kerry, incommunicado from his structured hierarchy, blurted out an answer. It's interesting to me, while making the point about the importance of planning in a campaign, that I end up noting that one of the most defining moments of the 2004 presidential race came down to unvarnished candidate against unvarnished candidate.

That's because, all planning and execution aside, in the end, candidates ultimately matter the most.

The Kerry campaign stands in sharp contrast to the Bush campaign's message discipline. As with any campaign, this is likely to reflect the nature of the candidate more than anything else. Senator Kerry has a history as a legislator of being "nuanced" on issues, and somewhat vague on his positions. This worked to his advantage when he sought to position himself as a "centrist Democrat" after securing his party's nomination. Despite Kerry's twenty years of a consistently liberal voting record, the media were able to cherry-pick enough statements and votes throughout the years to treat as legitimate the notion that the man the *National Journal* magazine ranked as the most liberal senator in the last session of Congress was somehow a centrist.

He also lacked any real personal mark on the legislative process. During his twenty years in the Senate, not a single bill had been passed in his name. He and his campaign attributed this to his incredible humility and his willingness to allow others to take credit for his work, but the fact is he was a legislative lightweight.

As we watched the Democratic primary unfold, the Bush-Cheney team figured there were four candidates in the field who had a chance to capture the nomination: Senators Kerry and John Edwards, Representative Dick Gephardt, and Governor Howard Dean.

Karl did a little, informal survey in the winter of 2003, and five of us thought Gephardt would be the nominee and four thought Dean. (President Bush was among the Gephardt speculators.) No one had guessed Kerry.

But we examined the policy and campaign histories of all four in depth, searching for clues of how to approach each should he be the nominee. The RNC research staff compiled voting records, news clips, and debate tapes. Edwards, Gephardt, and Dean were all pretty easy to get a handle on, but Kerry was enigmatic.

His voting record was liberal in the classic, Massachusetts Democrat sense, but it never felt to me as if I got to "know him." By the time he won the New Hampshire primary, however, I knew his voting record like the back of my hand.

As I sat in my basement watching him on the big-screen TV claim victory in the Wisconsin primary, he actually spoke to me. Literally.

"And so I say to George Bush, and Karl Rove, and Ed Gillespie, if you want to attack my record, I have three words for you: 'Bring it on!' "

I couldn't help but laugh.

"Oh, don't you worry," I thought. "We're gonna."

CHAPTER TWO

//

DEFINE OR BE DEFINED

The word the ancient Hebrews used for God was Yahweh, which translates to "that which cannot be named." They understood that if you can name something you can control it, and God was beyond their control.

The notion that if you can name something you can control it applies to politics today.

In naming John Kerry a flip-flopper, we controlled the race. Every time he was inconsistent or sought to move to the middle after twenty liberal years in the Senate, we hit him with the flip-flopper label. At the RNC, we had dolphin costumes made for college kids to wear at his public events. "Flipper" and "Flopper" would race back and forth and dance around at the back of Kerry rallies. Kerry even addressed them one time. "I see the dolphins are here today!" It drove him nuts.

In naming a rising lack of health insurance a "health care crisis," the Clintons controlled the debate over policy. Anyone who opposed their plan was against solving the "crisis." We finally defeated Hillary-care by defining it as "government-run health care."

And in naming Bob Dole "Newt Gingrich" in 1996, President Clinton controlled his re-election bid, by tying Gingrich's high negatives around the neck of the more popular Dole. (Democrats had spent a fortune driving up Gingrich's negatives, running ad after ad highlighting a careless statement he'd made that under GOP reforms, Medicare would "wither on the vine.")

If you can name something you can control it.

I have spent a lot of my time in politics naming things. I named the ten bills in the Contract with America—from the Tax Relief and Job Creation Act through the Personal Responsibility Act and the Common Sense Legal Reform Act. I wrapped the various policy proposals Elizabeth Dole had put forward throughout her campaign into "The Dole Plan for North Carolina," dubbed the Democrats' heated rhetoric in 2004 "political hate speech," and suggested President Bush call the difference between what John Kerry was proposing to spend and what the current budget called for a "tax gap."

"Define or be defined" is one of the most important rules in politics. As soon as John Kerry wrapped up his party's nomination for president, the Bush-Cheney team set about the process of defining him.

I gave a speech at the RNC Winter Meeting in which I laid out vote after vote John Kerry had cast as a United States senator against important weapons systems, but only after I acknowledged his service to our country in Vietnam.

The media were looking for us to somehow try to discredit Kerry's Vietnam service, but we believed that service deserved respect, and voters would rightly punish such a tactic. First of all, while President Bush's service in the Texas Air National Guard was honorable (and flying jets is not exactly risk-free duty), the president recognized that Kerry's service in Vietnam constituted a greater sacrifice. Second, while questions about his Purple Hearts had floated around his political career for decades, we had no reason to believe (and didn't seek any) that Senator Kerry had not earned them.

While we did not question the merit of his medals, the question of whether he actually threw them away in protest was a legitimate one.

On April 23, 1971, Vietnam Veterans Against the War staged a protest at the U.S. Capitol during which a number of veterans threw their medals over a chain-link fence. John Kerry was one of those who threw medals, but he admitted later in the course of a campaign that they were someone else's medals, not his own.

It struck us as revealing, and really stuck in the craw of Karen Hughes, an army brat whose father had been a major general in the United States Army.

"He threw somebody else's medals?" she asked in disbelief one morning on a conference call after reading a briefing book on his record. "How can you throw away somebody else's medals and pretend they're yours?"

It was a good question, but Kerry had an answer, which was that he'd never said they were his own medals. He said he couldn't help it if people had come to that conclusion on their own.

Except for one thing: He *had* said he'd thrown his own medals, and he'd said it in a 1971 interview on a Boston TV program.

And in April 2004, the crack research staff at the Republican National Committee found a tape of the thirty-three-year-old local broadcast.

RNC Research Director Tim Griffin and Communications Director Jim Dyke came into my office wielding the videotape one morning with big smiles on their faces. "You got time to watch something?" they asked.

It was a straight one-on-one interview on a small set, Kerry seated in a wooden armchair directly across from the interviewer, no table or anything between them.

"How many of your medals did you throw?"

"Seven, eight, nine medals."

There it was, plain as day, John Kerry claiming that the medals he'd thrown had been his own when in fact they were someone else's.

Why does it matter? Because he was a phony. He's free to do whatever he wants with his medals. They're his. But he's not free to pretend he threw them away in protest when he actually kept them.

"What do you want to do?" I asked.

"Kerry's doing TV this week," Dyke said. "I think we ought to shop it as an exclusive to the *Times* or the *Post* to get it in play and have him asked about it when he's on one of the morning shows."

It was a good plan, but neither the *Times,* where we shopped it first, nor the *Post,* where we shopped it after the *Times* said no, would take the story without attributing the RNC as a source.

Print reporters and their editors had gotten very touchy about sourcing in the aftermath of the Jayson Blair implosion at the *New York Times* the year before, and after a plagiarism scandal that resulted in heads rolling at the top of *USA Today* as well.

But this newfound standard of sourcing was frustrating. After all, this was a tape of a TV interview, not some surveillance tape from a private investigator. Stories are written all the time that don't identify who first pointed a reporter to something that is publicly available.

We refused to let them identify the RNC as the source of the tape. Instead, we provided it directly to ABC News in advance of a *Good Morning America* interview with Kerry. Anchor Charles Gibson aired the old footage, then asked Kerry about his claim to have thrown his medals.

Kerry was infuriated by the question, obviously embarrassed that his assertion that he'd never said he'd thrown away his own medals was now proved false. It was a sharp jab, and Kerry was very testy. The microphone was still live when he turned to aides after the interview and said, "God, they're doing the bidding of the Republican National Committee!"

It was a nice little hit, but then a strange thing happened. Howard Kurtz from the *Washington Post* called Dyke and said he had sources in the media who said that the video that aired on *Good Morning America* had been supplied to ABC News by the Republican National Committee.

Unbelievably, reporters who had declined the offer of exclusivity because we wouldn't allow them to source it were now going on background themselves to say they had been offered the tape!

In twenty years in the business, I'd never experienced anything like it. Like most Republicans, I hate the media, but I happen to like reporters. This was appalling to me, and it was my first indication that in 2004, the press was going to play by a different set of rules.

I call the major media outlets "the referees," because not only are they the arbiters of what warrants coverage, but they often assume for themselves the role of determining which political attacks are fair or unfair. Shopping video of an interview that had aired on television that clearly shows a presidential candidate misleading the public about actions he considered one of his qualifications for the presidency is completely within the bounds of fair play, but they were blowing the whistle not on Kerry for his blatant inconsistency, but on us for seeking to make it a story.

There were other double standards on display throughout the campaign, but none so stark as the treatment of the so-called "527s," those political organizations apart from the parties and the campaigns that were free to spend unregulated "soft money" on behalf of or against a candidate.

By May, 527s opposing the president, fueled by tens of millions of dollars from liberal financier George Soros and others, had spent more than $100 million against him. Our interpretation of the law was that such expenditures were illegal, and on May 5 we filed a complaint with the Federal Election Commission making our case.

Two weeks later, the FEC gave the 527s a green light, and Republican-leaning organizations soon entered the fray. It was at this point the pundits began to thunder in righteous indignation, especially after the Swift Boat Veterans for Truth aired their first ad in August.

Over $100 million in soft money had been spent attacking

the president by groups like MoveOn.org, the Media Fund, and Americans Coming Together with nary a peep from the media, but when the Swifties spent a couple hundred thousand dollars, news organizations suddenly remembered how bad soft money was.

The media were pressing President Bush to single out the Swift Boat Veterans for censure, pressing the White House and the campaign day after day to rebuke the anti-Kerry 527 for its ad. The media wanted to define Swift Boat Veterans for Truth as beyond the pale, outside the acceptable limits of political discourse. When Senator John McCain repudiated them, it only added fuel to the fire.

But there was no way we were going to rebuke them. First of all, in the same way we were unwilling to question Senator Kerry and his allies over their right to speak out about his Vietnam service, we were unwilling to question John O'Neill and his friends' right to speak out about their different view of it. This wasn't about who was right and who was wrong. Kerry and his supporters had placed Vietnam front and center in this election, and they couldn't assume that only the people who shared his assessment of the war and his actions in it were free to speak out.

Second, we would have been weasels. After months of assaults by 527s against President Bush had gone virtually without comment by the media—or the Kerry camp—for us to weigh in now against a group that was attacking Kerry would have dispirited Bush supporters. I don't know if that was the intent of the media as they pressed their case, but it certainly would have been the effect, and John Kerry had not been exposed to days and days of questions about whether he approved of the ads that had been run against the president.

This prompted me to circulate "The Rules" to the Breakfast Club:

1. Soft money in support of Democratic candidates is free speech. Soft money in support of Republican candidates corrupts the process.

2. Many Democrats are allowed to vote two or three times per election. Any Republican who objects to this is engaged in voter intimidation.

3. Calling a Republican president or vice president a "cheap thug," a "killer," a "liar," or a "coward" is debate. Citing a Democratic nominee's vote for higher taxes is a negative personal attack.

4. Government employee unions, radical environmentalists, and proabortion groups are public interest advocates. Small business owners, Second Amendment rights supporters, and prolife organizations are "right-wing groups" or special interests.

5. To repeat a Democrat's own statement is to distort his position.

6. Anything any conservative activist anywhere in the country says may be attributed to "the Republicans." Liberal activists speak for themselves, not the Democratic Party.

7. Michael Moore is to be taken seriously. (Seriously.)

8. Joe Wilson, too.

9. Cutting billions of dollars from intelligence agency funding is patriotism. Don't question anyone's patriotism.

10. Reporters who cheer a presidential candidate wildly at their association meeting will set aside those personal feelings when they return to work the next day, and will cover both campaigns objectively.

The Joe Wilson referenced in Rule 8 is the former ambassador who ignited the controversy over the president's line in the 2002 State of the Union Address that Iraq sought to purchase uranium from Niger.

Apparently, in the course of seeking to undermine his credibility, an administration official told columnist Bob Novak that Wilson was given the assignment of looking into the yellow cake matter because his wife, who worked at the CIA, suggested it.

Wilson's wife, Valerie Plame, not only worked at the CIA, but was an undercover operative. Since knowingly disclosing the identity of an undercover operative is a crime, an investigation was begun.

"I want to see Karl Rove frog-marched out of the White House," Wilson said at the time, charging someone with a crime with no evidence to back it up.

Wilson became omnipresent in the media, milking his self-perceived victimhood for all it was worth and becoming a cult hero to the left. He made charge after charge against the president and the administration. As party chairman, I would point out his history of contributing to Democrats, making the point that he was not as objectively nonpartisan as people might think.

One day I walked into the Green Room at MSNBC's studios at 400 North Capitol Street, and Wilson was sitting there. I sat down across from him and called into a radio show that had already been scheduled, and with him less than two feet from me began pointing out to the host Wilson's donor history with Democrats while he sat and fumed. It was fun.

"Is he not allowed to contribute to candidates," I was asked.

"Of course he is, and I'm allowed to inform your listeners of the fact."

"But he also gave to former president Bush."

"That doesn't make him any less political," I said. "It just means he changed sides."

On another show, I noted that "we are all influenced by our political preferences. I know I'm more likely to give the benefit of the doubt to my Republican friends and tend to be more skeptical of Democrats. It's just human nature."

Wilson later went on to serve as an advisor to the Kerry campaign, and sent out an email solicitation for campaign funds.

The Senate Intelligence Committee issued a bipartisan report in the summer of 2004 that unanimously rejected every charge Joe Wilson made, but you could hardly find it reported anywhere. Reams of newsprint had been dedicated to his charges, and in the month of July you could hardly turn on your television set without seeing him spouting off, but when Democrats and Republicans alike concluded that his charges were essentially made up out of whole cloth, the media did not find it worthy of reporting.

On the July 18 broadcast of *Face the Nation* with host Bob Schieffer, I pointed this out, saying:

"We just talked about the Senate Intelligence Committee report, which found that Joe Wilson, who led the attack against the vice president and the president for the—more than a year has been entirely discredited in bipartisan fashion, by the way, unanimously by the Democrats and Republicans on the Senate Intelligence Committee. They found that he fabricated stories, that he talked about seeing documents that he never even saw. He says that he used a little "literary flair." Pretty serious business to be using a little literary flair about. He said he misspoke when talking to the *Washington Post*.

"He was on this program, Bob; and in fact, CBS News itself, on thirty different occasions, has reported on his allegations, fifteen of him on camera, including this program, and yet at some point I think it would be helpful to have the viewers informed—and I've got the Senate Intelligence Committee report here—that he has completely been repudiated and let them know that those thirty reports, the fifteen times he was on camera he was basically making stuff up."

Bob Schieffer, one of the longest-serving and shrewdest hosts in the business, deftly deflected the direct challenge to CBS News, turning to my counterpart DNC Chairman Terry McAuliffe with a simple, "Do you think that's right?"

At which point McAuliffe didn't exactly stand by Wilson, saying: "I'll let Joe Wilson speak for himself. I saw the editorial he wrote yesterday in the *Washington Post*. He wrote a six-page letter to the Senate Intelligence Committee, so you know, I'll let Joe Wilson speak for himself . . ."

I interjected, "But the Kerry campaign is letting him speak for them. He is an advisor to the Kerry campaign and they continue to post his now-repudiated allegations on their website."

My public plea for setting the record straight on Wilson's charges fell on deaf ears. Very few stories were aired about the Senate Intelligence Committee's utter repudiation of Wilson's charges.

One of the biggest mistakes made during the course of the campaign was saying that the charge that Iraq was seeking to purchase uranium from Niger was a mistake. The fact is, what the president said in the State of the Union Address, "The British government has learned that Saddam Hussein recently sought significant quantities of uranium from Africa," was true. And what did he get for saying the line was wrong? Did those in the media or the Democrats who were so critical respond by saying, "Well, now that you've acknowledged that we'll just move on." Of course not. They treated that concession as proof that everything else the president said was wrong.

There is little margin in politics today for conceding a mistake. It's better to just bear down and press forward or change the subject entirely, especially if you're a Republican. When former Clinton national security advisor Sandy Berger admitted that, while serving as a policy advisor to Senator Kerry (whom many expected would have made Berger secretary of state if he'd won), he had not only stolen sensitive documents from the National Archives, but cut them to bits with scissors, it was treated with virtual indifference by the *New York Times*.

Now just think for a moment if Condoleeza Rice had committed the same crime. Think the *New York Times* might have played it a little differently?

Republicans are increasingly coming to view the media as little different from a special interest group. Responding to questions from reporters at the *New York Times* or the *Washington Post* is a little like responding to questionnaires from the League of Conservation Voters or the AFL-CIO. You can respond however you want, but in the end you're probably going to get screwed. They have their own agenda, and it's generally not a Republican one.

At the same time, the Republican National Committee is increasingly becoming its own media outlet. It has a quarterly magazine that goes to more than five hundred thousand donors and activists, an email list of over 15 million people, a website that gets between fifteen thousand and fifty thousand hits every day, and its chairman and spokespeople are constant guests on talk radio and the 24/7 cable networks. This allows the party to communicate directly with voters in a way not possible only ten years ago and helps bypass the hurdles constructed by the old media.

The rise of independent bloggers was an important factor in the 2004 elections. I'll never forget the first time I heard that the National Guard documents that were reported on CBS News's *60 Minutes* might be fakes. I was in Arkansas at an event when RNC Research Director Tim Griffin told me he'd heard from another reporter that they thought the documents were forgeries.

The forged documents are famous for having ended CBS News Anchor Dan Rather's career in embarrassment. They purported to show that a young George W. Bush had not fulfilled his commitment to the National Guard, but it turns out they were fake, and experts had questions about their authenticity before CBS aired the program. It seemed then and still feels now that the notoriously liberal network news outlet was seeking to influence the outcome of the election with a much-hyped late hit. Fortunately, it backfired because some eagle-eyed bloggers caught them in the act.

The fact is, bloggers, email, and talk radio sustained the Bush-Cheney campaign in the final thirty days of the 2004 election. If it had not been for the alternative media providing accurate information that was often at odds with the mainstream media (the MSM, as we've come to call it), John Kerry probably would have been elected president.

On October 17, there was this fascinating exchange on CNN's *Reliable Sources* program between host Howard Kurtz and *Newsweek* editor Evan Thomas:

CNN'S HOWARD KURTZ: It is a tight race. Do you believe that most reporters want John Kerry to win?

NEWSWEEK'S EVAN THOMAS: Yeah, absolutely.

KURTZ: Do you think they're deliberately tilting their coverage to help John Kerry and John Edwards?

THOMAS: Not really.

KURTZ: Subconsciously tilting their coverage?

THOMAS: Maybe.

KURTZ: Maybe.

THOMAS: Maybe.

KURTZ: Including at *Newsweek?*

THOMAS: Yeah.

KURTZ: You've said on the program *Inside Washington* that because of the portrayal of Kerry and Edwards as young and optimistic, that's worth maybe fifteen points. That would suggest.

THOMAS: Stupid thing to say. It was completely wrong. I do think that the mainstream press, I'm not talking about the blogs and Rush and all that, but the mainstream press favors Kerry. I don't think it's worth fifteen points. That was just a stupid thing to say.

KURTZ: Is it worth five?

THOMAS: Maybe, maybe.

I highlighted this in a memo to fellow Republicans and went on to warn them that we needed to be prepared to offset the impact of such bias:

> Anyone who has seen the coverage of the presidential campaign over the past month knows there is no "maybe" about it, the so-called "mainstream media" are doing all they can to help elect John Kerry, and over the next two weeks it

will reach a crescendo. You will play an important part of helping to get accurate information out to your friends and neighbors to offset the impact of their efforts, subconsciously or not, to add five-to-fifteen points (worth about 5-to-20 million votes) to Senator Kerry's tally.

In head-to-head polls since the debate, the President has opened up a two-to-eight point lead, but if you listen to the pundits, watch the television news or read your newspaper you get a different opinion.

On the same day *The New York Times* endorsed Senator Kerry, its magazine ran a cover story hit piece by Ron Suskind, a registered Democrat with a history of inaccurate reporting based on the same kind of rumors that were used in August's front page story speculating that Vice President Cheney wouldn't be on the ticket in the Fall.

Mike Allen, who covers the President and his campaign for the *Washington Post,* said in an online chat on Friday, "The mood is like a long car ride home from a tiring trip. Yes, the President and Mr. Rove both love surprises. Reporters would not be shocked if Osama Bin Laden turned up, or a cache of ugly stuff in Iraq was found."

An important reporter for the *Washington Post* actually believes that the President of the United States could— and worse, would—deliberately hold back the capture of someone whose capture is a national security priority in order to enhance its political impact.

And it's not just what you read.

A recent memo from the ABC News's Political Director told reporters, "Kerry distorts, takes out of context, and mistakes all the time, but these are not central to his efforts to win. . . . We have a responsibility to hold both sides accountable to the public interest, but that doesn't mean we reflexively and artificially hold both sides 'equally' accountable when the facts don't warrant that."

An assumption in black-and-white that distortion is central to President Bush's re-election, and a directive to not hold both sides "equally accountable."

NBC "political analyst" Chris Matthews, a strong Democrat, can not even hide his disdain for the President and Vice President and his support for Senator Kerry, and consistently takes sides.

And who can forget the CBS memos. While they have apologized for their mistake they never retracted their story, and the producer responsible for providing opposition research to the Kerry campaign remains in a news gathering and reporting capacity at the network.

Taken exclusively we might chalk these incidents up to bad judgment but taken collectively only a fool would not be concerned about media coverage in the final two weeks of this campaign.

So don't be surprised.

The Kerry campaign's political calculation relies on the media to report their baseless attacks and misrepresentations on Social Security, the draft, the flu vaccine, voter intimidation or whatever other headline of the day. They report the Kerry campaign accusations as "fact" and the Bush campaigns response as "denials."

We must remain vigilant and hold the press accountable because they have made clear they are not an objective third party but a participant with unvarnished opinions that are appearing on the pages of newspapers, magazines and television news nationwide.

So forward this email to your friends, family, co-workers and make sure they know to keep an eye out for the Kerry campaign political rhetoric in whatever forms it may appear.

Evan Thomas was right. The "journalists" at *60 Minutes* seemed to take it upon themselves to affect the outcome of the election, running the discredited Texas Air National Guard Story and reporting the flawed "missing munitions" story at the end of the campaign. The MSM was worth between five and fifteen percentage points to Kerry, but fortunately our ability to communicate around them in the world of the new media mitigated their impact.

Problems with the MSM continued through Election Day, and culminated with their errant exit polling data. Around 2:00 P.M., I began to get calls from friends and others around town despondent over reports of early exit polls. I got the following email from Sara Taylor at the Bush campaign.

RESULTS SO FAR—EXTREMELY PRELIMINARY—

POTUS (Bush/Kerry)

OH	49/50 (heavily female)
FL	49/50
VA	52/47
WI	48/51 (heavily female)
CT	40/59
IA	45/53
WV	54/45
MI	47/51
AR	54/45
MN	44/54

Senate (GOP/Dem)

FL	48/51
SC	51/47 (heavily female)
NC	52/47
SD	52/48 (slightly R sample)
KY	51/49

It was a punch in the stomach, and it was completely at odds with our take on the state of the campaign. Late afternoon the day before, I'd had the following email exchange with Karl Rove.

> **ME**: How you feelin'?
> **ROVE**: Good but hate all the bouncing around in the public polls, esp on FL
> **ME**: me too. Feel like we're flying blind in a lot of ways.
> **ROVE**: Okay—here it is from a rational perspective. In Mel's tracking, up 4. [Mel Martinez ran for and won the open U.S. Senate seat in Florida that had been vacated by retiring Democratic senator Bob Graham.] In NRSC, up 6. In ours, up 5 on Saturday. So when looking at the public polls, what should we think FL is?
> **ME**: I'm guessing 5.
> **ROVE**: Then we win FL and OH and the election.
> **ME**: we get 286 EVs. I feel better about FL than OH—I am recalibrating my pop vote to 51–48.
> **ROVE**: You are now where I am—all we won last time except (maybe) NH but plus IA and NM. Same as you on EVs and popular.

As it turns out, our analysis was dead-on. The president won the popular vote 51–48, got 286 Electoral College votes, Ohio was closer than Florida, we carried every state we did in 2000 except New Hampshire and won Iowa and New Mexico, which we'd lost in 2000. But at 3:00 PM on Election Day, we were doubting our predictions.

Most voters didn't have any idea, but many in the media and many of the people in the campaigns they covered assumed Senator John Kerry was going to defeat President George Bush, and it affected the tone of both the media and the campaigns for much of the day.

Exit polling information is important enough that both parties would pay for it themselves if the networks didn't. For the past three cycles, early exit data have been wildly inaccurate—and skewed against Republicans in every instance, making us scramble to offset any dampening effect on our voters.

The networks should cover elections, not participate in them. The premature calling of Florida for Al Gore based on exit polls before the polls had even closed in the state's (heavily Republican) Panhandle directly affected the 2000 election. The networks should abandon the practice of exit polling entirely.

If they insist on continuing it, they should enter into contracts that require their polling vendors to withhold all data until every last voting booth in America has closed so online reports and on-air body language cannot affect voter turnout. The data are only relevant in their complete form, so there is no negative journalistic impact from withholding early exits from the networks themselves.

Even with the growing importance of alternative media, if you're in national politics you have to be able to deal with reporters and the mainstream media, and there are some important lessons about how to do that.

The more you get, the more you get.

The more money you raise, the easier it is to raise more money. The more volunteers you recruit, the easier it is to recruit more volunteers. And the more press interest you generate, the more interested the press becomes in you.

I first learned this lesson working for Dick Armey. When I went to work for him, he was in his first month in office, having upset a one-term incumbent Democrat in the Reagan landslide year of 1984.

He had been an economics professor at the University of North Texas before running for Congress as a virtual unknown. Legend has it he was watching the House of Representatives on C-SPAN one night and turned to his wife Susan and said, "Honey, these people are idiots."

To which she replied, "Yep. You could be one of them."

Over twenty years later, I still don't know if that's a true story or falls into the category of what my family calls "Irish truth"—that is, so good it ought to be true.

Armey liked to point out that in the first poll taken for him in Texas' Twenty-sixth Congressional District, he had "2 percent name ID with a 5 percent margin of error," adding, "I came back from that meeting and asked my kids if they knew who I was."

He ran a classic anti-Washington, anti-Congress outsider's campaign, tapping the frustration of voters in a North Texas district teeming with new arrivals in search of high-tech jobs and escaping the high taxes of the industrial Midwest and decaying Northeast.

He hired me sight unseen. I interviewed with Denis Calabrese, his chief of staff, and Kerry Knott, his legislative director. I wanted to be a press secretary because I liked shaping message and working with reporters. I had been hoping that my current boss, Andy Ireland, would make me his press secretary. A little more than a month after the 1984 election, he had brought me back to Washington as a legislative assistant, and shortly after that his press secretary left. I expressed my interest to his chief of staff, with whom I had become pretty close.

I was young to be a press secretary for a five-term member of the House, but felt I had proven my acumen in the campaign. On top of that, I knew Ireland and knew the district and its issues, so there wouldn't be a learning curve. And I had proven my loyalty.

One Monday morning I walked into our staff meeting and

saw a new face, who was introduced to us as Mike Thomas, the congressman's new press secretary. I sat through the rest of the staff meeting in stunned silence, listening to Mike tell us a little about himself before we ran down the issues on the floor that week and the vote recommendations we would make to the congressman.

I've never known why I came to learn of the new hire this way, why I wasn't told privately beforehand that I didn't get the job I wanted, and I never said a word to Ireland or his chief of staff about it. I just kept my head down and performed my duties, but I didn't feel guilty about looking for a press secretary opening in another office.

As part of my job, I helped educate Mike about Ireland's congressional district, including the media that I understood so well from their coverage of the campaign. He gravitated more and more toward me in the process, and eventually found out that he was in the job I wanted. Mike Thomas turned out to be a good guy, and when he learned the circumstances of his acing me out for the job he was in, he felt bad. In working with me, he felt I would make a good press secretary. On the QT, he introduced me to his wife, Deborah, who had just been hired as office manager to the newly elected Armey. She, in turn, put me in touch with his chief of staff, Denis Calabrese.

Calabrese offered me the press secretary position before I ever met Armey. I got a call from him late one afternoon asking if I was free to come by and meet the congressman I had already agreed to work for, so at around 6:30, after the Andy Ireland office had vacated for the evening, I walked through the tunnel from the Rayburn Building to the top floor of the Cannon Building to meet my new boss.

Armey had essentially brought his entire campaign staff from Texas with him to Washington despite their wholesale lack of congressional experience. There was only one exception—David Hobbs, who had worked as a legislative assistant for Houston congressman Bill Archer.

I sat outside Armey's personal office as he finished a meeting with Calabrese, who eventually opened the door and invited me in. Dick Armey remained seated behind his desk as Calabrese introduced the brand-new congressman to his brand-new press secretary.

"Nice to meet you, sir," I said.

"I understand you're one of them assholes that works for Congress," Armey said, in my first exposure to his deep, gravelly voice and irreverent sense of humor.

"Yes sir," I replied. "And I'm proud to be one of your assholes now." This was the beginning of a ten-year working relationship and a friendship that lasts to this day.

The funny thing is, I had also interviewed with another freshman congressman from Texas, Mac Sweeney. Sweeney was a young, handsome congressman from Victoria, Texas, who'd served in the Reagan White House. The Texas media saw him as a rising star, the savviest of the "Texas Six Pack," the six Republicans who'd been elected in the wake of Reagan's massive win in the state. Armey was viewed as a novice, or worse, an oddity, too academic to be politically effective over the long term.

Before accepting the offer from Armey, I called over to Sweeney's office to tell them I had received another offer and would accept it unless Sweeney wanted me to work for him. I have thanked God ever since that they never called me back, and I ended up working for my second choice. The media assessments proved wrong. Armey rose to be the first Republican majority leader in the House in four decades, and Sweeney lost his seat in the very next election.

I was twenty-three and a congressional press secretary, a job I had never even dreamed possible for me. I remember staring at my new business cards, excited by the words "press secretary."

And it was exciting from day one. Literally. On my very first day in the job, I got a call late in the afternoon from an Associated Press reporter wanting to know why Armey had voted against a bill that had just passed the House.

I told him I was unfamiliar with the legislation and the congressman's reasoning, but would find out and call him back. Though new to the job, I was struck that an AP reporter would be calling, and wondered if this was maybe routine for the Texas delegation.

"Just out of curiousity," I said, "why are you asking why he voted that way?"

"Don't you know?" he asked. "The vote was 418–1."

"Uh-huh. And I take it Armey was the one?"

"Yep."

In Literature 101 it's what's known as "foreshadowing." From my first day working for him through my last, ten years later, Dick Armey was at the center of a lot of news, a lot of fights, and a lot of controversy.

Having cast his lone vote against "The Whistleblower's Protection Act of 1985," introduced by Representative Patricia Schroeder (D-CO), Armey caught the attention of the media, both in Texas and nationally. The bill provided a financial incentive to government workers who blew the whistle on fraudulent actions by their superiors that cost taxpayers money. There had been an extensive internal debate over the bill the night before (a debate I was not privy to since I was not yet on the staff), with no uniform recommendation on how Armey should vote.

On the subway on the way in to the office that day, Armey weighed the pros and cons of the bill in his mind, ultimately deciding that it was wrong to reward employees with a bonus for doing the job they were supposed to be doing in the first place. When the time for the vote came, he cast his "nay" and walked away—probably somewhere to grab a quick cigarette (during the campaign, he'd reverted to the habit he'd successfully abandoned in order to train for the seven marathons he'd completed).

Ordinarily, members "check the board" before casting their votes, looking up at the electronic listing of all House members marked by a green dot (yea) or a red dot (nay) to see how their colleagues are voting. Some simply look to see where the representative in the district next door has voted, or how their party's whip has voted, before casting their own, identical vote.

But Armey was new, and he weighed each vote on its own merits, based on his own staff's recommendation. He trusted them more than he trusted his fellow elected representatives, often saying, "I hire people who are more like me than me."

So he voted no on what every one of his colleagues considered a "no-brainer." The media were curious about why, and then ultimately impressed by the depth of his reasoning and his articulate explanation of his vote. And they liked the guts of someone less than two months in the job willing to be a lone vote against his colleagues.

"An Armey of One," Charles Osgood dubbed him on his *Osgood File* national radio program, probably the only such broadcast that year to feature a first-term member of the minority party.

It wasn't all positive. Democrats tried to dub him "Dr. No" for his votes against the bills they scheduled, and we did bow somewhat to reality in instituting a "five-vote" rule, which said if there were fewer than five votes against a bill Armey probably should not be one of them again.

By the beginning of the second year of his first term in office, Armey had made a decision that would bring him some measure of fame. Tired of paying seven hundred dollars per month (in 1985 dollars) for an Arlington, Virginia, apartment in which he spent only about eight nights a month, he decided to start sleeping in one of the small rooms in the House Gymnasium on the nights he was in town.

The House generally begins voting on Tuesdays after 5:00 PM, and ends Thursdays by 6:00 PM so most members can fly in Tuesday morning and fly home Thursday evening. At some point, it became the norm for members to keep their families back home, lest they be accused of "going native," and now a majority are part of what used to be called the "Tuesday-Thursday club," those members who are only in town on days the House is in session.

One of the perverse effects of this is an increased breakdown in civility. In the old days, the children of members of Congress went to the same schools and their families came to know one another. Democrats and Republicans alike would spend some time together over weekends. Now they only spend extended periods together on travel to foreign countries, and even those have been curtailed because the media treat them as "junkets." The decreased opportunities for socializing have correlated with a decrease in civility in the House. This is less the case in the Senate, which operates on a Monday-through-Friday schedule, with more whole weeks taken off (and more foreign travel).

In Armey's case, the decision to abandon his Crystal City, Virginia, apartment was an economic one. Having been in academia all his adult life, he needed every bit of the eighty-four hundred dollars annually to save for his five children's college costs. So he would wander down to the gym in the basement of the Rayburn House Office Building around ten every night after changing in his office from his business suit to a running suit. The gym had a number of small enclosed cubicles where members would sometimes go to lie down, and Armey simply claimed one as his own on the nights he was in town. He'd shower in the gym in the morning and return to his office around 7:00 AM to change back into a suit that hung in the closet of his office.

When word got out that a congressman was sleeping on a sofa in the House Gym, it became an object of intense media interest. Armey wasn't the only one who engaged in the practice, but he was the only one naïve enough to publicly talk about it.

I say naïve because it rankled the powers that be. Once it became known, we played it up, using it to reinforce the perception of Armey as an outsider uninterested in having a place in Washington, D.C. It was a net positive in his contrarian congressional district, but it did not help him in Washington.

The Democratic leadership, especially House Majority Leader Jim Wright of neighboring Fort Worth—and many in the Republican leadership as well—didn't like the fact that Armey was publicizing the existence of a House Gym. Gym membership doesn't seem extreme by today's standards at all, and many Americans would see it as a positive, understanding that it is in the public interest for their elected representatives to stay physically fit in the course of a job that requires long hours and constant travel.

Twenty years ago, however, it fit into an anti-Washington storyline of the perks of a spoiled governing class, along with "junkets" and speaking fees and free, premium reserved parking spaces at National Airport. On top of that, many of Armey's colleagues thought the footage of him trekking from his office in Cannon to the gym in Rayburn in his sweatsuit was unbecoming a member of the United States House of Representatives.

The combination of his good looks (think of a heavier Dean Martin), his Ph.D. in economics, his quotable speaking style, and his "quirkiness" à la sleeping in the gym made Armey a bit of a media darling for a freshman in the minority, tapping into and being tapped into by the burgeoning 24/7 media culture, helping to fill the need for content (and controversy) of the sprouting cable news shows.

As a new press secretary for a new member, I was fascinated by the fact that every time Armey went on a show, it seemed to spur an invitation from another show. Money may be the mother's milk of modern politics, but media exposure is a sweet nectar. It was then that I realized that when it came to getting press, the more you get the more you get.

With the proliferation of national and regional cable networks, this is even truer today than it was then, to the point where junior members of congress can get national exposure. Representatives J. D. Hayworth (R-AZ), Tom Cole (R-OK), Harold Ford, Jr., and Rahm Emmanuel (D-IL) all but double as on-air commentators.

It's a far cry from the days when "young turk" members like Representative John Leboutillier (R-NY) were excoriated by their colleagues for grandstanding. Newt Gingrich was the first to under-stand the impact of the new media in shaping Congress, urging junior members of the minority party to try to affect the policy debate on C-SPAN, which had moved the House floor into the living rooms of America.

> **Convincing a reporter to write a positive story is a lot easier than convincing one not to write a negative story.**

The corollary to "the more you get the more you get" is my belief that any decent press secretary can get his boss into the paper, but it takes a really good one to keep him out sometimes.

Negative press is the bane of everyone who has ever run for office. The media are simply drawn to bad news, finding it much more interesting than positive stories. There's an old saying that goes, "No news is good news." I think newspaper and network assignment editors have their own saying: "Good news is no news."

Negative stories require "tracking," working with the reporter as he or she follows leads, getting reports from sources about where they're heading. The traditional trajectory of such a story is the reporter gets on to something, begins "gathering string" and building a storyline. It culminates with the one-on-one interview with the subject of the story, where data points are presented for comment and quotations from often anonymous sources are presented for reaction.

Once a reporter and his editor get it into their heads they're going to do a major piece with a negative slant, it's hard to convince them otherwise. If you can effectively refute their premise with data or credible sources, fair reporters will drop a story or at least include your viewpoint to make the story more fair.

When it was reported that Enron CEO Ken Lay had called

Commerce Secretary Donald Evans seeking government intervention in the days preceding an expected downgrading of Enron's bond rating, many in the media assumed I had arranged the call. My firm represented Enron and I was friendly with the secretary, having worked for him in the 2000 campaign and briefly at the Commerce Department helping to set up his communications shop.

But I wasn't even aware of the call. A number of reporters asked about it, and I told them I had nothing to do with it. When they were able to confirm that fact through Enron and the Department of Commerce, they dropped it. They didn't, however, drop the story, which I had also encouraged them to do, noting that I thought the whole thing had been blown out of proportion since it wasn't out of the ordinary for the commerce secretary to take a call from a major CEO (and at the time Evans took the call, no one was aware of the magnitude of Enron's problems or the fraud involved). And the fact is the secretary told Lay no—so what's the story? But by the time this story was being written, the media were in a feeding frenzy over anything related to Enron.

There's a big difference between taking a call and making a call. Evans had taken a call, but he didn't make the call that was asked of him. End of story.

If it's hard to dissuade a news organization from airing a story, it's even harder to get one to admit a mistake on the air. It requires careful documentation, as evidenced by my experience with the *Today* show concerning a story about reaction to the first Bush-Cheney campaign ad of the 2004 election. The ad included a fleeting image of firefighters removing a victim of the September 11 attacks from the wreckage of the World Trade Center.

While in New York City's Washington Heights neighborhood for a press conference touting our voter registration efforts in the

Hispanic community, I was asked about objections to the ad that had been raised by some of the victims' families. I noted that I respect the views of all the families, but pointed out that not all of them objected, and in fact, in at least one instance those who did were part of organized opposition to the president's re-election.

This was a reference to a press conference that had been held only the day before, organized with the help of MoveOn.org, one of the 527s seeking to defeat President Bush. On the *Today* show the following day, however, my comment was wrongly portrayed as directed at all the families who had expressed concerns about the imagery.

I was upset by this, because it made me seem callous in the first instance and pretty slimy in the second, seeming to attack as politically motivated the legitimate concerns of family members of 9/11 victims.

I spoke with Tim Russert, Washington bureau chief of NBC News, someone I have dealt with for years and for whom I have a great deal of respect as a tough but fair journalist. He is also one who, having been on my side of the business at one point, understands the importance of one's reputation for honesty.

After our discussion, I told him I was going to put my concerns in writing so he could weigh them and share them with others in the organization. I also made clear that while I was not making my concerns publicly known at this time, I would be willing to do so and to let the public judge whether the reporting on the *Today* show had been fair or not.

This is the text of the letter I faxed to NBC:

March 12, 2004

This is to request in writing that the *Today* show publicly clarify its misleading reporting on my comments about the views of families of September 11 victims, as broadcast on Tuesday, March 10, 2004.

Norah O'Donnell's lead-in, "Now the chairman of the Republican Party claims the 9/11 families who objected to the ads are part of an organized anti-Bush coalition," gives viewers the false impression that my comments were directed at all such families who have expressed concerns about imagery in the Bush-Cheney leadership ad, when in fact they were specific to those families involved in the group "September 11 Families for Peaceful Tomorrows."

Since the reporter who aired this inaccurate account was not present at the event where I made my comments, I am providing you a videotape and transcript of the press conference exchange about the issue.

The relevant excerpt follows: "I think it's important to note, as I know one of the papers did here today, that the families that have raised concerns about this do not, are not representative, of all the families of the victims of September 11, and in fact actually are a small segment of that—those that are very anti-war, not only anti-war in Iraq, but were opposed to the military removal of the Taliban from Afghanistan. The press conference they held was sponsored and organized by MoveOn.org, an organization dedicated to defeating the President in his re-election, they put it together, and they are running ads themselves right now trying to defeat the President. So, it's not a surprise that they would bring in political allies in this regard."

Note that I begin by citing a story "one of the papers did here today," a reference to the March 9 *New York Post* editorial (enclosure) about "September 11 Families for Peaceful Tomorrows." I also cite "the press conference they held," which was organized by MoveOn.org—a clear and direct reference to the Peaceful Tomorrow's press conference of March 5, as anyone covering this story would know.

Indeed, when I made the point to Ms. O'Donnell that she should have noted that these remarks were specific to the

Peaceful Tomorrows group and that she should have gone to
them to respond rather than Ms. Kristen Breitweiser, Ms.
O'Donnell told me that Ms. Breitweiser was a member of
Peaceful Tomorrows and that is why she put her on camera.

One, despite her saying this, the context of Peaceful
Tomorrows was absent from the coverage, and two, Ms.
Breitweiser is not a member of that group. These are
egregious errors.

Ms. O'Donnell's acknowledgment that they sought a
member of Peaceful Tomorrows to respond to my comments
is clear indication that she knew I was referring to them in
my remarks. My staff has been told that there was some
miscommunication between producer and reporter that led
to inadvertently airing an interview with a survivor who is
not a member of Peaceful Tomorrows.

What is worse, NBC News knows full well that my
remarks were directed at Peaceful Tomorrows, as I spent a
good portion of my hour-long lunch with the NBC News
team in New York, less than two hours after the press
conference where I made my remarks, discussing this very
same matter.

As if there needed to be additional reinforcement to Ms.
O'Donnell's failed effort to interview a member of the
organization for her piece, my explicit discussion with NBC
News in New York the day before the *Today* show segment
aired could not have been clearer.

Treating my remarks as though they were directed to all
families of victims of 9/11 who have a concern about imagery
in the aforementioned ad rather than about a politically
active group or its members put me, and my party, in a
negative light. Juxtaposing them with a widowed survivor not
affiliated with the group I referenced only made it worse.

I realize that there are members of victims' families who
are not members of Peaceful Tomorrows who object to the

imagery in the ad, and I respect their feelings. I also respect the feelings of the members of Peaceful Tomorrows, but I do not believe they speak for all the families, which is the point I made in Washington Heights and at our lunch.

Tom Mazzarelli, Senior Producer of the *Today* show, told me yesterday a correction would be aired. I would appreciate NBC being true to its word.

I look forward to your timely response.

To NBC's credit, they did set the record straight the following morning, and I thanked Tim and others there for their fairness.

Some conservatives are notoriously leery of the MSM. My friend Mark Stephens cut his political teeth in Jesse Helms's "Congressional Club" organization, and he tells a great story about the famously aloof Helms press operation. The *Raleigh News and Observer* was working on a major story about Helms and seeking a sit-down interview, which Helms was resisting.

With the deadline approaching, the paper settled on a list of seven questions that had arisen from their reporting and faxed them on a Tuesday afternoon to Helms's press office with a request for a response by close of business Friday to accommodate a story in Sunday's paper.

At 5:50 PM on Friday, the *N&O* received a fax from Helms's press secretary.

"Why do you want to know?" was all it said.

Once the media come to a conclusion about someone, it's hard to change their perception. I've never known anyone whose public image and private persona were so at odds as Dick Armey's. To his family, his friends and his staff, he is the most gentle and kind person you could imagine. To the pundits and operatives in Washington, he was a smart but tough—even mean—partisan.

Much of this impression was shaped by the "Barney Fag" incident, an experience that makes me cringe as I type the words a decade after it occurred.

We were in the first one hundred days of our new majority. I had urged Armey to reinstitute as majority leader a weekly briefing every Tuesday for the radio correspondents, giving them sound bites they could use in their feeds.

Radio is an underused medium, and the weekly briefing allowed Armey to reach the millions of listeners who tune in to newscasts in their cars and at work. The briefings were enjoyable for both Armey and the reporters, who appreciated the re-establishment of a practice that had been abandoned by Representative Dick Gephardt (D-MO) when he had been majority leader.

On the first Tuesday in February as Armey was touting a vote on the Balanced Budget Amendment to the Constitution, one of the correspondents asked Armey about a book he'd agreed to write, and what was going to be done with the proceeds.

Newt had run into all kinds of trouble over a book deal a few weeks earlier, and Armey had decided to donate all his royalties to charity. He explained his decision to forgo the money and the political fallout, saying he didn't want to deal with "Barney Frank haranguing in my ear."

Barney Frank is the liberal congressman from Boston who revels in skewering Republicans on the House floor. He was respected by the Capitol Hill press corps for his intelligence and wit. He and Armey had worked together to reform farm subsidy programs in the previous Congress, and had developed a mutual respect.

Barney Frank was also the most prominent openly gay member of Congress.

As Armey said the words "Barney Frank haranguing in my ear," he mangled them, as was his habit. A linguist later told me that people like Armey sometimes get ahead of themselves, merging succeeding words—in this case, Frank and haranguing.

Less than an hour after the briefing had ended, I got a call from Thelma LeBrecht, the AP radio correspondent, asking me to come up to the House radio-TV gallery. "I have something you need to hear," she said.

When I walked into the gallery, the place was abuzz, and I immediately attracted a crowd that followed me back to Thelma's desk.

"What's up?" I asked.

"Listen to this and tell me what you hear," she said as everyone watched.

She played back the tape with Armey mispronouncing the Massachussets congressman's name.

"Yeah?" I said, starting to have a sense of where this was heading.

"What did you hear?"

"I don't know. He mangled Frank's name. He mangles my name all the time."

"It sounds like he said 'Barney Fag,'" said Bob Franken, CNN's congressional correspondent. Franken could be playful and he could be edgy. This was the edgy Franken.

"That's not what I heard," I protested.

"Play it again," another reporter asked. Thelma did, back and forth twice.

"Ed, have you ever heard Armey refer to Barney Frank as 'Barney Fag,' maybe just joking around in the office?" Vic Ratner, ABC's longtime radio correspondent, asked, with a helpful power of suggestion.

"Never," I said. "I have never heard him use that phrase or that word. I've worked for him for almost ten years, and I've never heard him say anything like it."

There is a supposition lurking just beneath the surface of many reporters that conservative Republicans, especially those from Texas or the South, are inherently bigoted, and while I knew Armey very well and knew he didn't have a bigoted bone in his body, I was swimming against a riptide now.

"I think we have to go with it," Franken said. "Whether it was a slip of the tongue or not, he said it."

"He didn't say it," I protested, heatedly. "It's not fair to run this when he's never used that word, and he didn't say it in this instance. He just mangled the name."

"If a congressman was talking about a black member of Congress and said, 'He sniggered,' but dropped the s it would be the same thing," Franken argued. "Fag is just as bad."

"I'm not arguing it's not a slur, I'm saying he didn't say it. How is it there were eight reporters in the room for his briefing, and yet none of them said anything at the time? Because it's not clear that that's what he said. You're playing it back, over and over, straining to hear it."

The radio correspondents looked at me with some sense of confusion about what to do, knowing I was right that no one had picked up on it in the briefing itself. I also sensed some feeling of pity for me. I implored them not to run with this out of fairness to Armey, and noted that if they did, it would be so unfair we would discontinue the radio briefings.

I left the gallery and headed back to the office, unsure whether the media would go with a report that Armey had slurred a colleague or not, but shortly after I got back CNN began running the audio with a picture of Armey, a graphic of a reel-to-reel, and a helpful transcription on the screen with the words "Barney Fag" where Armey had mispronounced the name. I was not sure then and can't say with certainty now, but it sounded to me at the time as if the tape had been slowed to make it sound more clearly like "Barney Fag."

All hell broke loose. The phones started ringing off the hook. I couldn't find Armey anywhere; he was cloistered somewhere working a floor vote. This was before BlackBerries or omnipresent cell phones. I instructed my deputy Michelle Davis to find Armey, get him back to the office, and not let him talk to any reporters until I had a chance to talk to him.

I stopped by Tony Blankley's office for some advice. Blankley was the savvy press secretary to House Speaker Newt Gingrich. He is one of my best friends, but as my luck would have it that day, he was out. I was going to have to handle this on my own.

My first thought was that Frank's own reaction to the story was critical, and I wanted to be the one to put this all in context for him. I called over to his office and learned that he was in a committee hearing, so I rushed over to the Rayburn Building and found him there, sitting on the members' dais.

In politics, body language is often more important than the words that are spoken.

I walked up the side staff aisle, made my way behind the committee Democrats, and knelt by Mr. Frank. I was a little out of breath as I introduced myself and asked him if he could spare me a moment. We walked back to the members' lounge and found a private room.

I sat across from him and told him what was going on. I told him Armey would have contacted him himself, but I couldn't find Armey and he didn't even know all this was going on. I assured Congressman Frank that I had never heard Armey use that phrase, and that in fact, Armey respected him even though they disagreed. (It was true.)

He listened quietly, nodded, said he appreciated my coming over, and got up and went back to his committee work.

What I didn't realize was that I was stoking the story. C-SPAN was televising the hearing Frank was in, and their cameras caught me going into the hearing room and pulling Frank out of the hearing.

I had provided fresh footage for the story, which CNN began airing along with the audio. Worse, my body language was bad. Awful, really—rushing around breathless, heated with reporters. The scent I was throwing off was fear, and the press was picking up on it.

I did not serve my boss well that day. My reaction helped trigger a feeding frenzy. A press secretary has to be calm and reassuring even under the worst of circumstances, which this was. But I wasn't.

I finally caught up with Armey back in his office and explained to him what was going on. He was dismissive of it. "That's ridiculous," he said.

"You're going to have to address it," I said.

"Why?"

"Because everyone thinks you used a slur against a colleague."

"But I didn't."

"You need to find Frank and talk to him," I said. He picked up the phone on his desk and asked the Capitol operator for Barney Frank's office. This time Frank was there, and he agreed to meet Armey on the floor during the next vote. He had withheld making a statement to the press until Armey had a chance to talk to him. Whether it was graciousness or calculation—letting the story run for a while until it needed a kick to move it further along—I'll never know, but the decision to have them meet on the floor to talk only provided the press cameras more footage, with Armey and Frank seated beside each other on a back bench in conversation.

"How'd it go," I asked as Armey came off the floor.

"I think he understands," Armey said. I hoped he was right.

The press was now clamoring for Armey to appear before them. I tried to satisfy them by releasing a statement from Armey, saying that he had only mangled his words and had not used a slur against a colleague.

It wasn't enough. They wanted him on camera, and were demanding he come up to the radio-TV gallery. I told them I'd think about it, which they took as a yes. It was getting late in the day, and I felt it was now in Armey's interest to make a public statement, but I was worried about the mood in the press gallery, which was rapidly turning ugly, especially among the print and TV reporters who were not in the room when Armey gave his briefing. For them, there was no sense of doubt about the story.

The perception of the media as liberal is most accurate when it comes to social issues. They're not great on tax cuts, they're pretty bad on matters of national security, but when it comes to abortion or gay rights, they are very much on the left, and in this case objectivity had gone entirely out the window.

I decided Armey should go to the floor and make a statement after regular business had been completed, and made that suggestion to him. Armey's legislative director, David Hobbs, objected, saying he had some things he had to do relative to floor scheduling. "If we don't deal with this now," I snapped, "he's not going to be doing any more floor scheduling."

We walked over to the floor, reporters shouting questions to Armey as he made his way, stone-faced. "He's making a floor statement," I said, running interference. "You can take from that."

In the cloakroom, we talked about what he would say. I was surprised by how cool, almost sanguine, he seemed. I felt good about it, and thought we'd get closure out of his statement.

The seats in the press gallery were full when he took to the lectern in the well of the House. He started slowly, but I could see and hear the emotion in him begin to well up to the surface. He was clearly pained that people would think him a bigot.

"This morning I mispronounced the name of my friend and

colleague Barney Frank in a way that sounds like a slur. The media and others are reporting this as if it were intentional, and it was not.

"I take strong exception to the airing of the tape and even the transcribing of a stumbled word as if it were an intentional attack."

His voice quaking, he repeated the sentence again for emphasis.

And then he repeated it a third time.

As I watched from the side of the House Chamber, I began thinking less like a press secretary and more like someone feeling sorry for a friend in pain.

Again, the body language was more important than the words themselves. The press took his emotion not as the response of someone who felt wronged, but as the response of someone caught doing wrong.

After Congressman Frank released a statement that wasn't at all helpful, I asked Representative Steve Gunderson, a gay Republican from Wisconsin who was a deputy whip, if he would be willing to talk to reporters and attest to the fact that Armey had never evidenced hostility toward gays. He did, and his support for Armey helped ease things a little that day.

But real damage had been done to Armey's standing. The *New York Times* on Sunday ran a lead editorial calling on Gingrich to dump his number-one deputy. Liberal columnists pounced. They used the now-accepted view that the House majority leader had used an antigay slur to tar the entire House Republican Conference.

I felt that I had let my boss—and friend—down, that I was unable to stop the story. I shared my self-doubt with Tony Blankley the next day.

"By all accounts you fought like a tiger for your man," he said.

"I think I got too hot," I said.

"That may be. It's hard not to sometimes, though."

A few months later, the Senate Democratic whip, Wendell Ford of Kentucky, used the "N word" in an interview. There was hardly a peep about it. No calls for resignation, no thundering from civil rights groups, no recriminations among his colleagues. Here was the number-two Democrat in the Senate, of nearly identical stature to the number-two Republican in the House, dropping a racial slur in an interview, and it was treated as a yawner. In the same way suspicion lurks below the surface toward conservative Republicans, deference lurks toward liberal Democrats.

When I was a press secretary on Capitol Hill, I used to say I don't believe in reincarnation, but if I did, I'd want to come back as a Democratic press secretary. That's a good life. You say it, they print it, no follow-up questions.

Despite my concerns about anticonservative bias, the press plays an important role as watchdog, and even the threat of bad publicity keeps people in check. Shortly after the Ninety-eighth Congress convened in 1991, Minority Leader Bob Michel tapped Armey to serve as the ranking Republican on the Joint Economic Committee. The JEC was a congressional backwater, an anachronistic entity that had been eclipsed by the creation in 1973 of the House and Senate Budget Committees. In fact, Armey's selection for the committee was a consolation prize for not being chosen ranking Republican on the House Budget Committee.

The JEC had been established in the 1940s as the congressional counterpart to the President's Council of Economic Advisors. It had no oversight or authorizing jurisdiction, but as ranking member, Armey inherited office space and committee staff, and he named me minority staff director.

Making his press secretary staff director was seen as another quirky decision by Armey, since the JEC was staffed almost entirely by professional economists. People understandably wondered how someone with an undergraduate degree in politics was qualified to oversee a staff of Ph.D.s in economics, and the majority side openly sneered at the notion, razzing their Republican counterparts over having a "flack" for a boss.

But there was, as usual, a method to Armey's madness. The JEC minority staff was already full of people who could make widgets. He wanted somebody there who could sell the widgets. And he wanted somebody there who would be loyal to him.

Kerry Knott, who had taken over as chief of staff when Denis Calabrese moved back to Houston after Armey's first year in office, notified the sitting minority staff director of the change that would be taking place. Doug Koopman was disappointed, but proved to be a team player. He called me to introduce himself and invite me over to his office to brief me on the lay of the land.

I told Knott I was going to go over to Doug's, but he cautioned me against it.

"Why?" I asked.

"You shouldn't go traipsing over there to meet with him. He needs to come over here."

Besides college interns, I hadn't had much experience running a staff. Though only a year older than me, Knott was much more conscious of the need to project authority when you are starting in a new position in a new environment.

I soon learned that the Republican staff at the JEC had a terrible case of "Stockholm syndrome"—they had come to identify with their majority captors. The Democratic staff director was Steven Quick, and he was used to Republican staff directors who didn't issue anything without his approval.

I made a courtesy call to his office to introduce myself, and he immediately set out to break in this new pony of a staff director.

"The majority controls the imprimatur of the committee, so the minority staff cannot issue its own reports," he informed me.

"What if we do?" I asked, just out of curiosity.

"Well, you can't."

"But what if we do?"

"It's not done. It would violate the rules of the committee."

"What happens if the ranking Republican violates the rules of the committee?" I asked, shifting the discussion away from him and me as staffers to the prerogative of a member of Congress.

"Well, obviously we have no control over how the Republican leadership would handle one of their ranking members' violating the rules of the committee, but you should understand that the committee chairman controls all funding and payroll, and while we are obviously deferential to the wishes of the ranking member, at the end of the day it is the chairman who authorizes who can and can't work for the committee."

"You mean if the Republicans put out our own report, Senator Sarbanes could fire me?"

"I'm sure it would never come to that, but he has that authority."

"Wow," I said, growing excited. "I'd be a household name in this town, wouldn't I?"

"What?"

"Are you kiddin' me? If the Democratic chairman of this committee fired me as the Republican staff director, I'd be a household name, don't you think? I'd be all over the news. People would write editorials about it. I think it'd be pretty big, don't you?"

At first he seemed a little confused, but slowly he realized he wasn't dealing with another economist. Maybe the logic of Armey's putting a press secretary in charge of his side of the committee made some sense, after all.

English beats math.

In the fall of 1995, House Republicans and the Clinton administration had the now infamous Federal Budget Showdown, resulting in the now even more infamous government shut-down.

It's a classic example of winning a battle but losing a war.

The spring of 1995 was a heady time for House Republicans, after having gained control for the first time in forty years and moving the Contract with America with efficiency greater than anyone could have hoped or expected. But threaded throughout votes on welfare reform and tort reform and other Contract legislation was a growing battle over the budget.

The House passed a constitutional amendment requiring a balanced budget, but it fell short of passage in the Senate when Republican senator Bob Packwood of Oregon joined six Democrats in switching their past positions in favor of the amendment to vote against it.

Despite this defeat, Gingrich, virtually unilaterally, declared that Republicans would balance the budget anyway. Not only that, he said we would do so in seven years.

There had been a heated internal debate about making such a promise, and I was in the House press gallery with Gingrich when he made the policy pronouncement. I thought he'd misspoken, and rushed out to call Kasich to come over and clear up any confusion.

Kasich joined Gingrich at the podium in the gallery and said he'd heard the talk about balancing the budget and agreed that that was the goal, but wanted to be clear that the committee was not drafting a seven-year timeframe.

But Gingrich hadn't misspoken, he was driving policy through the press. He had determined that unless there was actually a "zero" at the end of the process, the public would not accept the pain of entitlement cuts (or reductions in the rate of growth, as we disciplined ourselves to say). Right there in the House press gallery, he committed the conference to the goal, and Kasich along with him.

His theory proved correct about the magic of the zero. The political pain of deficit reduction had for decades proven unbearable, but it had been thirty years since the country had actually had a balanced budget. Americans would be willing to accept cuts, however, if at the end of the process there was actually a balanced budget.

This had the effect of changing the political dynamic entirely, and by April, Clinton himself had acquiesced to producing a balanced budget. We were no longer debating if the budget would be balanced, but how.

That shifted the debate yet again, and Clinton began to regain his political footing after being off-balance since the November elections. We were winning so long as we were for a balanced budget and he wasn't, but once he claimed the same goal but through different means, we began to lose the PR war because we put too much of our focus on process.

Clinton's revised budget was deemed to be in balance by the Office of Management and Budget (OMB), an arm of the White House, and it had clearly engaged in some good ol'-fashioned blue smoke and mirrors—accounting gimmicks and optimistic economic assumptions—to achieve balance. In addition, it didn't achieve balance until year ten, whereas our budget balanced in seven years as calculated by the Congressional Budget Office, which we considered much more objective and reliable than the OMB.

Having browbeaten Clinton into agreeing to balance the budget, we decided to browbeat him further to balance it on our terms. Thus was born the great rallying cry, "CBO and 7!"

We poured all of our energy and messaging into who should count the beans and for how long.

Meanwhile, over at the White House, they settled on a different rhetorical formula: M^2E^2—for Medicare, Medicaid, Education, and the Environment. They emoted over health care for the elderly and the poor, children in failing schools, and the need for clean air and water, while we affixed our green eyeshades tightly to our foreheads and explained baseline budgets and revenue projections versus reductions in the rate of increase and the need for the expenditure column to equal the revenue column.

We sounded cold and technocratic. They sounded warm and

compassionate. They were speaking English, and we were talking math.

When communicating with voters, English beats math. Clinton went on to rehabilitate himself and routed Bob Dole in 1996, rather than being the one-term president Armey had once told him to his face he would be.

Ever since then, I have always taken care to make sure Republican officials add the "because clause."

"We need to cut taxes, BECAUSE tax relief will spur investment that will create jobs."

"We need to reform Medicare, BECAUSE we can provide health care more affordably while saving the program for future generations."

The "because clause" helps make sure your candidate is talking about people, not numbers.

A picture's worth a thousand press releases.

During his time in the Reagan White House, communications impresario Michael Deaver used to watch the evening newscasts with the volume off, knowing that what was said was much less important than what was shown.

During the 2004 Republican Convention in New York, John Kerry used some of his downtime to partake in one of his favorite pastimes.

Windsurfing.

Yep, windsurfing.

The picture of him off Nantucket in skintight nylon shorts hanging on to the crossbar of a sail attached to a surfboard tacking back and forth across the bay did more to convey how out of touch he was with blue-collar workers than anything we could have done. The footage was so compelling the Bush-Cheney campaign used it in a mocking campaign about Kerry changing positions with the blowing winds.

In the 1992 campaign, the Clinton team had done a very good job defining a health care crisis. After winning the election, President Clinton put First Lady Hillary Clinton in charge of coming up with a plan. After months of secret meetings, the Clinton White House unveiled a massive health care proposal that featured a lot of new regulations and bureaucracies, and centered on an employer mandate.

As chairman of the House Republican Conference and a Ph.D. economist to boot, Dick Armey took a leading role in opposing its enactment. As the conference's communications director, I asked my old friends at the Joint Economic Committee to do not only an analysis of the job-killing aspect of the employer mandate, but literally draw up how the proposed new system would look on a flow chart.

We ran the resulting diagram, reproduced here, along with the glossary of terms contained in the bill in an October 13, 1993, *Wall Street Journal* op-ed. This image did more to convey the onus of "government-run health care" than months of floor speeches were able to do. It was reproduced all over the place, and we had a big blowup of it created that Armey and others could use on the House and Senate floor and on television interviews.

The Clinton Health Care Bureaucracy: "Simplicity" Defined

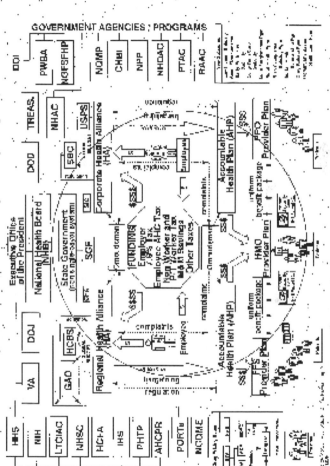

CHAPTER THREE

//

THE RECOUNT

I n the early morning hours of November 3, 2000, Cathy and I stood in the nearly freezing rain outside the governor's mansion in Austin waiting and waiting for Vice President Gore to concede. Finally, at 4:00 AM, we gave in and walked back up Congress Avenue to the Stephen F. Austin hotel and crashed until about 10:00 AM.

The next morning we got to the headquarters at about ten-thirty, but it was pretty deserted. At around 2:00 AM, I had told the communications staff they didn't need to be in until noon the next day.

I realized that this had been a mistake after talking to John Fund of the *Wall Street Journal* editorial page. "Do you know the Democrats flew a chartered plane full of lawyers down to Florida in the middle of the night?" he asked over the phone from New York.

"No," I said. "Why?" I was still naïvely thinking that this thing would wrap up that day.

"They're going to create chaos, raise all kinds of questions, throw up all kinds of motions, force all kinds of recounts until they can figure out a legal strategy to get it all into court."

I have to admit, I thought John was being a little paranoid, but this would not be the last time he proved incredibly prescient on this front. John Fund was among the first to foresee the frightening convergence of electioneering and litigating that is becoming a regrettable hallmark of the American political process.

By now, the phones had begun ringing off the hook with reporters wanting to know what we were doing about the recount. I
went to a meeting in the main conference room where the lawyers
had begun to assemble. Bush-Cheney Campaign Manager Joe Allbaugh was there with top campaign attorneys Tom Josefiak and Michael Toner and a few of the more junior lawyers I didn't know by
name.

It was in this meeting that I first heard the phrases "dimpled
chad," "dangling chad," "swinging door chad," "undervote" and
"overvote," all of which were explained to me by Josefiak and
Toner.

A dimpled chad, for those who don't remember it all as vividly
as I do, is a chad that has been punched but not punched through,
with only an indentation resulting. A dangling chad is partially
punched through, but not fully disconnected from one of the corners, and so dangles precariously close to being a vote. A swinging
door chad is punched through on one side but not the other, remaining attached in a way that allows you to open and shut it like,
well, a swinging door.

An undervote is a ballot on which no candidate's line is
punched through, and an overvote is a ballot on which two candidates have their lines punched through.

"A team of lawyers just left Austin for Palm Beach County to
handle the recount," Tom said. It was now dawning on me that this
election was not going to be over today. Maybe not tomorrow, and
maybe not even next week.

Karen Hughes, the queen of communications strategy and
confidante of then-governor Bush, dispatched Tucker Eskew, one
of the best regional press secretaries in the campaign, to Palm Beach
County to handle the media that were gathering there. I was now
spending most of my time sitting around Austin, not sure what to
do. The action was increasingly shifting to the ground in Florida.
Karen was back, and though she was spending most of her time at
the Governor's Mansion, I had vacated her office, where I'd been

"holding down the fort" while she had been on the campaign plane, and been relegated to one of the cubicles back in the press shop.

On Thursday, November 9, Karen asked me if I would go to Miami the next day to link up with constitutional lawyer Ted Olson and handle the media surrounding our filing of *Bush* v. *Gore*. At the time, I didn't realize the significance the case would have in the election, not to mention history.

"Of course," I said. "But when that's done, do you think I could fly back to Washington instead of Austin?"

As a wife and mother, Karen understood that I was pained by the continued separation from Cathy and our kids, none of whom had anticipated the "overtime." I had deployed the Harry Potter nightly reading sessions the whole time I was in Austin, but John, Carrie, and Mollie were growing tired of it.

"Yes," she said with a smile.

I rushed back to my pool house apartment and packed everything I had for Miami—and ultimately home. I popped into the "big house" to say good-bye and thank you to my gracious hosts Pat and Julie Oles, and left the next day for Miami.

We filed *Bush* v. *Gore* in the federal court house in Miami on Saturday, November 11, and Ted took questions on the steps afterward. I did a little postpresser spin and headed back to my hotel room to grab my bags and catch the first flight I could back home.

Cathy, John, Carrie, and Mollie were as happy to see me as I was to see them, but our joyful reunion was cut short three days later by a call from Joe Allbaugh.

"Ed, we need you on the ground in Miami," he said in his deep Oklahoma drawl.

"When?"

"Tomorrow."

It's always tomorrow. Never "some time next week."

"I'll be there," I said, and I hung up the phone. I found Cathy in the family room with Mollie and pulled her aside to tell her the news. We broke it to the children at dinner.

They were disappointed, but by now had grown accustomed to my popping in and out during the course of the campaign. After they left for school in the morning, I left once again for the airport.

The night before the Miami-Dade recount began, about a dozen Bush campaign operatives went to Joe's Stone Crab Restaurant in South Beach, where we were joined by the well-respected U.S. Representative John Sweeney of New York.

Sweeney had been executive director of the New York Republican Party. He's one of the few members of Congress who is at his core a political operative himself. New York politics is not played as a finesse sport, and Sweeney is the kind of guy who could really check a player into the boards. I was glad he was there.

I laid out the game plan for the next day. We would open up with a press conference at eight-thirty before the count commenced, putting down markers for what constituted a fair process. At around 2:00 PM we would come back out for another briefing for the cameras, providing clips for the evening news packages assessing how the process was going and how it was measuring up against the yardstick we established in the morning. At 5:30 PM we would do a recap, with the message we would want to be in the final wire wrap-up and in the morning papers. We could ratchet up from morning to afternoon and from afternoon to evening, if we needed to.

"I know what I'm going to say tomorrow morning," Sweeney said while we were breaking open Alaskan King Crab legs. "I'm going to say that Joseph Stalin said, 'It doesn't matter who casts the votes, it only matters who counts the votes.' And these people are worse than Stalin."

Everyone loved the quotation. In a city with a population of Cuban-Americans with a great deal of passion about Fidel Castro's Stalinist dictatorship of their native island, it would be powerful, but I thought it bordered on incendiary.

"That's a great quote, John," I said, not wanting to dampen his enthusiasm. "But I'm a little worried that if we open up with

Stalin at eight-thirty in the morning, it's going to be hard to ratchet up at two o'clock."

Sweeney smiled. He has a classic, big grin like the cat that just ate the canary. "You Bushies are a bunch of wimps," he said (and I'm paraphrasing).

He ended up holding the Stalin quotation until the 5:30 PM wrap-up.

And by then, I had no trepidations about it. It was completely justified. Watching the recount process atop the Stephen P. Clark Miami-Dade Municipal Center was surreal. There were tables all around a big room. At each, a Democrat and a Republican sat across from each other reviewing ballots, with a "neutral" observer who would tally the votes they agreed upon. If there was a dispute over a ballot, that ballot was sent to another table at the front of the room, where the three elected Dade County election observers would arbitrate the disputed ballots.

Behind the three election officials sat lawyers for the Gore campaign and the Bush campaign, who in turn could challenge the decision of the three officials (literally calling out "challenge!" after the three had made their judgment) and a pile of disputed ballots were set aside for later court challenge. The commissioners would hold the ballot up to the light, checking for penetration of the chad, however slight, to discern "the intent of the voter." A Bush vote was cast on line 6, and a Gore vote on line 8.

The first commissioner would discern the intent she saw, calling out her number. "Eight," she'd say, passing the ballot to her right. "Six," the next commissioner might say. The third would then break the tie, invariably with another "eight."

After they held the ballot up to the light, I kept expecting them to hold it to their temple, like Johnny Carson as "Karnak the Maginficent." "And the answer is . . . 'eight'!"

The counting tables were like a Vegas casino, replete with "pit bosses" who would wander from table to table overseeing the recount.

Our lawyer was Kevin Martin, who'd come in from Austin.

Each county had a three-part team, with a political director, a legal director, and a communications director. In Miami-Dade, I was the communications director, Kevin Martin was the director of the legal team, and Ken Mehlman was the political director. The political director was first among the equals, responsible for the entire operation.

Kevin Martin is now the chairman of the Federal Communications Commission (FCC). Ken Mehlman went on from Florida to become White House political director, then Bush-Cheney '04 campaign manager, and later succeeded me as chairman of the Republican National Committee.

Ken is an excellent political strategist with a great sense for messaging, but he made his bones in the business as a box checker—someone who would begin every day with a list of things to get done and a box next to each item to check upon completion. And he didn't leave the office until everything had been checked.

He personifies the axiom "if you want something done, give it to the busy person." As a result, his list would just get longer and longer every day, but at the end of the day, each item's box would be checked.

As chairman of the Bush-Cheney campaign, he was masterful. He shared credit, took blame, and tore down the turf markers people beneath him were always trying to erect.

One day in the midst of the recount, I was standing out in front of the Municipal Center with Sweeney, and I bummed a cigarette off him. When I was younger, working on Capitol Hill, I would bum cigarettes off friends at happy hours after a few beers. Armey said once my brand was "OPs"—Other People's. But it had been a long time since I'd smoked a cigarette, having in Cathy a wife who was a very positive influence on me. ("You can smoke that cigarette or you can kiss your wife later. Your call.")

It was late, and Ken was leaving the building for his hotel when he spotted us. "When did you start smoking?" he asked, surprised.

"Just now," I said.

When we began the '04 campaign together, Ken promised me that I wouldn't need to start smoking again when it was over.

After we determined who would be in the room and identified who would be our lawyer, I pulled Ken aside in the hallway outside his room.

"Are you sure we want to go with Kevin in the room?" I asked. Kevin Martin is a great guy, a good friend, and a brilliant lawyer, but I was concerned that his niceness and quiet demeanor might be a detriment to us in this setting.

"Yes, why?" Ken asked.

"Well, Kevin's a solid lawyer, but I think we need a real hardass in there tomorrow."

"Don't worry," Ken said, chuckling. "Kevin can be a hardass."

And Ken was right. I couldn't help but smile as I watched Kevin the next day, in a very soft-spoken but firm manner, say "challenge" over and over again, ignoring the squinted eyes directed at him by the three officials from the Board of Elections.

While this hand recount was going on, a machine recount was also taking place on another floor of the building. They barred us from being inside the room where the machine recount was taking place, however, so we had to watch it through a glass window, like fathers looking at newborn babies in a maternity ward.

The ballots were sitting in long gray postal service trays, where they would be fed through the machines. They'd come zipping out the other end, and chads were flying around the room like confetti on New Year's Eve. By the end of the process, the floor was covered with chads.

Of course, each chad that came flying out in the recount process represented a newly cast vote (where no chad had been previously punched—thereby upgrading an "undervote" to a vote) or a newly disenfranchised vote (where a chad had been punched only to have another chad punched in the same race, degrading a vote to an "overvote").

To top it all off, one of the staff inside the room dropped a tray of ballots. Ballots were littered all over the floor. Staffers were stepping on some as they were scooping others back into the bin. My stomach churned as I watched people's votes being treated like candy wrappers on a movie theater floor.

I couldn't believe it, and felt sure nobody would believe it if I told them. I called Ken and asked him to send somebody over with a video camera to capture this on tape, which he did.

I took the tape and jumped in a cab and raced to a private video production house to feed the tape out via satellite. After I did, I went across the street to a dingy restaurant to get something to eat. It was three-thirty, and I hadn't eaten since having an apple in my hotel room at 7:00 AM.

At the end-of-the-day wrap-up in Ken's hotel suite, one of the lawyers mentioned the fight over absentee ballots from those serving overseas in the military, giving a rundown of the legal tussle between the Bush and Gore teams over counting those votes, some of which had been cast before Election Day but for various logistical reasons had not gotten back to Florida before deadline.

I was incredulous. "So these soldiers and sailors and airmen cast their votes, but somewhere along the way the Department of Defense did not get them where they were supposed to be on time?"

"Right."

"And the Gore lawyers are seeking to disqualify those votes?"

"Right."

"You've got to be kidding me! The guy who wants to be commander in chief is trying to disqualify the votes of the men and women fighting for our right to vote over some technicality?!"

Ken smiled.

The next morning, I called Bob Novak who broke the story

on CNN that day. It marked a turning point, especially after vice presidential nominee Joe Lieberman later refused to support the tactic.

After two weeks in Miami, I lined up my protégé Jim Wilkinson, who was then press secretary to Dick Armey, to relieve me of my campaign duties in Miami. Karen Hughes was again understanding, and I was able to get home about a week before the Supreme Court ruled on *Bush* v. *Gore*. I watched with Cathy on our TV as Vice President Gore conceded and President-elect George Bush accepted the final outcome of the election.

CHAPTER FOUR

EXECUTION IS CRITICAL

Every campaign is a race against the clock, with Election Day the certain ending point. Given the limited time available, every decision, or lack of one, is important. In a campaign, not deciding an issue is the same as making a decision—a decision to maintain the status quo.

People who are willing to serve as prime movers, willing to stake out a position and drive the decision-making process are invaluable. They are also expendable, which is why not everyone is willing to play the role.

Politicians like to have someone they can identify as responsible if things go wrong, and a willingness to advocate decisions makes you a candidate for culpability. The best way to avoid that is to make sure you're right at least most of the time.

The most important role anyone can play in the political process is the nexus between ideas and action. Campaigns and policy-making are full of interesting conversations that consider every conceivable angle and every potential outcome of a given action, but at the end of every ethereal discussion there must be a concrete decision.

A political campaign is a forest of decision trees. Do we hold a press conference or not? Do we go up with an attack ad or not? Do we schedule the event in Raleigh or Greensboro? If you let that moment go by without a yes or no decision, you have allowed stasis to take effect, and have allowed yourself to become a victim of circumstance.

Politics in its purest form is much more art than science. There are no "correct" answers. There are axioms, such as, "When, in a multi-candidate field, two of the candidates begin attacking each other the beneficiary is a third candidate." When Howard Dean and Dick Gephardt began attacking each other with ads in the Iowa caucuses, I knew they would both drop as a result, and thought John Edwards would be the prime beneficiary. I was wrong about Edwards—Kerry was the prime beneficiary—but I was right about Dean and Gephardt.

Stasis is the enemy of every campaign, front-runner or spoiler, and sins of commission are more forgivable than sins of omission. Better to make a mistake through action than because of inaction.

There are a few defining moments in presidential campaigns, windows of opportunity when you know the country is really locked in on things. Once the nomination is wrapped up, a challenger has three such opportunities: 1, announcing a running mate; 2, convention and acceptance speech; 3, debates.

The incumbent only gets the latter two (barring a sitting vice president being dumped from the ticket).

As I have pointed out, Kerry blew his acceptance speech opportunity. His VP announcement went well (though it had as a by-product the effect of cementing an unflattering image of Teresa Heinz Kerry when she pulled young Jack Edwards's thumb from his mouth).

One mistake the Bush-Cheney campaign made in 2004 concerned the presidential debates. Thinking the meandering Kerry couldn't clear his throat in less than a minute and a half, we insisted on short answers—two-minute responses followed by one-minute rejoinders. We demanded that there be a visible red light when time ran out, so the television audience could see Kerry going over his allotted time.

Unfortunately, the format had the effect of disciplining the ordinarily rambling candidate. Rather than running over his time, Kerry's answers were crisp, well informed, and well delivered.

On the flip side, Bush entered the debate in a poor state of mind. When Dan Bartlett walked into the viewing room offstage after leaving the president before the debate began, he looked at me and rolled his eyes while shaking his head no.

I took it to mean we were in for a long night.

We were in a strong position going into the first debate, and I was hoping President Bush might land a haymaker that could put the race away. This was not a time for caution, but it's hard to override that instinct when you're up in the polls with the election less than thirty-five days away.

That instinct was reinforced by an article in *USA Today* the day of the debate highlighting how gaffes posed the biggest risk to presidents in debates. Gerald Ford hurt himself in a debate with Jimmy Carter in 1976 by saying Poland was not under Russian dominance. In 1980, Jimmy Carter came off as less than serious in answering a question about nuclear arms control when he said he had been discussing the matter the night before with his twelve-year-old daughter, Amy. And Ronald Reagan put concerns about his age front and center in 1984 by meandering through his closing statement in a debate with Walter Mondale, talking about driving along the Pacific Coast Highway as his time ran out.

The president had read the article and it reinforced a natural tendency to play it safe. But in playing it safe, holding back from swinging away, he looked repetitive. *Saturday Night Live* brutally lampooned his point that prevailing in Iraq was "hard work." He didn't roll his eyes or audibly sigh as Gore had done in his disastrous 2000 first debate, but on the split screen Bush looked pretty disdainful of his opponent.

Nor was it as bad as Jack Kemp's vice presidential debate with Al Gore in 1996. That evening in St. Petersburg, Florida, Haley Barbour and I settled into the viewing room with the Dole-Kemp camp to watch the two vice presidential candidates debate.

Within minutes it was apparent that Kemp was not prepared. Haley leaned over to me, put his yellow legal pad up between his mouth and my ear, and said in his Yazoo City drawl, "Kemp suuuuuuucks."

I flashed back to that moment when, less than twenty minutes into Bush's first debate with Kerry, Dan whispered to me out of the side of his mouth, "How bad you think it is?"

"Pretty bad," I said. "But we'll survive."

We did, but barely. More than 60 million viewers had tuned in, an astounding one in five Americans, and Kerry had not come across as a wishy-washy flip-flopper. The biggest advantage in a presidential debate is to a challenger running against an incumbent, in that the public sees the two on the same stage and it shrinks the stature gap. Reagan capitalized immensely on the advantage in 1980, and Kerry did the same in 2004.

For the first time since their convention, the Kerry team found their footing. Worse, much of the Bush-Cheney and RNC communications staffs spent the night in Miami and flew back Friday morning, while the Kerry campaign team had flown back Thursday night after the debate. They were crashing the airwaves the following morning, aggressively spinning their "win" while our people were stuck in airports and on planes.

There are times when a campaign has to dig deep and push back hard.

The president wasn't happy with his performance, but he wasn't happy with ours either. And he was right. It's at such moments that you have to dig deep and push back hard, but we were flat-footed. We failed to execute. By the weekend, however, we had steadied ourselves and BC '04 was up with an ad that homed in on Kerry's comment in the debate that the United States should meet a "global test" before committing American troops to combat.

On CNN's *Late Edition* the Sunday after the debate, I reinforced our paid media. "Who passes or fails you on a global test? The French, the Russians, the U.N. passes you or fails you on a global test before we would take action under a President Kerry. That is a very disturbing point," I said to Wolf Blitzer.

The "global test" attack allowed us to tread water until Vice President Cheney debated John Edwards in Cleveland the following Tuesday night. Cheney's 2000 debate with Senator Joe Lieberman may go down in history as one of the most clear-cut debate victories in modern history. It was so pronounced that Lieberman was hardly heard from again in that campaign. That history made us optimistic about the VP debate, even though Edwards was a smooth-talking trial lawyer.

Edwards held his own in this instance, but Cheney righted our ship. He was strong, and looked much more authoritative than the younger, smaller Edwards. He was stern in his responses, and Edwards even seemed sprightly. I told RNC Communications Director Jim Dyke afterward that my favorite part of the debate was "when the Skipper whacked Gilligan with his hat."

The vice presidential debates gave the campaign a morale boost at a critical time, but by the second and third presidential debates, the race had fallen into a dead heat, and neither of them changed the dynamic, though President Bush closed strong in the final debate in Phoenix.

In my view, three presidential debates are probably one too many these days, but the Commission on Presidential Debates seems stuck in the three presidential, one vice presidential debate rut.

The Commission on Presidential Debates itself has become a self-perpetuating and self-important entity. It's an anachronism and it should be eliminated. It was founded at a time when there were only three broadcast networks and no internet. The public demands at least one presidential debate and one vice presidential debate, but the campaign committees can negotiate them directly and find acceptable sponsors and venues. It's done all the time in House, Senate, and gubernatorial races.

Debate venues are the rare moments when the two presidential campaigns come into direct contact. There are hospitality tents or suites set up by the host facility, and the media and the campaign and party operatives all come together in a state fair–like atmosphere.

At the second 2004 presidential debate, in St. Louis, Terry McAuliffe and I actually ended up having dinner together at a stand-up table across from a buffet line. I hadn't seen him much since the first debate and asked him where he'd been.

He jokingly complained that "Lockhart's hogging all the TV time!" Joe Lockhart, Clinton's former White House press secretary, had recently joined the Kerry camp and was doing much of their television commentary.

"That's nothing," I said of the then-portly Lockhart. "He was just in here and he was hogging all the cookies!"

If we'd been eight-year-olds, milk would have run out of our noses, we were laughing so hard. Adam Nagourney from the *New York Times* spotted us and wanted to know what we were laughing about, so I told him. To my chagrin, he reported the comment in his paper, and I felt bad about it.

Lockhart was gracious when I saw him after the final debate in Arizona less than a week after the *Times* piece ran.

"Don't worry about it," he said. "I thought it was funny." He handed me a cold beer his staff had brought to celebrate the end of debate season.

McAuliffe used to joke that he spent more time with me in 2004 than he spent with his wife. We were constantly in studios together. "The Macker," as he's known in political circles, is a much nicer guy in person than he comes across on television.

In question-and-answer sessions at Republican events, I would frequently get asked, "How can you stand going on TV with Terry McAuliffe?"

I'd say, "I just figure for every minute I spend in a TV studio with Terry McAuliffe, I get three minutes in heaven!"

Terry and I went to the same small college, the Catholic University of America in Washington, D.C. He graduated four years ahead of me and we had mutual college friends.

One of the duties of a party chairman is on-air sparring with your counterpart. Terry and I enjoyed it, didn't take it personally, and tried to be good-natured about it (though I think his elbows are sharper than mine).

The Sunday shows used to invite both chairmen on (they tend to rotate them, so you end up doing one per week), and if both accept the invitation there's a debate. If not, one gets to go on unanswered. It's a way of forcing both chairmen out.

In April 2004, my youngest daughter, Mollie, received her First Holy Communion, which is a major event in a traditional Irish Catholic family like mine—and Terry's. I didn't want to have to do television the day of her celebration, but couldn't miss it if Terry was going to be on. The Sunday before, we were on one of the shows and afterward, as we were walking out of the studio, I told Terry about Mollie's celebration the following week.

"You think you could take a pass next week?" I asked. "Then I could."

"No problem. Enjoy the Communion!"

It was a nice gesture, and I recount it so my Republican friends can better understand how I really can stand going on television with him.

My fondness for McAuliffe is similar to how I feel about MSNBC's Chris Matthews, as I once described it on Don Imus's syndicated radio show.

"I have a love-hate relationship with Chris," I said. "I love him, and I hate myself for it."

The Sunday shows have wrongly allowed current DNC Chairman Howard Dean to refuse to appear jointly with RNC Chairman Ken Mehlman. I don't blame him, as Ken would kick his butt, but the networks should not allow one of the two party chairmen to dictate the rules of engagement.

I never thought I'd see the day when Terry McAuliffe would be the voice of reason in the Democratic Party, but compared to his successor he's a veritable statesman.

At his first staff meeting at the DNC, Dean informed everyone that he didn't want to be called chairman, but governor. From his first day on the job, he has given voice to a very angry segment of the Democratic Party, saying, "The Republican Party is basically a White Christian party," "Most Republicans have never worked an honest day in their lives," and, "I hate Republicans and everything they stand for."

I can only respond by saying, "I love Howard Dean." As outgoing chairman of the Republican Party, I didn't get to pick the next chairman of the Democratic Party.

But if I did, I'd have picked Howard Dean.

Sometimes inaction is the right course, but it should be a conscious decision.

In early 1996, soon after I had started at the RNC under Haley Barbour, he wanted the House Energy and Commerce Committee to exercise its jurisdiction over interstate telecom fraud to investigate Lawton Chiles's Florida gubernatorial campaign for phoning the state's elderly voters and telling them that Jeb Bush would cut Social Security benefits if he won the 1994 governor's race. It was a blatant lie—no governor even has such authority—and the tactic surely constituted interstate commerce (the calls were made from North Carolina into Florida).

I met with House Energy and Commerce Committee Staff Director James Derderian ("J.D.") and his committee's chain-smoking press secretary Mike Collins about the idea of calling the Chiles campaign before the committee to investigate the false charges of Social Security cuts.

The reason was obvious: We wanted to shine a spotlight on a tactic we were sure would be replicated in the '96 congressional races and against our Republican presidential nominee.

They listened and took the case back to their boss, Chairman Tom Bliley of Virginia.

A couple of days later, Mike came by my office with their answer. They had concerns. Energy and Commerce was not like other oversight committees in the House. The minority had rights by the committee's rules to call almost as many of witnesses as the majority. John Dingell, the wily congressman from Michigan and former long-time chairman of E&C, was now the ranking Democrat, and he knew the rules well.

"We may not be virgins either," Mike said. Some Republicans might have used some questionable tactics in past campaigns that we might not want to have brought to light in such a hearing. I had known Mike a long time. He'd been communications director of the National Republican Congressional Committee, the NRCC, which is responsible for keeping and winning House seats every cycle, before going to the Energy and Commerce Committee to work for its chairman, Tom Bliley. I had a feeling he knew what he was talking about when he said some Republicans might not want to face scrutiny over campaign calls.

I understood, and agreed that the risk was probably not worth the reward. Now I just had to tell Haley. I knew he wouldn't take it well. The Republican committee chairs in the new majority were always coming up with reasons why they couldn't pass this bill or hold that hearing, even though it would be politically advantageous. But in this case, the political merits of going forward were questionable.

As I laid out Mike's concerns, I could see a look of disdain creep across Haley's face.

After summing it all up, I said I agreed with Mike that it was not worth going forward. To bolster my case, I acknowledged that the committees were always wimping out, but in this case, Mike made sense.

"And Mike's a total political hack," I said, hoping to reinforce the merits of my recommendation. Then, thinking that sounded a little too crass, I added, "And I mean that in the best sense of the phrase."

Haley looked at me and said, "Ohhhh, I took it in the best sense of the phrase."

Knockouts usually come from a counterpunch.

Executing on defense is often more important than executing on offense. It requires sharper reflexes. Two examples—one somewhat minor and silly, one significant and perhaps decisive—from Dole '02:

At a Labor Day event, Bowles operatives sent union "volunteers" to hold up signs protesting Elizabeth Dole's support of NAFTA. I'm sure they thought it would rattle her.

"Ooooohh, they have to pay for this," I said afterward to campaign manager Mark Stephens and his deputy, Brian Nick.

Bowles had made a major issue of Dole's support for NAFTA in the campaign, even though as President Bill Clinton's chief of staff he had been critically involved in its enactment. Ironically, his wife, Crandall, is a textile heiress, and part of their joint fortune came from Spring Industries, perhaps most famous for Spring Maid towels. We had responded to his criticism that Dole's support of NAFTA cost North Carolina textile jobs by pointing out not only that he had supported the treaty himself, but that his own family's fortunes rested partly on Spring Industries' moving their towel and washcloth production overseas.

At the next Bowles rally, people entering the event were handed white hand towels with "Bowles for Senate!" printed in big black letters to wave in the air. Bowles's wife spotted one from the stage and elbowed Bowles, pointing out the towels in the crowd with a big smile. Dole supporters throughout the crowd were holding the towels above their heads like banners, with the "Bowles for Senate!" side facing the stage, and Bowles acknowledged them with a thumbs-up.

But then our people began turning them around to show the other side, which said in big black letters, "Made in China."

Bowles's smile faded fast.

The incident did not garner much attention, but word of it spread like wildfire through the Dole organization and our people loved it. It was great for morale, and in the closing weeks of a hard-fought campaign, that's worth more than eight hundred gross rating points of a new ad going up.

What wasn't good for our morale in the last week of the 2002 Dole campaign was the need to respond to a late-in-the-game attack on our candidate for not caring about North Carolina hurricane victims. It was an attack against the former head of the American Red Cross that was so over the top it backfired and contributed to her margin of victory.

Fortunately, we had seen it coming. About a week before Bowles launched the ad, he'd been sending one of his campaign staff to Elizabeth's events to hand out a one-pager to reporters making the charges that would air in the ad, which was that while North Carolina was still reeling in 1999 from hurricanes Fran and Hugo, Mrs. Dole had held a fundraiser in Charlotte for her presidential primary campaign while ignoring the needs of her fellow North Carolinians.

"This feels like a script," I said, handing the smear sheet to campaign manager Mark Stephens in the Salisbury campaign office we shared when I got back from the road that night. "We better get something in the can."

Our research team documented how much money Elizabeth had raised on behalf of the hurricane victims, as well as the hundreds of millions she'd raised for countless other disaster victims while head of the American Red Cross. Fred Davis, the very talented ad producer for the Dole for Senate Campaign, went to work immediately on a spot we could rotate in right away if need be.

Before the hurricane spot hit, Fred had worked up another closing ad that Bob Dole had talked him into that I was agonizing over. There was concern in the campaign that we were damaging Elizabeth Dole's "brand" in running contrast ads against Bowles, and that voters had truly grown tired of the negativity in the Dole-Bowles race.

Voters always tell pollsters they hate the negativity, and for more than a decade I dismissed such poll results. There's no bigger difference between voter attitude and voter behavior than in this area. Voters mean it when they say they can't stand "negative" ads, but at the same time they often take more information away from well-done negative ads than the positive ones, and that information affects their vote.

I also think there is a difference between a true "contrast" ad, one which highlights the differences between the positions of the two candidates on a given issue, and a personal "attack" ad, which simply denigrates the opponent. More important, I believe voters think there's a difference (or at least respond to them differently).

Pundits love to bemoan the proliferation of negative ads. I've heard it said that Burger King and McDonald's don't seek to gain market share by attacking one another because they fear instead of consumers choosing one over the other, they'd choose Kentucky Fried Chicken or Subway.

The political marketplace is different. First of all, it's only a one-year advertising cycle (at most). Second, there are only three options, really: Vote for me; vote for the other guy; don't vote.

But Elizabeth Dole was a unique candidate, and a "pox on both their houses" mentality among voters would hurt her more than Bowles.

So I watched with interest Freddie's new spot. The ad was a Bob Dole voiceover about the wonderful qualities of Elizabeth

Dole, with lots of great shots and stills interspersed. The kicker was at the end: As the voiceover said, "Take it from me, someone who's lived with her for years," the camera cut to the Doles's dog, Leader (which is how you address a Senate or House majority or minority leader), whose lips were made to move through computer graphics as if he were the one saying the words. It was hilarious. Bob Dole has a great sense of humor, and he loved the spot, and after more than a year of not offering unsolicited advice (but offering plenty that had been solicited), urged me to think about running it.

I thought it might feel like a cleansing shower to voters in the homestretch, and remind them that Elizabeth Dole was the one they wanted representing them in the United States Senate. I showed it to a few confidants, all of whom liked it but all of whom noted it was a risk in such a tight race. I decided against it and picked up the phone to call Bob Dole to inform him of my decision.

After he graciously deferred to my opinion, I said, "Leader" (former officials retain their last, highest title), "I know if we lose this election my party's 1996 nominee is going to think I blew his wife's race by not running this ad. I'm prepared to accept that. If we were two points down I'd probably run it, but we're two points up. It's margin-of-error, but up. I don't want to risk wasting a spot."

The next day, Bowles launched the hurricane spot in eastern North Carolina, and within hours we had our response in rotation.

Elizabeth wasn't aware of it yet when she called to revisit the dog spot.

"Bob has great instincts. Can you talk to him one more time about the Leader spot before you decide?"

"Elizabeth," I said, somewhat short for the first time in more than a year with her, "Bowles just went up with the hurricane attack. We can't be talking about talking dogs anymore!"

"Oh, gosh," she said. "I can't believe he would do that."

"He did, and we're going to make him regret it."

"Okay, good," said the Steel Magnolia.

And we did. We went up immediately "down east," the eastern region of the state that had been devastated by the hurricanes, with ads denouncing Bowles for his desperation tactics.

On election night, as we enjoyed the victory, Elizabeth Dole doubled over in laughter as she shared the story of the internal ad debate with the rest of the staff, taking special delight in doing her best imitation of this New Jersey boy saying, "We can't be talking about talking dogs anymore!"

CHAPTER FIVE

It's Not About You!

I remember the beginning of Elizabeth Dole's 2002 Senate campaign vividly.

"The Democrats are going to hammer you," I said, leaning over the small, round meeting table in her softly lit office in the Watergate complex. "The first ad they run will accuse you of wanting to 'privatize Social Security.'"

Dole listened intently. I was in only my second meeting with her after agreeing to serve as her general strategist, and I was pointing out that the position she had taken in the 2000 Republican presidential primary in favor of allowing younger workers to direct a portion of their payroll tax to private investments could be a vulnerability in a state where 26 percent of the voters on Election Day are sixty-five or older.

"How wed to this position are you, Elizabeth?" (While everyone else on the campaign called her "Mrs. Dole," she had invited me early on to call her Elizabeth. I was initially uncomfortable calling an American icon whom I'd just met by her first name, but every candidate needs someone in his or her campaign to interact with as a peer. By the way, nobody but her oldest friends actually calls her "Liddy.")

"Well, we can't do nothing," she said. "The system's going to go broke under current circumstances. Personal accounts are the best policy."

"When you're explaining you're losing."

George Will once wrote, "It's axiomatic in American politics that when you're explaining you're losing." It was an axiom I had committed to memory, and I knew we were going to spend a lot of time explaining her position if she held to it. "It's a tough position in this state," I said, pressing her. "We can explain it, but we'll spend a fortune doing so. I'm just asking if it's a fight we really want to have?"

She looked at me as if she felt sorry for me. There was an awkward pause in conversation as I waited for her answer. As I did, I couldn't help thinking that decades after the fact, I could still see how it was she'd been Queen of the May at Duke.

"Well, Ed," she finally said, "we're just going to have to educate the voters."

I knew at that moment she would be the next senator from North Carolina.

Though the issue presented a potential vulnerability, President Bush had run on the same concept two years earlier and turned the "third-rail" ("touch it and die") conventional wisdom on its head, winning seniors despite Al Gore's Social Security "lockbox" onslaught.

Her conviction and willingness to fight for that policy answered the only concern voters might have had in the backs of their minds about her, which was, "Sure, Elizabeth Dole is smart and popular, but does she have principles she believes in?"

Candidates define issues, and issues define candidates.

Elizabeth Dole's support for Social Security personal accounts in a state with a high concentration of senior voters proved she was a woman of principle and made clear she had depth as well as charm. In fact, her Social Security position combined with her support for the North American Free Trade Agreement (NAFTA), in a state wracked by cheap textile imports and furniture from Asia, was really gutsy.

Elizabeth Dole had been the first woman to ever serve as secretary of transportation. She had been secretary of labor, head of the American Red Cross, and a viable presidential primary candidate in 2000. As the wife of the legendary Bob Dole of Kansas—the former Senate majority leader, presidential nominee, vice presidential nominee, and chairman of the Republican Party—she had seen a lot of politics up close. She knew full well the potential cost of her position on these difficult issues, but she had faith in her convictions and faith in the voters.

Erskine Bowles had a tough task from the get-go in trying to win a statewide race against Elizabeth Dole, but he was also saddled with his service in the White House of Bill Clinton, a figure overwhelmingly disdained by North Carolina's voters in 2002.

But Clinton was popular with a key part of the Democratic Party base—African-American voters, who comprised about 19 percent of the vote in North Carolina. In his effort to hold his liberal base while still trying to appeal to the huge chunk of conservative Democrats in the state, Bowles had to be vague on a lot of issues. As a result, it was a lot easier for him to be against Dole than to be for his own policies.

We turned this to our advantage by basically asserting he was for nothing, and the "Bowles Plan" to save Social Security, a blank slate, came to embody this. By the end of the campaign, Dole had turned her plan to save and reform Social Security into a major asset, holding up the flopping pages of her detailed proposal in one hand and "the Bowles Plan"—a blank piece of paper—in the other.

By the last week of October, people were rushing up to her at campaign rallies thrusting blank pieces of paper at her and asking her to "sign my copy of the Bowles plan."

There is a perception that people go into politics only because they want to be important, they want to have "power." While this is undoubtedly true in many instances, most people who go into politics understand it's not about them. Good candidates run because they want to do something, not because they want to be something, and good political operatives understand that the people who actually put their names on the ballot are the ones who are important. Campaigns are about the principles in which you believe and the principals for whom you work.

There was a time in politics when political strategists and tacticians were more mercenary, willing to sell their stock in trade to the highest bidder. A mail piece was a mail piece, an attack ad an attack ad. Whether it helped elect somebody who was for higher taxes or lower taxes, for abortion or against abortion, mattered less than the retainer fee. Political operatives were like lawyers—everybody was entitled to representation.

That's not the case anymore (with the obvious disclaimer that there are exceptions to every rule).

Politics is about something greater than self.

I was fortunate to learn early on that politics is about something greater than self. I learned it from Andy Ireland, when in 1984 he changed parties to run as a Republican for the first time in seeking a fifth term in his U.S. House seat.

After four terms in the House, Ireland was very popular in the Tenth Congressional District of Florida, and could have been re-elected virtually without challenge in 1984 if he'd stayed a Democrat, considering that his district was composed mostly of Democrats.

Democrats would have pulled the lever for him as their party's nominee, and Republicans would have voted for him because he was a "twofer," voting with Reagan yet enjoying the parochial benefits a member serving in the majority can bring.

But Andy Ireland saw 1984 as an important year, too big to ignore the widening gap between the Democratic Party of his youth and the much more liberal party it had become. To run as a Democrat in a year Ronald Reagan was carrying the banner of the Republican Party and Walter Mondale was carrying the banner of the Democratic Party didn't feel right to him, even though doing so would have meant re-election without breaking a sweat.

On March 17, St. Patrick's Day, he announced to a crowd of supporters that he was changing parties and would run in November as a Republican. He announced it six months before Florida's primaries so his former party had time to field a candidate to oppose him in November.

Some people walked out of the event, disgusted. To some conservative Democrats, he was throwing in the towel in the fight over the direction of their party. To more liberal Democrats, he was plainly and simply a turncoat. Republicans, on the other hand, welcomed him with open arms knowing that he could deliver a House seat to the GOP column.

To Andy Ireland, risking re-election to his certain House seat was not about him. It was about a simple fact: The Democratic Party in which he found himself was not the one he'd joined decades earlier. He decided to confront that fact himself, and then ask his constituents to do the same.

In that process, he forced me to do so as well.

As an Irish Catholic born in New Jersey the year John F. Kennedy was inaugurated as the first Catholic president of the United States, I all but had "Democrat" stamped on my birth certificate.

And yet, I related much more to Ronald Reagan in 1984 than

to Walter Mondale. The threat of communism and its oppression of the Catholic faith drove much of my perspective. As a child sitting in the pews of St. Ann's in the Pines, I would hear occasional Sunday pleas from the pulpit to pray for the Catholics trapped behind the Iron Curtain. As early as eighth grade, I had written an essay on the threat posed by the spread of communism. One of my favorite books as a teenager was *The Jesuit,* a fictional thriller about a priest organizing underground masses in the old Soviet Union, and I found Pope John Paul II's rise from communist Poland to the chair of St. Peter inspirational. The concept of individual freedom was the central organizing principle of my politics then as it is today.

The Scoop Jacksons in the Democratic Party were a vanishing breed by 1984, as the party was moving further and further to the left. In announcing his party switch, Ireland said, "I didn't leave the Democratic Party, the Democratic Party left me." Then–Speaker of the House Tip O'Neill only reinforced Ireland's point in his response to news of the party switch by saying Ireland "wasn't much of a Democrat anyway."

Andy Ireland changed parties, and I changed with him, joining at twenty-two the party I would chair twenty years later. My boss and I personified the Reagan Realignment—a middle-aged southern conservative and a young northeastern ethnic Catholic who no longer felt comfortable in the party of their heritage. Michael Deaver, Reagan's brilliant communications strategist, once told me that President Reagan called the party switching that took place during his presidency "a prairie fire" because "you can't stop a prairie fire" and there was nothing the Democratic Party could do to stop the defections that swept through the Old South and blue-collar enclaves of the industrial Midwest and Northeast.

Some of the most successful Republicans in politics have been those who were once Democrats, beginning with Ronald Reagan himself. Other examples abound: former U.S. Representatives

J. C. Watts and Billy Tauzin, Senator Richard Shelby, and former senator Phil Gramm.

When Andy changed parties, there was the obvious question: Do I remain loyal to my party or my boss?

It was not an agonizing decision. I loved Reagan. When he raised a pint of Guinness in a Boston pub, he spoke directly to thousands like me: "Come on in!"

I admired my boss for making the leap. President Kennedy once said, "Sometimes party asks too much." I changed parties and never looked back. I chose to be loyal to my boss over my party, but more important, to myself. Only one member of the Ireland staff quit over his decision. Not all changed parties themselves, but all remained part of his team.

Congressman Ireland's decision to change parties resulted in his race being targeted by the Democratic Congressional Campaign Committee. It was my first campaign, and it was exciting. I was responsible for coordinating the people and the activities in three of the four counties that composed his district—Manatee County on the Gulf Coast and Hardee and DeSoto counties in Florida's "heartland."

I remember returning to my little apartment (so small it had a "Murphy Bed" that folded down out of the wall) one evening after Ireland had left for his home in Winter Haven. He had been in my part of the district for two days of nonstop campaigning. As I got to the door of the building, I leaned over the stoop to throw up in the bushes. The gallons of coffee, long hours, fast food, and constant adrenaline of the past two days had gotten to me. I shivered, wiped my mouth on my sleeve, and thought to myself, "Man, I love campaigns!"

Had Ireland remained a Democrat, his race would have been

what it always had been—a sleeper. He put his entrenched seat at risk for something he believed in, because it wasn't about him. It was about the ideas that affect our nation.

As it was, he won handily. His opponent was a fairly competent county commissioner from Manatee County, the part of the district where I was based, which made my knowledge of the area (and her) important to the campaign. Ironically, Pat Glass, the Democratic nominee, eventually became a Republican herself.

While it was apparent she would be the nominee in November, Florida has a late primary (September), and Glass was legitimately contested for the Democratic nomination. The local media wanted to engage the Ireland-Glass race in the summer, but Ireland insisted he would wait until the Democratic voters decided whom he was to face in the general election before engaging any one of the Democratic candidates. It was a lesson I learned and applied eighteen years later in the Dole Senate race.

In order to win, you have to be willing to lose.

Andy Ireland and Elizabeth Dole were willing to lose, and in politics it is often the case that in order to win you have to be willing to lose.

A recent, dramatic example is Senator John Kerry. When it came to the central issue of the 2004 presidential campaign, the war in Iraq, Kerry adopted policies not necessarily because he believed them to be right, but because he thought they would make it easier for him to win the presidency.

A few weeks before the '04 election, I talked about this with ABC News's George Stephanopoulos. Every week, five of us on the Bush-Cheney team each took ten media pundits to reach out to with our take on the state of play in the race, and George was on my "Fab 50" list that week. George had been a top political advisor to former president Clinton, and still has very good political antennae and strong contacts with the Democratic establishment. That, combined with his Sunday morning show and the fact that he moves around quite a bit and tends to influence other journalists, rated him regular weekly contact from the campaign.

When Stephanopoulos was at the Clinton White House and Dick Armey was House majority leader, Armey once told him, "George, you're good at what you do." In vintage Armey fashion, he added, "But what you do ain't good!"

During the contentious budget negotiations between the White House and the Congress in 1995, George and I were the two policy/press guys in the room of negotiators—cabinet secretaries and House and Senate leaders and committee chairs and support staff. I remember Kasich turning to Tom DeLay on the first day, nodding toward Stephanopolous, and saying, "What's he doing here?"

DeLay nodded toward me and said, "It's okay. We've got one, too."

One what, I wasn't sure, but I took it as a compliment.

George's political and policy experience are valuable to him in his current role, and I think he generally tries hard to be objective. I have less concern with him and Tim Russert of NBC than some of my Republican brethren because I think the experience of having worked in the process is worth a lot, and they are actually less cynical as a result of it.

That said, it's unlikely that a top-level Republican operative would be welcomed at the news division of one of the major networks on the other side of the revolving door, with Fox being a possible exception. It's equally worth noting, however, that while such a move at Fox would be criticized by others in the media, it's accepted at ABC.

Over lunch one day at the Capitol Hill Club next door to the Republican National Committee, Stephanopoulos shared his personal speculation that the reason Kerry was so inarticulate in explaining his Iraq policy was that if he had voted what was in his heart he would have voted against the war resolution and in favor of funding the troops in combat once committed, rather than the other way around.

It was an astute observation. In my view, Kerry had made a political calculation early in the political process that he could not be to the left of Joe Lieberman, Dick Gephardt, and John Edwards when it came to the vote on the Iraq War Resolution, but when Howard Dean began picking up steam in New Hampshire and Iowa, he tacked to the left by voting against funding for the troops after having said on CBS News's *Face the Nation* that it would be "irresponsible" to do so.

President Bush's approach to Iraq was exactly the opposite. He was willing to make unpopular decisions and stand by them in the face of withering criticism and falling poll numbers. In the end, the candidate who'd been willing to lose won, and the candidate who tried to calculate how not to lose, lost.

That's not to say candidates should not be determined to win. To the contrary, they must be. And it's not to suggest that they should be unwilling to take into account the views of the voters. Campaigns are a constant stream of information that flows in both directions, and it's important that candidates listen to the people they seek to represent.

For example, Elizabeth Dole did change one position she had taken in her presidential primary run, which was her earlier support for certain gun restrictions. She knew this could be problematic in a state with a strong tradition of support for Second Amendment rights. She weighed mountains of evidence carefully, listened to progun supporters, researched the issues, and consumed studies, notably the work of John R. Lott, Jr., formerly of Yale, who demonstrated with empirical data that areas with fewer gun restrictions had fewer incidents of violent crime and sexual assault.

By the time she came out in opposition to gun restrictions, she was not only versed in the policy details, she had internalized the position. It was hers. It was a reversal, but it was a reversal she believed was right. She wasn't just mouthing somebody else's policy, but espousing what she believed.

I'm not naïve enough to think the political dynamic wasn't an incentive for her to reevaluate her stance, but I also have no doubt that if she could not have gotten her mind around it she never would have gotten her heart into it.

One-third can beat two-thirds.

During the last two weeks of the Dole campaign as we rolled across North Carolina on the "Eliza-Bus," I continued what had become a Pavlovian response of waking up every night around 2:00 AM to check the tracking numbers, which would come in on my email at around 1:00 AM. I'd wake up, go online in my hotel room, and pull down the fresh polling data, which showed where the two candidates stood and how many undecided voters were still left. If the numbers were good I'd go back to sleep. If they were bad, I'd toss and turn until it was time to get up. Down the stretch, the race was tightening, as we knew it would, but I was concerned about the trendline.

"The Bowles people think they've caught you on the one-yard line," *Wall Street Journal* political reporter John Harwood told me a couple of days before the election.

"It's closing," I said, "but they're not going to catch her."

"How come?"

"Elizabeth was in Dunn last week and two hundred people showed up to see her. Bowles was there yesterday and only about sixty people showed. I don't care what the polls say, we have the intensity."

Polls don't capture intensity. There are issues on which I'd rather be on the side with one-third of the voters than on the side with two-thirds, because the one-third care passionately while the two-thirds may share an opinion but not care deeply about it. Polling data do not accurately reflect the dynamic of intensity; it's only reflected in your gut, and that November in North Carolina my gut felt good.

One of the things that fascinated me about Elizabeth was that in those last two weeks heading into the election, she never asked me how she was doing in the tracking data. Tracking data are the results of daily polling that's done at the end of a campaign, usually the last four weeks or so. It lets you see how a candidate is performing with certain demographics and in specific regions. The nightly "track" is added to the previous two days of data and the three days' worth are averaged out to provide a more statistically accurate rolling poll, or "the roll." A bad track will bring the roll down, and a good track will bring it up.

One day, about a week out, as we were getting jostled back and forth by the rocking of the bus, I asked her, "Don't you want to know the track?"

She just shook her head no, determination in her face. "It doesn't matter. We wouldn't change anything anyway."

A moment later, though, she couldn't help herself. "What was it?" she whispered. I held my thumb and index fingers slightly apart to indicate it was close. She just rolled her eyes and never asked again. I guess it would have just been a distraction, and she was focused on her message, riding the Dole Plan home down the stretch.

The bus trip was a great way to close. It gave us a place to be every day, it generated news in the local markets, and it let us drive message. Our candidate was a machine, flat outworking her opponent. And we had a blast, except for when my cell phone antenna broke and I could not get a signal for long periods of time.

I was going through cell phone withdrawal, getting frustrated every time a call would get dropped midconversation. After I had slammed the phone down on the tabletop one time too many, Elizabeth politely informed me that we were going to be within twenty miles of Salisbury later that day, and maybe I should get off the bus, get my cell phone fixed, and catch up with her later on the trip.

She kicked me off the bus!

I wasn't keeping things loose. I was injecting stress. Once I got my antenna fixed, and my attitude along with it, I flew out to meet the bus two days later.

Cathy and the kids had made a CD and sent it to me for the trip. It included songs like "Magic Bus" by The Who, James Taylor's "Carolina on My Mind," "Runnin' Down the Highway" by the Doobie Brothers and "The Wheels on the Bus Go Round and Round" from a kiddie album. We played it over the PA system as the bus rolled up State Highway 52 into Salisbury for the final stop the Saturday before Election Day. Everyone was in a great mood. This had the feel of a winning campaign, regardless of close tracking numbers, but we had no idea the race would break open the way it did.

The day before the election we flew a small plane into all six media markets in the state. Elizabeth Dole was prepared to accept victory or defeat. Either way, she felt good about the campaign she had waged. Along the way, her instincts proved more important than any polling data we had.

On Election Day 2002, the networks' exit polls leaked out on the internet (as they always do), and they had Dole losing to Bowles by six percentage points. It didn't make any sense. There's no way she could have been doing as well as we knew she was doing in Wake County and other bellwether areas and be so far behind.

She hadn't seen the reports, but Bob Dole had, and he was crushed. I told him I didn't believe the exit data, that I thought we were going to win, close maybe, but a win. As it turned out, Elizabeth Dole was the first Republican open-seat candidate to be called a winner by the networks that night. It came so early, it made me nervous, fearing it would jinx us.

As is custom, Dole's campaign manager Mark Stephens had swapped phone numbers with Bowles's campaign manager that day for concession call purposes. I asked Mark if he wouldn't mind giving them my cell phone number instead of his.

"I'd like to get the scalp," I said.

Mark was happy to have the call come in on my phone, which it did.

"This is Erskine Bowles. Is Mrs. Dole available?"

"One moment, please," I said with a grin as I walked the phone back to Elizabeth's office, where she was sitting, working on her speech. I handed her my cell and left the room.

Bob Dole told me that Elizabeth's win was the sweetest victory he'd ever experienced, and he meant it. After years of his own campaigns and elections, after having been chairman of the Republican Party and having won primary after primary to garner its presidential nomination, nothing was better for him than his wife's win.

If you're like me, you see power couples or celebrity marriages on television and wonder if they're real or more like a business arrangement. If you've ever wondered that about Bob and Elizabeth Dole, I'll let you in on something: It's real.

The Wednesday after Election Day, the entire campaign staff gathered in the Salisbury office. Bob and Elizabeth were both there. I asked everyone to come together because I wanted a few moments to thank all the young workers and share some thoughts with them.

"I have been through a lot of campaigns," I said, doing my best to play the "gray beard" at forty, a role made easier by the fact that just about everyone else in the room was under thirty. It was a classic campaign where young people had come from all around to form its core. There was a "frat house" that about eight of them lived in. Others stayed in the same apartment building.

"And this was one of the best. You all dug deep, worked hard, stayed loyal. And we won. Bottom line, though, is our candidate beat their candidate. Elizabeth Dole flat outworked Erskine Bowles. Thank you for that, Senator." The staff erupted in applause for their newly elected senator. It was the first time anyone on the campaign team called her "senator," as nobody had violated the standard campaign taboo of calling the candidate by the title before voters had spoken.

"Years from now, you'll be at some dinner in Washington and somebody will introduce you to the person next to you, not knowing that you already know each other. And they'll say, 'Oh, how do you two know each other?' And you'll say, 'We were in the Dole Senate campaign in '02.' And you'll both smile.

"I worked for Bob Dole in 1996, and I'm proud to be a Bob Dole guy. And now I'm proud to be an Elizabeth Dole guy, and everyone in this room is an Elizabeth Dole guy. Even if you're a woman, you're an Elizabeth Dole guy."

When you tell someone you're their "guy," you are making a commitment. In addition to being an Elizabeth Dole guy, I'm an Andy Ireland guy, I'm a Dick Armey guy. I'm a Haley Barbour guy. I'm a John Kasich guy. I'm a George W. Bush guy.

They all know it, and they know it is a matter of honor to me. Someone once told me, "In politics, you don't change bosses, you accumulate them."

Much of the analysis leading up to the 2004 presidential election completely missed the intensity dynamic. Lots of stories were written about the Democrats' ground game, which the Democratic National Committee essentially contracted out to so-called "527 groups" like Moving America Forward and MoveOn.org. The other side spent hundreds of millions of dollars trying to manufacture synthetically what was growing organically on our side.

But thanks to President Bush's strong leadership, the RNC built the greatest ground game in the history of our party, registering 3.4 million new voters and enlisting 1.4 million volunteers.

In the last ten days of the campaign, I went from phone bank to phone bank and volunteer center to volunteer center in our target states, and I was moved by what I saw. The two places people are actually excited to see me come through the door are my home and Republican Party phone banks (and in the case of my home, that's mostly my dogs). Volunteers like to hear from the national chairman, and I was more than happy to fire them up.

I'd close my remarks by saying, "Every day, each one of us in this room counts on George W. Bush to do the right thing. And he does. For the next few days, George W. Bush is counting on each of us in this room to do the right thing. Call your neighbors, your family, and your friends. Make sure they vote on Election Day."

Some women would get teary-eyed at the thought of the president counting on them, which he was. I was not exaggerating. These volunteers would thank me for coming to thank them, but I was inspired by them. Many of them were putting in twenty to twenty-five hours a week, on top of a forty-hour workweek! And they were incredibly effective. We ended up meeting 129 percent of our door-knocking goal and met 120 percent of our phone-calling goal. Our volunteers directly contacted over 30 million voters.

They were much more motivated than the kids who were walking neighborhoods for Kerry to pocket eight dollars an hour. Money can't buy you love, and in politics, love trumps hate. According to an Annenberg Survey taken shortly before the election, 81 percent of Bush voters were voting for the president because they supported the president, while only 41 percent of Kerry voters were voting for Kerry because they supported Kerry (as opposed to opposing the president).

The best thing in politics is to run as who you are on things you believe in and win. The worst thing is to run as who you're not on things you don't believe in and lose.

If you run as who you are on things you believe in and lose, you can live with yourself—but if you run as somebody else on things you don't believe in and lose, it can haunt you for the rest of your life with the nagging thought, "What if I'd just been myself?"

It's hard to imagine now, but when Hillary Clinton ran for the late Daniel Patrick Moynihan's Senate seat in 2000, it was not a forgone conclusion she could win.

When Rudy Giuliani opted out of the race to focus on beating prostate cancer, Republicans found in U.S. Representative Rick Lazio a strong candidate to oppose her. Rick was perfect for the state. With a Long Island district, he had generated enough press to have positive name identification in the country's biggest media market. He represented a new generation of Republican leadership for the state, and his moderate, "proenvironment" stance would appeal in the bedroom communities outside New York City. His record of bucking his leadership in support of organized labor was appealing to upstate and western New Yorkers in places like Syracuse, Buffalo, and Ithaca. He had a record of accomplishment on issues like the minimum wage and affordable housing that added gravitas to his youthful demeanor.

Rick is a friend, and I was excited about his Senate bid, and asked only one thing of him: Talk to me before you hire a media consultant.

During my tenure as communications director at the RNC, I had reason to work with a number of ad guys on our side of the aisle, and I was struck by how widely varying were their talents and their fees. A statewide New York race costs a fortune (Lazio and

Clinton each spent $30 million in 2000), and I wanted to give him some guidance on negotiating placement fees, and also share with him some of my thoughts on who would be best for the contest.

I wanted to urge him to hire Greg Stevens, who'd done Tom Keane's successful bids for New Jersey governor, helping to elect a moderate Republican in a neighboring Dem-leaning big state. Greg had a knack for blending light humor into his attack ads, which I thought would be a very valuable trait in a race against a former First Lady.

I learned after the fact that Rick had decided on Mike Murphy, who'd just come off guiding Senator John McCain's nearly successful presidential primary bid.

Mike, or "Murph" as he's known in the business, is very creative and strategically smart, but he has a strong personality that he can overwhelm a candidate. In a lengthy profile piece in the *Washington Post,* he once said, "I fell in love with the meat," the "meat" being Senator McCain.

Given the success of McCain's "Straight Talk Express," the campaign bus that became a rolling press availability in Iowa and New Hampshire, and the fact that New York is a liberal-leaning state, it's understandable that it might have made sense to put Lazio on a bus across New York and dub it the "Mainstream Express." But while McCain had over time established himself as a reform candidate through his advocacy of new campaign finance laws and gun controls, Lazio was perceived, rightly, as a fairly establishment New York political figure, even if he was often at odds with the more conservative national leadership of his party. In fact, he served as assistant majority leader to Dick Armey, with responsibility for cajoling his fellow moderates to vote with their more conservative leadership.

All of a sudden, Rick Lazio the young but substantive legislator who could use his influence with the Republican majority in Congress to help his fellow New Yorkers became Rick Lazio, the reformer running against Congress. Instead of talking about the housing and finance issues in which he had developed expertise, he was talking about the evils of the political system and the need for reform. The good-natured, back-slapping legislator was replaced by a more hard-edged outsider.

The persona reached its zenith on September 13 in the only debate between the two Senate candidates, when Lazio crossed the stage to confront Mrs. Clinton with a pledge he wanted her to sign on the spot that neither candidate would spend any further "soft" (nonfederal) money for the remaining six weeks of the campaign. She handled it as any pro would, refusing to sign anything on the spot.

Instead of damaging her, however, his encroachment into her personal space alienated voters, who felt he had been rude. I got the impression from the repeated airings of the exchange that Rick wasn't all that comfortable in the moment.

As we all know, Hillary won. And I'm not sure that even the most brilliant campaign that played to Lazio's obvious strengths would have changed that outcome. But Rick took the loss hard, and I believe that he did so because he had doubts about his own campaign and wondered "what if" he'd only been more himself.

Mike Murphy is a very good strategist who has won a lot more campaigns than he's lost, and he might like to have this race to do over again in the same way I'd like to do over again some of the things I've highlighted in this book. He has not been as visible in his races as he was in 2000, in contrast to Democratic consultant Bob Shrum, who became the focus of the "Shrum Primary" in the 2004 presidential election.

Political pundits have a variety of yardsticks by which they measure how even unannounced candidates for a presidential nomination are faring long before any votes are cast in Iowa or New Hampshire. They look at largely irrelevant early polls, money raised, travel schedules, and talent signed up.

In 2003, the media created the "Shrum Primary," watching

which of the potential Democratic nominees he'd sign up with. The early speculation was that he would join John Edwards's camp, but he ended up with John Kerry. "Shrummy" started out as a speech-writer and evolved into an advertising producer and general strategist. His flair for self-promotion is evidenced by the fact that of the eight presidential campaigns he has been involved in, his candidate has won exactly zero times. And yet the punditry waited with bated breath for his decision in '03.

"Talking about political process is never good."

It's self-serving and harmful to the candidate when a political consultant makes visible his or her role in a race. I've seen consultants quoted in articles to the effect that "I'm positioning Jones as the centrist in this race."

Haley Barbour, one of the greatest party chairmen ever on either side of the aisle, taught me that talking about political process is never good. The media love it, but the public doesn't like seeing it. It contributes to cynicism and wastes a message opportunity. Talking openly about political process makes it about you, and it's not about you. Instead of saying, "I'm positioning Jones as the centrist in this race," or saying on background that "our polling shows that Jones can win if he's seen as the centrist in this race," what you should simply say is, "Jones is the centrist in this race." State it as immutable fact, not political calculation.

Putting commitment to principles and policies and overarching goals ahead of one's self is not always as easy in practice as it is in theory. When Newt Gingrich and Dick Armey became the leaders of the House Republican Conference in 1993, they established a working relationship that was unique among House leaders, essentially unifying their two staffs and setting aside the kinds of personal rivalries that are inevitable in such situations.

Their remarkable collaboration helped lead Republicans in 1994 to their first majority in the U.S. House of Representatives in forty years. Armey put it this way: "Newt and I agreed to set aside our egos. I agreed to set aside Newt's, and he agreed to set aside mine."

A little over four years later, Gingrich would lose his historic speakership largely because he forgot that it wasn't about him. He began acting on whim, reversing decisions that his leadership team had agreed on only a day before.

He lost what discipline he had when it came to dealing with the media and would say things that got us "off message." By the time he left the House, his colleagues had come to the conclusion that the burden this lack of discipline imposed was not worth the trade-off.

In the summer of 1997, a group of younger House members had grown so weary of Gingrich they tried to figure out a way to remove him as Speaker. Eventually they were joined in the effort by members of Newt's own leadership team. When the plot failed, there were recriminations all around. Armey was accused of supporting their effort and then reversing himself, a charge he vehemently denies.

After the electoral debacle of 1998, when our majority was reduced to only a five-vote margin, and in the wake of the failed coup attempt, House Republicans were antsy and the scent of a shakeup was in the air. It was so strong, in fact, that Gingrich decided not to seek the Speakership again and to abandon his House seat, before his colleagues took an opportunity to replace him involuntarily.

Armey, badly damaged by the fallout from the failed coup, was too weak within the conference to make a run at Speaker, and Representative Bob Livingston of Louisiana, who was chairman of the powerful House Appropriations Committee, quickly wrapped up the job.

Armey was vulnerable, and Representatives Steve Largent of Oklahoma, the Hall of Fame receiver for the Seattle Seahawks and a favorite of the most staunch conservatives in the conference, and Jennifer Dunn, the telegenic moderate from Washington State, each announced bids for majority leader.

Two spots down the leadership ladder, Conference Chairman John Boehner faced a formidable challenge from J. C. Watts, also from Oklahoma, the only African-American Republican in Congress.

Watts had proven himself a very effective messenger. I remember when he was a freshman being interviewed by CNN's Bernard Shaw, who asked him how Republicans could continue to push for budget cuts when polls showed public approval of Republicans in Congress falling precipitously, which could mean defeat in the fall.

"Bernie," Watts said in his amiable way, "the title Dad is more important to me than the title Congressman, and I'm going to do what's right for my children and the children of this country."

It was beautiful.

About a week before the conference election, Illinois representative J. Dennis "Denny" Hastert, Tom DeLay's chief deputy whip, asked for a private meeting with Armey. Rumors had been rampant for some time of members urging Hastert into the race as a consensus candidate, and we feared Hastert was coming to discuss the idea with Armey.

The two were friends. Though a loyal deputy to DeLay, who reviled Armey after the coup episode, Hastert, in typical fashion for him, maintained a good relationship with Armey and had committed to support him against Largent and Dunn.

The two men talked one on one for nearly an hour in Dick's spacious office on the third floor of the Capitol. Afterward, Armey confirmed that our fears had been realized.

"He said he didn't think I could win, and he asked me to release him from his commitment and support him as a consensus candidate," Armey said.

"What did you say?" Kerry Knott asked him.

"I said if I didn't have the votes, I would do exactly that, but I have the votes."

He would have, too. Armey would have rather seen Hastert be leader than Largent or Dunn if he thought that was the only choice.

Obviously in the course of an hour, they talked about a lot more than that, but that was the gist of what clearly could not have been an easy conversation for either of the two men.

Since leadership contests take place in order from top to bottom, the majority leader's race was the first contested race on the ballot the morning of the organizational conference. The practice in a leadership race is that the votes are cast by secret ballot, tallied, and the lowest vote-getter drops out and another ballot is distributed until someone gets a clear majority—in this case 113 votes.

As a result, leadership elections often hinge on the second ballot, which is much more difficult to count. We knew Armey did not have the strength to win on the first ballot, and he consequently expended a lot of effort appealing to Largent votes as the more conservative of him and Dunn—and Dunn votes as the more reasonable between him and Largent.

But in a confounding twist, there were four write-in votes cast for Denny Hastert on the first ballot, meaning that the three declared candidates would all be on the second ballot, with Hastert dropped out.

Armey and Dunn survived the second ballot, with Largent getting the least of the three.

By this time, all bets were off. It's impossible to get a hard count in these races, and you have to assume 10 percent slippage from whatever your commitments are, as members hate saying no to their colleagues.

Boehner and Armey were good friends, their staffs were close—Boehner's press secretary succeeded me as Armey's press secretary in the majority leader's office—and most of the members who were voting for Armey for leader were also supporting Boehner for conference chairman, the job in which Boehner had followed Armey (with Armey's support).

As the third and final ballot was being prepared and distributed, a number of Boehner's friends and some of his colleagues in the Ohio delegation pulled him off to the side. One of Armey's aides overheard them.

"They were trying to get him [Boehner] to throw his support to Dunn, saying that if Armey lost, the conference would have gotten its scalp and he would be more likely to hold on to the conference chairmanship."

It was a legitimate strategy, and it might have worked, but Boehner stood firm. "We're voting for Dick," he said. "We committed to him, and he'd be better as majority leader."

It is to this day one of the most principled, selfless things I have ever known a politician to do.

Armey won on the third ballot, and I have no doubt that both Denny Hastert and John Boehner voted for him on the first, second, and third ballots because their word is their bond.

In the next race up that morning, John Boehner lost the conference chairmanship to J. C. Watts. He took his loss with grace and dignity, went on to be a strong and effective chairman of the House Education and Labor Committee, and in 2006 was elected to succeed Tom DeLay as majority leader, winning on the second ballot.

Shortly after Armey held on to his leadership position, Bob Livingston shocked the political world by announcing that he was stepping down after *Hustler* magazine publisher Larry Flynt had dug up some dirt from Livingston's past. Within hours, J. Dennis Hastert emerged as the consensus for the Speaker's job. He was elected by acclamation, no one even challenging him for the House's top spot. Speaker Hastert and Majority Leader Boehner won their jobs because their colleagues know they are men of honor, and when they make a commitment to someone you can take it to the bank.

Loyalty, loyalty, loyalty.

Here's the commitment: As long as you remain ethical, I will be with you through the end, through thick and thin. I won't cut and run. I won't go "on background" with a reporter and pee on you. I'll skip a paycheck if our cash flow is off. When everyone else says you're losing, I'll say you're winning. I'll be there at the printer's at midnight making sure the mail piece is right. I'll tell your cousin he can't have a job. I'll be with you until the last dog dies. I am with you until you release me.

Any decent political operative can quote you *The Godfather.* ("Fredo, you're my brother and I love you, but don't ever take sides against the family again.") Our candidates are like dons and we're all Luca Brasis.

This is the code that is at the center of the political enterprise. Ken Walsh, who has covered the White House for *U.S. News and World Report* for more than a decade, asked me in 2001 shortly after President Bush was sworn in how the president "demanded such loyalty from all of you."

"That's what you all don't understand," I said. "He doesn't demand it, he commands it."

As chairman of the Republican National Committee, I frequently had the privilege of being around the president and the First Lady, and I generally did the same thing every time: I left them alone.

I didn't need to "chat" with the president, didn't need to share what I thought might be a "fascinating insight." I was his guy, and as such, the most important thing I could do was not impose on his scarce time.

He and Mrs. Bush were always incredibly gracious. "How you doin', Eddie," he'd ask.

"Fine, sir. Thank you," was all I'd say.

After I'd been in the job for about eight months, Cathy and I were invited to ride in the presidential motorcade to the RNC gala in March 2003. What I didn't know at the time was that we would not only ride in the motorcade, but ride with the president and the First Lady.

"Awesome" is a word that has been cheapened by overuse, but there's no other way to describe how Cathy and I felt as we sat in the president's limousine with Mrs. Bush and him.

As we rode the two miles to the Washington Hilton, the president and First Lady made Cathy and me so at ease it was like we were on a double date.

"How old are your children?" Mrs. Bush asked as the limo began easing out of the White House grounds.

"Twelve, nine, and seven," I said.

"Twelve, ten, and seven," Cathy said, correcting me. (Carrie had just had a birthday.)

"You've got to know your children's ages, Eddie," the president chided.

As we rode up Connecticut Avenue, it was readily apparent that George W. and Laura Bush are also a real couple. He digs her and she digs him. They were fun to be around as they waved to the impromptu crowds that had gathered on the sidewalks as their motorcade went by.

The president didn't need to invite us to ride with him, but I suspect he knew that those ten minutes helped make the long hours that come with being party chairman in an election year—and the frequent separation from your spouse that goes with the travel—a whole lot easier to live with.

After the 2004 election, I took my eighty-three-year-old father to one of the White House Christmas parties so he could meet president and Mrs. Bush and have a picture taken with them.

"It's nice to meet you, Mr. President," my father said, shaking his hand after going through the receiving line. My father came to this country from Ireland as a nine-year-old boy with nothing but the clothes on his back, and never dreamed that one day he would be face-to-face with the president of the United States.

To my father's surprise, the president said, "We met before, didn't we?"

They hadn't. My father was confused, but I wasn't. I knew right away why he said it. My dad didn't know it, but I had asked for him to be in the greeting line for the president when he went to my native Burlington County, New Jersey, only three weeks before the election. Unfortunately, my father ended up going into the hospital for shortness of breath and had to have his pacemaker adjusted on the day of the presidential visit, and my brother took his slot.

Flying up on *Air Force One,* I saw the president's briefing book for the event, which noted that one of his greeters would be Jack Gillespie. The hospitalization came too late to change the brief. At the White House in December, he just assumed my dad had been one of the many who'd met him at the event in New Jersey.

I can understand his not realizing my dad hadn't been in one of the many crowds of tens of thousands of people he'd seen in the last months of a grueling campaign, but it's remarkable to me that he would have remembered that tidbit from a two-month-old briefing book.

One other anecdote from that White House picture. Cathy's parents were also with us, and as the president greeted them he asked where they were from. "Texas," they said, with some pride.

"Where?" the president asked.

"Dallas."

He turned to Cathy and said, "I didn't know you were a Dallas girl."

At that moment, the photographer snapped the picture.

"Yes, sir," Cathy said, as we began to move on so the couple behind us could get their picture.

But the First Lady stopped us. "Wait a minute!" she said. "He was talking when the picture was taken," she said, referring to the president. "Can you take another one?" she asked the photographer.

We reassembled for the photo, and just as it was to be taken she teasingly chided the president. "No talking this time!"

This was the last of ten White House Christmas parties, where over ten thousand photos were taken of the president and the First Lady with guests, but Mrs. Bush knew it was the only one that Cathy's parents and my father would have, and she wanted it to be perfect for them.

After Cathy and I had our picture taken with the president and Mrs. Bush at the 2004 senior staff Christmas party at the White House, I began to worry that maybe he and Mrs. Bush might mistake my deference to his time for coldness, or worse, rudeness.

The concern prompted me to write the president a personal letter, thanking him for entrusting me to head the Republican National Committee, and for his leadership of our great country. I wrote him that his discipline, his devotion to his wife and daughters, his commitment to principle, and his faith in God set an example for all Americans, but especially those of us who are honored to work for him.

I told White House Chief of Staff Andy Card of my concern, and asked if he'd make sure the president got my letter before he left for Crawford for Christmas. "First of all," Andy said, "I'm sure the president doesn't think you're rude, but get me the letter anyway. He'll like to read it."

When I saw the president again two days before his second

inauguration, I broke my own rule of not imposing on his time. Before introducing him to the members of the Republican National Committee for my last time as chairman, I said to him backstage, "Mr. President, may I take a moment to thank you for letting me be a part of your re-election."

Before I could finish my thought, the president reached his hand behind my head and pulled my head to his shoulder. "I know, Eddie," he said. "You did a great job. Thank you."

I knew he'd read my letter. In retrospect, I suspect Andy was right. The president and Mrs. Bush probably don't have time to waste wondering if I had been "cold," and even if they did, it's not their nature to think that way.

But I felt better having written it, because I'm one of his guys. The president at one time was one of his father's "guys." He lives by the code himself, and it permeates his organization. His people are loyal not only to him, but to one another.

For years, there was speculation in the media and in political circles of a rivalry between Karl Rove and Karen Hughes. The fact is, Karl and Karen are like brother and sister. They can disagree over tactics or message, but if anyone were to badmouth Karen to Karl or Karl to Karen, they'd find themselves on the receiving end of walking papers in fairly short order. "Bushies" understand that loyalty to one another is the same as loyalty to the president.

Karen Hughes has one of the best "ears" of any political operative I've ever worked with. Despite having served at the right hand of the president of the United States and serving at the very top echelon of our State Department, she always sees the world through the eyes of the working mother she is. She's smart, fierce, straightforward, and funny, with a big, booming laugh.

President and Mrs. Bush command loyalty from people like Karen because they are inherently good and decent people. Let me give you another example, this one about Mrs. Bush.

About two weeks after I had returned from the recount in Miami in 2000, I got a call at my firm, Quinn Gillespie and Associates, from a young woman at the Presidential Inaugural Committee.

"How many computers and phones are you going to need?" she asked in earnest.

"What?" I asked, confused.

"I'm in your office and we've installed your computer and phone, but how many more are you going to need for the communications staff?"

That's how I learned that I would serve as communications director for the Presidential Inaugural Committee for the forty-third president of the United states.

"Twenty phones and fifteen computers," I said.

Karen Hughes called two days later, and I acted surprised when she asked me if I'd serve in the role. I knew Karen had tasked me with the job because I could move paper quickly and without need of her approval, having absorbed her style during my time on the campaign. Everyone else from Austin was in the midst of facilitating the transition or adapting to their new jobs in the administration.

I cleared everything without bothering Karen, except for the official biographies of the president-elect and vice president–elect and the incoming First Lady and Mrs. Cheney, which were to be in the official inaugural program that would ultimately go into the National Archives.

For that, I wanted a clear "CYA" paper trail, so I called Karen.

"Fax the president-elect's to Crawford, and the incoming First Lady's to the Governor's Mansion," Karen said. She gave me a fax number, and I fired off Laura Bush's draft biography with a cover sheet addressed only to "The First Lady's Office," noting that there was a tight deadline and it would be appreciated if someone could get back to me later that day. I put my cell phone number on the page, made a copy of the entire fax package, and took it with me as I left to coach my son's fourth-grade basketball game.

Since June, I had been in Philadelphia for the convention, Austin for the campaign, and Miami for the recount much more than I had been in Alexandria for the family, so I was determined not to miss a game. I had the draft bios beneath my lineup sheet on my clipboard as I entered the gym at Bishop O'Connell High School that Saturday afternoon in January.

As my boys lined the wall of the gymnasium along the baseline waiting for the game ahead of ours to finish, the cell phone on my hip vibrated. I was surprised when I answered to hear, "Ed, this is Laura."

"Oh, hi, Mrs. Bush. How are you?"

"I'm fine. How have you been?"

"Fine," I said, a little nervous to be talking to the next First Lady of the United States ("FLOTUS," as she would be referred to in countless memos and emails over the next eight years).

"I've got a few edits to the biography," she said, as I pulled the draft to the top of my clipboard and began moving from the gym to a nearby staircase where I could take notes.

Just then the game clock buzzer loudly sounded to signify the end of the current game.

"Where are you," Mrs. Bush asked, hearing the obnoxious sound on my end.

"I'm at my son's basketball game," I said, "but it's not a problem. I have the bio right here and I'm happy to take edits."

"No, no. That's not necessary. How long will your son's game last?"

"About an hour, but it's really not a problem."

"We're just packing here, Ed. Why don't you call me at this number in two hours? Do you have a pen handy?"

"Yes, ma'am," I said, as she gave me the number.

I called it when I got home after John's game, and Laura Bush answered. She had given me the direct line to the residence.

"Is this a good time?" I asked. When she said it was, we proceeded to go through her official biography to ensure its accuracy.

When we finished, I couldn't help but tell her how much I appreciated her letting me call her back. "I didn't even get a chance to tell you, I wasn't just at my son's game, I was coaching it!" I said.

"Well, whether you were coaching or just watching, it was much more important than what we just did," Laura Bush said.

And she meant it. To Laura Bush, a father being at his son's fourth-grade basketball game at a high school gym is more important than making sure the biography of an incoming First Lady is accurate before it goes into the National Archives of the United States of America.

It's just one example of why the easiest applause line I would later use as chairman of the RNC was ". . . and we need to make sure Laura Bush gets four more years as First Lady!"

The president and Mrs. Bush's commitment to family permeates the White House, where the staff are encouraged to be with their spouses and children. It's not unusual to see kids in and around the White House, their parents having brought them in with them.

After I had been in the chairman's job about a year, I asked Andy Card if there might be some time on the president's schedule for him to take a photo with John Patrick, Carrie, and Mollie. I was increasingly on the road, and I wanted them to get some reward for having to miss their dad. The president understood, and an Oval Office visit was scheduled within a couple of weeks.

The day of the visit, there was another act of violence in Israel, and President Bush held a press conference with Israeli prime minister Ariel Sharon on the South Lawn. I called Andy that morning and said maybe we should reschedule our visit since things were so hectic.

"Ed, things are always hectic here," Andy said matter-of-factly. "We're going to keep this on the schedule. Let's not disappoint the kids." Each of them treasures the pictures from that day.

Governor Barbour

Haley Barbour is one of the greatest political minds of our time. I learned more from him in one year at the RNC than I learned in twelve years of school and four years of college. One of the better moments of my chairmanship was being with him the night he was elected governor of Mississippi.

I flew into Jackson the day of the election. The week before, Haley's campaign had given me a list of county party chairmen in the state who were working their volunteers' fingers to the bone making calls on Haley's behalf. Getting a call from the national party chairman helped energize these county chairs, so they could energize their volunteers.

On Election Night, Haley felt good, and so did his very talented wife, Marsha, who'd been his partner throughout the campaign. "Mr. Chaaaaairman," she'd say to me in her lilting southern accent. "I love calling you Mr. Chairman. I hated calling Haley that, but I love calling you it."

But Election Night was dragging on without a concession call, even though Haley had built up a substantial lead over incumbent governor Ronnie Musgrove. "I don't understand this," I said. "There's no way he catches you at this point. He's gotta call soon."

"He's hoping I fall under fifty," Haley said.

Under Mississippi law, if no candidate gets 50 percent of the vote, it goes to the state House to decide, each representative acting as an elector in a statewide electoral college. There had already been some speculation about whether some of the Democrats in the majority would vote their districts or their party if they were in conflict.

By midnight, I had to go to bed. My flight out was at seven the next morning, and I had a 6:00 AM wake-up call.

But at twelve-thirty my cell phone rang, and it was Todd Bachman, my "body guy," which is what politicos call that young aide you always see traveling with a party chairman or elected official who takes notes for follow-up, makes sure you get from place to place on time, and handles all the miscellaneous things that arise on the road. When I was chairman I used to joke, "I used to be a guy, now I've got a guy."

"Haley's about to make his victory speech," Todd said. "I thought you'd want to know."

Of course, I did (as Todd knew I would or he wouldn't have called). I threw on my pants and shirt and jacket and went down to the ballroom just as Haley took the stage. I watched from the back as he gave a very substantive, agenda-oriented speech.

As he finished, he turned to Marsha to give her a kiss. She reached up and pinched his cheeks in a genuinely spontaneous, adorable moment. He grinned big as can be. I knew right away it would be the shot in the papers the next day.

I was going to go back to my room, but decided I had to at least call him "governor" before leaving. After all, that's what I'd come for.

I worked my way to the front of the room, near the stage where Haley had just delivered his speech. I wasn't sure how I'd get to him, but he was leaning down shaking hands with his supporters and I was trying to make my way through the crowd to say good-bye.

He spotted me from about twelve feet away, and I saw him whisper to one of the state troopers who'd now been assigned to him and point to me. The burly officer came over to the edge of the stage and called me to him, reached down, and pulled me up on the stage with him.

"The governor would like to see you," he said. I got to Haley and Marsha just as they were about to descend the stairs leading backstage.

"Congratulations, Governor!" I said, hugging him.

"Let's go get a drink, Gillespie."

"You bet."

We worked our way out the back door and into a waiting SUV, two troopers in the front, Marsha between Haley and me in the middle backseat. We drove around to the back of the hotel and entered a back door, scooted down the hallway, and found his suite.

"I've been saving this," he said, pulling out a bottle of Jameson's from the bar in the room, knowing it's my preferred brand.

It was late, and I was worried about getting up for the plane in the morning, but I'm a Haley Barbour guy and I wanted to celebrate with the man who'd been my boss, business partner, mentor, and friend, and who was now a governor.

The three of us sat in his room for a wonderful, quiet moment and savored a little whiskey and a big victory.

"Thanks for all you did, Ed. Every time we asked for something, you delivered."

I didn't tell him the standing order I'd given months ago to RNC Political Director Blaise Hazelwood: "Whatever Haley asks for, the answer is yes."

("That's so cool," she had said, understanding the code, herself.)

Politics is like an old trade, with apprentices, journeymen, and masters. I was a journeyman when I went to work for Haley, and a master when I left. My friend and former business partner Ed Rogers had worked for both Haley and Lee Atwater, and had possession of the large blue leather chair that both had used during their tenure as chairman. I saw it at a reception in the Barbour Griffith and Rogers offices not long after I'd been elected chairman, and told Ed I'd like to use it as my own during my chairmanship.

"I'd be honored for you to," he said.

There was a plaque on the back of it commemorating the tenures of two of the most effective chairmen the Republican Party had ever seen, and I promised him that I would return it to him in good condition, and if President Bush were to be re-elected I'd add my name and tenure to the plaque.

In January 2005, I sent the chair back with all three of our names on the plaque on the back of the chair, though I still don't think I belong in the company of the other two.

Haley was an old-fashioned party boss, elected in his own right to lead the committee when Republicans were completely out of power in 1993. He had such control of the party that when Bob Dole became our presidential nominee, he kept Haley in the job rather than risk alienating a wide swath of Republicans (including a good number of governors and members of the House and Senate) by replacing him with one of his own people, as is customary.

Loyalty is a two-way street. While I was serving as RNC chairman, Senator Elizabeth Dole won a tough contest for chairmanship of the National Republican Senatorial Committee (the campaign arm of the Senate Republican Conference) against Senator Norm Coleman of Minnesota. The race pitted two of the most talented first-term senators against each other, each with distinct merits for the job. Elizabeth won by one vote.

I had not been able to help her at all, neither providing counsel nor talking to senators on her behalf, since it would have been inappropriate for me to do so as RNC chairman. I was happy for her, though, when I saw her at the Senate policy lunch the day of her victory. After the lunch broke up, I gave her a hug, and she asked me to walk back to her office with her to discuss staffing the NRSC. She and Mark Stephens and I were meeting in her office when we were interrupted by a staffer informing the senator she needed to go back to the Capitol for a meeting of the leadership team.

After she left, I told Mark it had been difficult for me to watch our friend in such a tough battle and not be able to be involved, and to have to monitor from a distance.

"We know that, Ed," Mark said in his deep southern drawl.

"She and I talked about it a couple weeks ago, and we agreed it wouldn't be right to ask you to help. I told her if she asked you to make a call, you would, because you're an Elizabeth Dole guy, but that you shouldn't do that in your position. And she didn't want to put you in those alligator jaws. There were times we were tempted to call, but she always ended up saying, 'We have to keep Ed out of this.' "

That is class.

Later that day, I talked to a reporter for *Roll Call* about Senator Dole. He agreed to a ground rule that would make it clear I was not involved in her leadership race, but was commenting only as someone who had worked closely with her. I pushed back on a few negative questions about her, including the charge that she could be indecisive. I told him that Bob Dole had given me a lot of sage advice over the years, but perhaps the best advice he ever gave me was when I first went to work on his wife's campaign and he told me, "Ed, if you say yes to Elizabeth early it will save you both a lot of time."

I was surprised the next day by the emphasis the reporter put on my comments, including the headline on the jump page ("Gillespie says Dole Knows how to Win"), and while he had honored his commitment to note that I had not been involved in the NRSC contest, I was quoted as one of her "political inner circle."

I immediately picked up the phone and called Senator Coleman, with whom I had developed a warm relationship during the Bush-Cheney '04 campaign, in which he had been one of the president's most effective surrogates.

"Senator, I just saw *Roll Call* and I wanted to tell you directly that I was not involved in Elizabeth's race. She is a great friend and I admire her a ton, but it would have been inappropriate for me to have helped her while serving as RNC chairman."

"I appreciate that, Ed," he said. "And I'm glad to hear that because I had been told that you were, but I wasn't ever sure. It's Washington, and people say stuff like that."

"I wouldn't do that. And if I had gotten involved, I would have told you. I would have owed you that."

"You don't owe me anything. Somebody flipped on me in the end, and I know who it was. You're a good guy, and I trust you. Let's stay in touch."

That, too, is class.

I call her Senator now, not Elizabeth anymore. She has told me not to, but I told her, "I appreciate that, but you worked hard to get that title. And frankly, so did I."

One of the great things about politics is the people you get to meet, and becoming friends with Elizabeth Dole and her remarkable husband, Bob, has been a joy.

Someone once asked Cathy, "How does Ed like working for Elizabeth Dole?"

Cathy said, "He likes it so much if she were any younger I'd be nervous!"

Consultants are important to a campaign, but there are some who think they could put a monkey in a navy blue suit, and if he'll follow their plan he'll get elected. It's not the case. Candidates matter. They matter a lot. In a close race, the candidate's performance is decisive on Election Day.

CHAPTER SIX

//

CUTTING CORNERS CAN
CAUSE BLEEDING

Haley Barbour says that in politics, "Everybody eventually gets their turn in the barrel." Mine came in 2001. It began with a call from *Time* magazine's Michael Weisskopf. "If you've got anything you want to get out, I'll be fair to you, but you ought to get it out."

Michael Weisskopf is an exceptional investigative reporter. To the extent people outside Washington know of him today, it's because he lost his right hand in Iraq when a grenade that had been thrown into the Humvee in which he was traveling exploded as he was throwing it back out of the vehicle, saving the lives of three U.S. Marines with whom he was traveling, as well as his own.

I had dealt with him repeatedly over the years, first when he and his beat partner, David Maraniss, extensively covered the Republican takeover of Congress in 1994 and later when he covered the campaign finance scandals of the late nineties including charges of Chinese money laundering at the Republican National Committee (charges that proved to be false).

Michael is one of the few reporters I have dealt with who routinely has more information than I do. Reporters and sources trade information all the time. The truth of the matter is, I have learned as much from reporters as they have learned from me over the years, picking up intelligence on what the Democrats are up to, how much money an opponent has on hand, what amendment they'll be offering. You have to give information to get information, but reporters know a whole lot more than they write about in their newspapers or broadcast in their stories.

The difference with Mike was he often knew more about stuff I was supposed to know about than I did.

Whenever I get a message that Mike Weisskopf called, I get the same uneasy feeling you get when you see a police car in your rearview mirror. Your first thought is, "Was I speeding?" If somebody in Washington is breaking the rules, a call from Weisskopf is likely to be coming their way.

Inevitably in the practice of politics and public affairs, there is temptation or even pressure to cut corners, to skirt the spirit if not the letter of the law or the rules. Such corner cutting rarely goes undiscovered, and is never worth the risk.

> **The people who go farthest in the political profession are those who play by the rules.**

This was reinforced for me in the fall of 2001, when Enron, the giant energy company, collapsed in spectacular fashion. Enron was a client of Quinn Gillespie and Associates (QGA), and given my role in the Bush-Cheney 2000 campaign the spotlight was quick to fall on my representation of the company.

The week we signed Enron as a client, it was featured in a *Fortune* magazine cover story as one of the ten best-run companies in the country. We were proud to have won out over a number of other firms that had vied for their business, and considered them a marquee client. We had no idea that their success was illusionary, based on a very complicated recipe of book-cooking, and were as surprised as anyone by the company's implosion.

I had as much to do with the company's bookkeeping as I have to do with Daimler Chrysler's new car designs, to draw an analogy to another QGA corporate client. Putting my name in the story,

however, enabled newspapers to put the names Enron and George
W. Bush in the same sentence.

The media were hoping that this financial scandal would also
be in some way a political scandal, and if I had done anything inappropriate that would have gone a long way toward making it one.

In 2001, I had organized the 21st Century Energy Project
(21CEP) to advocate enactment of the administration's commonsense energy policies. I recruited into this coalition a number of
market-oriented groups like Americans for Tax Reform and Citizens for a Sound Economy (which has since merged with Empower
America to become Freedom Works), as well as policy analysts from
think tanks like the Cato Institute and the Heritage Foundation.

The 21st Century Energy Project was organized as a "C-4,"
named for the section of the tax code (501 c. 4) that allowed for the
creation of nonprofit entities to advocate enactment of certain public policies. 21CEP's purpose was to energize grassroots support for
energy legislation, book policy experts on TV and talk radio, and
run ads in members' districts in support of the bill. I served as president, and officers of the board came from some of the groups par-
ticipating.

I announced its formation at the National Press Club and unveiled an ad that mocked opponents of the administration's policies
as trapped in the seventies, replete with disco music and images of
long lines of cars waiting for gas.

The media are skeptical of such ad-hoc coalitions because
they can be subject to abuse (as Jack Abramoff and his partner in
crime Michael Scanlon proved), but the 21CEP played by the rules.
Its membership consisted of long-standing and legitimate think
tanks and conservative groups that are philosophically opposed to
government-imposed price controls because such controls lead in-
exorably to government rationing.

After Enron imploded, every record of contact between QGA
and the company and between QGA and anyone in the administration concerning energy policy was collected by the Senate Govern-

ment Reform Committee, chaired by former Democratic vice presidential nominee Joe Lieberman.

Every email, phone record, and Word document was pulled together and turned over, including the organizing documents for the 21st Century Energy Project. After months of scrutiny and a committee report that was fifty-one pages long, I was barely mentioned.

Know the law.

Oregon Congressman Wes Cooley was one of the freshmen who'd washed ashore in the House of Representatives with the Republican tidal wave that was the election of 1994. (RNC Chairman Haley Barbour jokingly referred to freshman Representatives Steve Stockman of Texas, who'd defeated House Judiciary Chairman Jack Brooks, and Michael Patrick Flanagan, who'd defeated Ways and Means Chairman Dan Rostenkowski, as "Congressman Flotsam" and "Congressman Jetsam.")

Cooley had a bad habit of exaggerating things, particularly his own life story. Oregon has a "truth in campaigning" statute that makes it illegal for politicians to deceive voters over their qualifications for office. One of the things Cooley had exaggerated was his military record, asserting combat experience when he'd only been a paper pusher. It was enough that the state was investigating whether he was in violation of the statute.

As the negative stories and his legal fees mounted, it became apparent that the embattled rep was unlikely to survive the '96 cycle even though he was in one of the more favorable congressional districts for a Republican. Bill Paxon, the smart and effective chairman of the National Republican Congressional Committee, had tried unsuccessfully to get Cooley to retire after his one term rather than seek re-election. Newt, Armey, and Haley were all frustrated at the prospect of losing a seat that should be Republican.

One night I went over to meet Cathy at a fundraiser for her boss Joe Barton at the American Trucking Association, a couple of blocks down First Street from the Cannon House Office Building, and ran into Wes Cooley there. He seemed as though he'd been there awhile when he pulled me aside and asked me why everyone wanted him to go.

I made the case that, "however unfair it might be," the negative publicity had hurt him with his constituents. He launched into a detailed repudiation of one of the "exposés" purporting to show that he had exaggerated his record as a motorcycle race competitor. We sat side by side on a sofa by a big, tinted-glass window drinking cheap wine as the catering staff broke the room down, and he told me of his exploits in various competitions around the country.

"That's great, Mr. Cooley," I said. The wine had given me a "what the heck" attitude, so I figured I'd take a shot at the same thing our leadership had been urging for weeks.

"Mr. Cooley, don't you want to go out on your own terms? Not give the Dems and the Oregon press the satisfaction of defeating you?"

He stared out the window and didn't say anything for a long time.

I excused myself, figuring I'd only made him angry. He nodded good-bye, and I thought that was the last time I'd ever talk to Wes Cooley.

The next day, however, he called to ask if I would come by his office. Once I was there, he told me he'd been thinking about what we talked about the night before for some time, and he was leaning toward not running again, but he had some issues he wanted to be addressed. I was excited that somehow I was in the middle of brokering an exit deal where people much more experienced and savvy than me had been unable to.

Cooley had three requests: One, he wanted to serve as Speaker Pro Tem, to have a video of him gaveling open a session of Congress to give to his grandchildren; two, he wanted the party to cover his legal fees, which were about to break six figures; and, three, if Bob Dole were elected president he wanted to be appointed director of the Bureau of Land Management.

He went into great detail about why item three was so important, something about the bureaucracy totally screwing up mining policies in the West. He was passionate.

"Mr. Cooley, obviously I'm not in a position to make promises, but these certainly seem to be reasonable requests, and I'll take them to the chairman and the leadership and let you know what they say."

I left his office in the Longworth Building and ran-walked back to the RNC, rushing to Haley's office. He grabbed his white legal pad and wrote down the three demands with his black Mont Blanc pen. When he finished, he looked up at me and said, "Well, I'm sure Newt will go along with number one. And I can get some of the bigger state parties to kick into a legal defense fund, but only up to two hundred thousand dollars. As for number three, it's a felony to offer anyone a federal position in exchange for seeking or abandoning a bid for federal office. But tell him if Dole wins, I'll write him a strong letter of recommendation," he said, laughing.

Later that day I pulled Paxon aside after a leadership meeting and told him what had happened. The Capitol is dotted with alcoves, and he and I stood in a Capitol corridor about twenty feet from the entrance to the House floor in one of the recessed windows that ran from floor to eighteen-foot ceiling, assured a measure of privacy by the rich gold curtains that hung in front of it.

"Great work, Eddie," Bill said. Just as I'd finished briefing him, Speaker Gingrich was sweeping by and Bill called him over. "Tell him what you just told me," he instructed.

The Speaker began smiling as I gave him the data dump.

"Well, I'll let him open the House if Haley'll pay his legal fees and get him a job!" he said, laughing at having the easiest of the lifts.

"Haley will round up legal fees of up to two hundred thousand dollars," I told him, "but it's illegal to promise anyone a federal job in exchange for running or not running for office."

"Well, see if the first two are enough," he said.

It took me a full day to get Cooley on the phone, and I was worried when he didn't return my call that he had changed his mind about leaving. But he called the next day, and I told him I had his answers and would like to get together to discuss them.

Oddly, instead of asking me to come to his office or offering to come to the RNC, Cooley asked me to meet him on the East Front of the Capitol, on the House steps. "I'll pick you up in my car."

I stood at the bottom of the House steps of the Capitol, waiting and wondering why he was driving his car. An older-model American car pulled up, with tinted-glass windows so I couldn't see inside, but the Oregon congressional plates gave him away. It slowed to a stop and I hopped in.

As Cooley headed out East Capitol Street into some of the roughest neighborhoods in the city, I actualy began to feel a little scared.

"Well, have you got some answers?" he asked.

At that moment it occurred to me that maybe Wes Cooley was wearing a wire, that he was involved in some kind of sting operation in exchange for the Oregon authorities' dropping the charges against him. Maybe he figured we'd go for the job deal, and then the Oregon guys would get bigger fish like Barbour, Dole, and Gingrich. Suddenly, I felt I was in something way over my head. I was glad the answer to the job question was no, however.

"The Speaker would be happy to have you open the House for a session to get you on video serving as Speaker Pro Tem," I said, checking the first box.

He smiled. "Good."

"And Haley will help raise money for your legal defense fund, but only up to two hundred thousand dollars. But he also said if you don't run again, the authorities are likely to drop your case anyway, so it should end up covering everything."

"Okay."

We had turned around and were heading back now toward the Capitol.

"As for the Bureau of Land Management job," I said, "it turns out it's illegal for anyone to promise a federal job in exchange for someone running or not running for federal office. It's a felony, Mr. Cooley."

I spoke clearly and precisely so the microphone would pick it up, wherever it might be hidden.

But I realized there was no microphone when Congressman Wes Cooley looked at me in exasperation and said, "I know that! Why do you think we're riding around in my car?!"

I couldn't believe my ears. I was dumbstruck, but also relieved that I wasn't somehow a target of some kind of corruption investigation (even though I hadn't done anything).

"Well, if Bob Dole gets elected, Haley Barbour will have had a lot to do with it," I said, pressing forward now with my original mission of trying to get him to leave Congress. "And I'm sure he will be happy to put in a good word on your behalf."

With that, he pulled up in front of the RNC and let me out. "All right, let me think about it," he said. He got out a week later.

You have to know the law. Haley's understanding of the law served him well in the summer of 1997 when the Senate Government Affairs Committee launched a full-scale investigation of campaign finance activities in the '96 election cycle.

After becoming chairman in 1992, Haley founded the National Policy Forum, a party-oriented "think tank" that could serve as an incubator for policy proposals that could be used by GOP candidates to run on. After Clinton's defeat of former president Bush in '92, there was a sense among party leaders that after three Republican presidential terms, we had gone a little flat.

Clinton had capitalized on that sense, drawing on the Democratic Leadership Council (DLC) for ideas to give his campaign a feel of freshness and ingenuity. Haley wanted to have a clearinghouse for some of the thinkers in our party to come together with ideas for market-oriented health care policies, welfare reform, crime, trade, and national security policies. It was constituted as a C-4, and therefore allowed to accept unlimited, nonfederal "soft" dollars. He started the organization with seed money from the RNC.

In the midst of the '96 campaign cycle, confronted with the onslaught of spending by the labor unions and other liberal groups, Haley had the NPF repay the RNC its seed money. What caught the eye of the media and later congressional investigators was the fact that a Taiwanese national by the name of Ambrose Young had provided funding to the NPF before it repaid the RNC, which made it appear as though the NPF was funneling foreign money into the national party.

Democrats were in a world of hurt over Clinton fundraising practices in '96, especially raising money from Chinese nationals. It was within this cycle that Al Gore attended a fundraiser at a Buddhist temple, accepting thousands of dollars from monks who had taken vows of poverty, and said there was "no controlling legal authority" over soliciting campaign contributions from his West Wing office. When the story of Haley's meeting with Ambrose Young broke, Democrats jumped on it as a way of making the campaign finance scandal seem to be a bipartisan one.

But Haley had done nothing illegal, as became apparent in the course of the hearing. He gave a virtuoso performance that even the *New York Times* acknowledged in its July 25, 1997, edition:

"I understand politics a little bit," confessed Haley
Barbour, his throaty Mississippi drawl instantly suffusing the
Senate hearing room with the air of a master player of big-
money campaigning, an ardent pro who knows when he is
being challenged to watch his back and hold his own. . . .

Mr. Barbour took his seat before the microphone as one of
the most successful party chairmen in modern times, the one,
in fact, who had helped finance the stunning 1994 election
victory that enabled the Republican senators assembled before
him to sit on the majority side of power at the hearing table.

Nimbly as a dealer cracks the cellophane from a fresh deck
of cards, Mr. Barbour soon worked the minority side of the
table with his opening remarks, sending Senator John Glenn
of Ohio, the ranking Democrat on the committee, into a
deep, silent scowl by alluding to an old scandal—the savings
and loan affair that once dogged Mr. Glenn and others with
conflict-of-interest charges. Mr. Glenn suffered only the
lightest of Senate criticism as a result, but the accusations
proved harrowing. . . .

This was to be turnabout day for the Democrats, who
have been pressed for the past two weeks in having to defend
President Clinton from charges of big-money campaign
abuses in his re-election drive. But Mr. Barbour came
prepared with state-of-the-art graphics and detailed
knowledge of the Democrats' own venturings along
the fine rich line of fundraising law arcana.

Spinning in the hallway outside the hearing room after it was
over, I told reporters the Democrats' chief counsel looked like his
dog had just died.

Put it out there.

When Karl Rove invited me to lunch in the private dining room off the White House Mess in the Summer of 2002, I had no idea what he wanted to talk about, but didn't ask before saying "sure."

Not surprisingly, he had begun thinking past the midterm to the president's re-election. "What do you think of Ken [Mehlman] as campaign manager?" he asked.

"I don't think you could get anyone better," I said.

"I agree. Marc Racicot [at the time, chairman of the Republican National Committee] is going to be campaign chairman."

"That's good. He'll be perfect."

"Do you have any thoughts who might be good to replace him?"

I thought for a moment, then threw out the names of a couple of former House members. Karl agreed they were worth considering, but wasn't sure they'd be right for the job. I looked down at the shrimp on my plate, trying to decide if I should say out loud what I was thinking.

I decided to. Without looking up, I said, "I've always thought I could do that job."

When I did look up, Karl was smiling and nodding his head yes. He then made clear that this was a preliminary discussion, saying that the "Leader of the Free World" would make the decision when the time came. But I figured that even the preliminary discussion had not taken place without the president's knowledge. For the next seven or eight months, Karl and I would have periodic conversations about the RNC. The prospect of following even indirectly in Haley Barbour's footsteps as RNC chairman was daunting to me, but at the same time exciting.

Finally, in May 2003, Karl asked me into his office. "The president would like to give you a call," he said. "Should he?"

"I'd be honored. I'd love to do it. But before he does there's something you need to know. After I had graduated from college and had moved back to New Jersey, I drove down to Washington one night to pick up my car from D.C. It was sitting in the parking lot of my apartment building with a blown transmission, and a guy who used to come into my father's bar was a mechanic and he volunteered to take his tow truck down one night and get it.

"We left together from the bar, which was stupid. We had both been drinking. By the time we got to the Baltimore Washington Parkway it was after midnight, and he was starting to fall asleep at the wheel. I had to drive, but I'd never driven a tow truck before, and it turns out they're illegal on the parkway anyway.

"So we got pulled over, and I was charged with a DUI, and received probation before judgment. After six months of probation, the charge was dropped."

"That doesn't disqualify you," Karl said.

"Well, unfortunately, there's more. There were diet pills in the glove compartment of the tow truck, and I was charged with possession of a controlled dangerous substance. That charge was dropped as well."

"I appreciate you telling me about it," Karl said. "I'll raise it with others, but I don't believe it's going to make any difference."

There is no formal vetting process for a top political spot like RNC chairman or campaign chairman as there is for a government job. There is no background check for RNC chairman, but I knew that if I were under consideration for a government job this arrest would have surfaced, because it had in 2001 when I was vetted for the Presidential Inaugural Committee. It surprised me then because I had been told years before that after I successfully completed my probation the record was "expunged." I thought that meant there was no record, but apparently—for those of you who have had your record "expunged"—it doesn't. It didn't disqualify me from serving on the Inaugural Committee, but since this was a top political post and I now knew that a record of the incident existed somewhere, I felt the White House should know about it.

I also raised it with White House Chief of Staff Andy Card, wanting to get more than one perspective on it. I wasn't trying to get myself disqualified, but I didn't want to run the risk of taking the job and then have some reporter dig up the information (or have some Democrat oppo researcher feed it to a reporter), then have the White House embarrassed by me.

I actually agreed with Karl's assessment. I didn't think an arrest of more than twenty years ago would matter, but I also knew it wasn't my judgment call and that the president, in the person of his top staff, was entitled to the information and to the knowledge that it could some day come out in a newspaper somewhere. The bottom line is, you've got to put it out there for others to know before moving forward with a position of importance.

It was a painful thing to raise. Making it public now is not easy to do, either. But it supports my rule that loyalty is paramount, and it would have been disloyal to President Bush for me to have accepted such a position without making sure that I had been properly vetted.

I have to say, it wasn't easy. Not only did I really want the job, but *Roll Call* had reported that I was likely to be tapped for it. I tried to hold the story back, noting—accurately—that I had not been offered any job (but adding that I would be happy to stuff envelopes if it would help re-elect the president).

It had become known in concentric circles at the White House that I was the pick, which is how it found its way into *Roll Call.* Karl, Ken, Andy, Dan, Cathy, and I had known of the very real possibility for a year and there was never a word of it anywhere. Had the president gone with someone else at that point it would have been embarrassing to me, but you've got to put it out there in a situation like that.

As I went in to talk to Andy about it, I couldn't help but remember an earlier discussion he and I had had about a top job.

After the 2000 campaign, Andy asked me if I was interested in serving as assistant to the president for legislative affairs, the job known as "the president's lobbyist."

I talked to my partner Jack Quinn about it. Taking the posi-

tion would have meant severing all ties to Quinn Gillespie. With
the White House, the House, and the Senate all in Republican
hands, the firm would not do as well with its name Republican taking his name off the door. At less than one year old, it might not
even survive.

Having served as President Clinton's White House counsel,
though, Jack understood the pull of a senior White House position.
We looked through the client roster, tried to figure which would
stay regardless, and decided the firm could carry on. Knowing it
represented a financial blow to him, Jack encouraged me to take the
position in a display of selfless personal loyalty.

Cathy, too, agreed I should do it. We analyzed our financial
commitments, what we had in the bank, and what the job paid and
figured we had enough in savings to draw down on to make it
through two years in the job. Though I had been in the private sector for four years, we largely still lived as though we were on government salaries anyway—with the exception of a beautiful house we'd
bought on the Potomac. We were mortgaged to the hilt, but our
Oldsmobile was paid for and we were leasing our minivan.

The thought of my being the president's top legislative person
was exciting to Cathy and me. When we worked on Capitol Hill
for junior members of Congress, the names of the legislative liai-
sons would float around, and they were big deals. Bea Oglisby, who
worked for President Reagan, was a household name on Capitol
Hill. We'd actually met and gotten to know a little bit former president Bush's head of legislative affairs, Fred McClure, because he was
a Texas Aggie like Cathy, and Joe Barton represented Texas A&M in
his district. It was like knowing a celebrity to us.

I called Andy in Crawford, where he and Karl and Karen were
helping the president through the transition, to accept the position,
but he wasn't in. I left him a message to give me a call back.

Jack and I decided we needed to ease the QGA staff into the
idea that my return to our still-only-one-year-old firm might be
short-lived. We gathered in our office's common area after work for

chips and Cokes and wine and Guinness, and broached the idea. Some were happy for me, but others were concerned. There were some people who only recently had joined the firm, and the Republicans who did had come there for me, not Jack. Some felt the firm couldn't survive my departure.

"That didn't go so well," I said to my partner after the meeting broke up.

"They'll be okay," he said, but I wasn't sure he was sure of that.

I left QGA that night in time to coach my son's seven o'clock basketball practice. It was a chilly night, cold enough to see your breath. There's a bell tower in the grassy center of the circular drive in front of the school. As John and I walked toward our car after practice, I looked up and saw that the floodlights aiming up at the cross atop the bell tower had the effect of projecting the cross high into the sky. It was a really cool effect, like a Bat-signal for Catholics.

Just then, as if out of nowhere, John said, "Thanks for coaching my basketball team, Dad." It was a very nice, very out of the ordinary thing for an eleven-year-old boy to say.

"You're welcome, son," I said. "I like coaching your team."

I really did. I started thinking how we'd need to get a new coach when I went to work at the White House. I wondered who would do it. I had a co-coach, but he could not make the time commitment to be the coach. We'd have to figure that out.

I was lost in thought as we drove home from St. Louis School after practice, thinking about who would coach the team. Then I started thinking about how I would tell the boys, and mostly how I would tell John. I looked over at him in the front seat. He'd just started riding in the front seat since I'd gotten back from Florida, big enough now that the air bag was not dangerous to him.

He was staring out the window, lost in his own thoughts. I liked riding in the car with him after our practices, when it's dark outside and it's just the two of us. Sometimes we talk about serious things, sometimes we talk about silly things. Sometimes we don't talk at all.

I had been gone so long. First Philadelphia. Then Austin. Then Florida. The kids had been very happy when I came home from filing *Bush* v. *Gore,* and crushed when I left again for Miami-Dade. Being the White House congressional liaison essentially meant moving to the White House for the next two years. The senior staff meets every morning at seven-thirty. The House and Senate are in until all hours of the night.

It really wasn't fair to the kids, and it wasn't fair to Cathy. The lobbyists and public relations specialists at QGA were grown-ups, but John, Carrie and Mollie were ten, eight, and five. As I got closer to home, I got closer to deciding against taking the job after all.

Like many Irish Catholics, even devout ones like myself, I'm not Pentecostal in nature. But I started thinking that maybe seeing that big cross beamed into the sky while hearing John say, "Thanks for coaching my basketball team, Dad," was some kind of sign. By the time I got into bed, Cathy and I had agreed it would be best for the family for me to say no when Andy called back.

Which happened a little after 8:00 AM the next day, as I was pulling out of the McDonald's drive-thru on Route 1 just before the ramp onto the Wilson Bridge.

"Sorry it took me so long," he said.

"No problem, I know you're crazed right now. But I've got to tell you, you're going to wish you had called last night, because last night I was calling to tell you I was taking the job—but this morning I can't."

"Why not?"

I explained about my concern about being away from the children, and he said we could make the hours manageable, but I knew—as he probably did, too—that I wouldn't cheat the job of the necessary hours if I ended up taking it. I don't doubt Andy would have tried to make it work, but it's not my nature to leave early when others around me are working late. I even confided in him about the sign of the cross!

He was disappointed, as was I. "I hope this doesn't keep me off the list for future consideration," I said. "I would really like to serve the president some day."

"Don't worry about it, and you already have," he said. "We'll need new blood at some point."

"Andy, I want you to know if anyone asks about this I'm going to say I was never offered anything, since the president himself never asked."

"I'm going to say it was the background check," Andy said with a laugh. He was busting my chops, but I thought to myself as I hung up my cell, "That might be more right than he knows."

Lobbying.

So I returned to my firm, which grew considerably because I was one of the few people from the Bush campaign who did not go into government.

A reporter once asked me how to describe my firm, Quinn Gillespie and Associates, for a story he was writing.

"It's a public affairs firm," I said.

"I guess you don't want to call it a lobbying firm, huh?" he asked, suggesting with a certain amount of smugness that I was somehow trying to conceal that QGA does lobbying.

"You're welcome to call it a lobbying firm if you want, but a third of our revenue comes from communications strategy and public relations."

As with any profession, lobbying is perceived through a lens crafted by the worst in its ranks. Most lawyers are hard-working, professional people who provide an important service in their community, but lawyers as a whole bear the burden of a perception perpetuated by the "ambulance chasers" in their ranks. Most used car dealers honestly help people who can't afford a new car get affordable transportation, but they're identified with the minority in their ranks who unload lemons on unsuspecting consumers. And most reporters are honest and abide by the highest standards of journalistic ethics, and for every Jayson Blair or Mary Mapes there are thousands of honest and fair reporters.

Most lobbyists represent honest companies, industry associations, union members, or groups of people with a common interest and do so with integrity, but are lumped in with the guys who unfairly bilked millions from unsuspecting Indian tribes.

The growth of Washington lobbying is the natural by-product of the growth of the federal government, which is too large and too regulatory, and of a tax code that has grown too complicated.

I didn't go to Washington in hopes of becoming a lobbyist, and I don't actually know anyone who did. But after thirteen years of long hours and low pay on Capitol Hill and in campaigns, and after Mollie Brigid came along behind John Patrick and Carrie, the prospect of leaving a long hours-less money job for a less hours-long money job got more appealing.

When Republicans took control of the House in 1994 and I became communications director for the new majority leader, I found myself hearing from lobbyists pretty frequently because they not only provide background information on policy, they also often provide polling data and focus group results to demonstrate the popularity of a proposal with voters.

After one meeting it occurred to me that the person urging me to look favorably on a certain bill probably made twice what I was making. It dawned on me that I could make more money *knowing* Ed Gillespie than I was making *being* Ed Gillespie.

My transition to lobbying was made all the more easy by the fact that Haley Barbour wanted me to join him when he returned to his firm, Barbour Griffith and Rogers.

There is a sense that lobbyists should not be necessary in an open democracy like ours, but the fact is getting something done in legislative and regulatory processes often requires a greater understanding than most Americans gain from Social Studies or Politics 101 classes.

In theory, you shouldn't need a lawyer to participate in our legal system, but more often than not it makes sense to retain one. I could have sold the rights to this book without an agent, but I don't really understand the publishing industry. Anyone should be able to call an assignment editor at a TV station or a reporter at a newspaper to pitch a story idea, but the same types of organizations that hire lobbyists hire public relations firms to handle such tasks. You could put your own ad in the paper to sell your house, but it makes more sense to do it through a realtor. In theory, talented actors should be able to get roles without benefit of an agent, but they hire one.

The rap is that lobbyists trade on their relationships with government officials, but the axiom "it's not just what you know but who you know" doesn't apply only to the field of government relations. It's pretty much true of every field I just mentioned. Lawyers shmooze judges at Bar Association meetings, PR agents take editors to dinner, and realtors are constantly expanding their connections with potential sellers and buyers.

The implicit, negative assumption is that members of Congress, mayors, governors, subcabinet secretaries, commissioners on independent agencies, and White House staff wouldn't adopt some of the positions they do except for being "in the pocket" of some "special-interest group" or "high-powered lobbyist."

The media perpetuate this notion, filtering virtually every domestic policy debate through the prism of money and "influence peddling." The supposition is that how members of Congress vote follows their political contributions, never that political contributions follow how members of Congress vote. But do liberal politicians really vote in support of labor unions because they get money from their political action committees, or do labor unions give liberal politicians money from their political action committees because they support their policies? Do conservative politicians get money from "big oil" because they favor deregulation and oppose excise taxes, or do oil companies contribute to conservative politicians because they favor deregulation and oppose excise taxes? (And why are oil companies always "big oil" but labor unions never "big labor"?)

Transparency is critical to the process of campaign financing and lobbying activities, and they should be covered by the press, but the media today focus so much on this aspect of the policy process that it crowds out legitimate discussion of truly substantive and consequential issues. It's true that doctors favor reform of medical liability laws and trial lawyers oppose it, and it's true that the American Medical Association (AMA) gives money to those who support medical liability reform and the American Trial Lawyers Association (ATLA) donates to those who oppose it, but is that really the most important aspect of this debate? (Disclosure: Quinn Gillespie has worked to pass medical liability reform on behalf of the American Hospital Association.)

Good doctors are closing their doors, fleeing their practices. In some parts of the country expectant mothers drive more than sixty miles to see an obstetrician. Rising insurance rates are driving up the cost of health care. At the same time, there are many who have suffered from real instances of malpractice. There are merits on both sides of the issue, and it is felt in communities all across the country. But thoughtful articles analyzing the policies in question are the exception to the rule, while whole forests have been felled to provide the newspaper space devoted to the relative influences of the docs and the trial bar.

The rules of politics apply to lobbying as well. Any lobbyist who provides bad information to a member of Congress or administration official will burn an important bridge. A partisan lobbyist like me would never urge a member of Congress of my own party to take a position that would hurt him or her with constituents back home or make it harder to get re-elected.

I have taken on some tough issues on behalf of clients, but

have always been comfortable representing them. For years, I used as my benchmark, "Can I tell Dick Armey this is my client and this is the position I am advocating and not have him think to himself, 'Gosh, what happened to Eddie?' "

My firm has argued vigorously for the U.S. government to drop tariffs against Mexican cement and Canadian lumber imports, but in spite of my free trade point of view, I advocated on behalf of steel companies and the steelworkers union for tariffs against illegally dumped foreign steel because I concluded that foreign steel companies were in violation of our trade laws, and because I have a fairly wide populist streak that leads me to believe this nation needs a vibrant steel industry.

Despite being a fiscal conservative, I argued on behalf of the National Air Traffic Controllers Association (NATCA) against privatizing air traffic control towers because I think they play an inherently governmental role, as we saw starkly on September 11, 2001, when they landed over three thousand planes in less than two hours. I also worry about the economics of having the airlines responsible for manning the towers, given how many of them seem to be constantly revolving in and out of Chapter 11. There is a public safety role that should be immune from the kinds of cost-cutting pressures found in the private sector.

Naturally, I have wondered if I would have taken these positions had I not been paid to do so, but I have turned down potential clients because I was not comfortable with their positions. QGA declined to work on behalf of government funding for stem cell research beyond the limitations of President Bush's policies because of my prolife views and those of others in the firm, and we have not represented tobacco clients because many of the Democrats in the firm are uncomfortable doing so.

Being a lobbyist often affords you the opportunity to learn about things you otherwise would have no reason to know of. In 1997, I was approached by the Independent Truckers Association to work on restoring the business meal deduction for those individuals covered under the Department of Transportation's Hours of Service rules, which applied to interstate truckers and skippers on the St. Lawrence Seaway.

Real truckers and seamen with legitimate business expenses for their food on business trips had been caught in the net of tax reformers in the same way dolphins are caught in tuna nets from time to time.

By the 1980s, corporate America was seen as abusing the business deduction, and the "three-martini lunch" was part of the rallying cry for major tax reform. Anyone or any group that stood against its passage risked being dubbed a special-interest spoilsport, but policy-makers restored the deduction for those blue-collar transportation workers, and I'm glad I was able to help restore what we dubbed "the chicken-fried-steak break."

Transparency is the most important rule of lobbying. If I find myself talking to an elected official about something that touches on a client interest, I make it a rule to note that "I have a client interest in this," and err on the side of caution even with tangential connections. In talking with one high-ranking Republican about the need to be the party that gets things done, I suggested the importance of the Republican Congress being results-oriented and enacting Social Security reform, secondary education standards, tax simplification, an energy bill, and a telecom update. In so doing, I noted that I have clients who want to see energy and telecom bills pass. I would have listed these issues without a client interest, because they are likely to be accomplishments of the Congress anyway, and I wasn't advocating the specific policies my clients cared about, but didn't want him to think I was hiding something.

The vast majority of lobbyists advocate policies they believe in for clients they respect in an honest manner, but there are some who try to game the system to their personal advantage. It's a shame that Jack Abramoff is who most people would probably think of today when asked their image of a lobbyist. But Abramoff's business practices were against the law for a reason, and the fact is he is going to jail for his unethical practices.

In the same vein, I don't know a member of Congress who would exchange his vote or the sanctity of his position for a million dollars, but apparently there is at least one who can be wrongly influenced for a French toilet, as was Duke Cunningham, the former congressman from San Diego now serving eight years in prison.

As former president Clinton was leaving office, he issued a number of controversial pardons on his way out the door. The most controversial was the pardon of Marc Rich, a billionaire financier living in Switzerland who'd left the United States after being charged with illegally trading oil in violation of government sanctions.

Rich's lawyer and the man who pressed his case with President Clinton was Clinton's own former White House counsel Jack Quinn. Jack Quinn is also the Quinn in Quinn Gillespie and Associates.

Our firm did not represent Rich. He was Jack's client from his time at the law firm Arnold and Porter, and when he left Arnold and Porter he continued as lawyer to Rich in his personal capacity. When we started our firm together, Jack told me that he had a client he wanted to continue to represent on the side, and warned me that he was a controversial figure but said he felt strongly that his legal case was just.

Rich's case was controversial, but had it remained in the standard legal process Jack's representation never would have become an issue. It was the pardon that elevated it.

Though he acted within the bounds of the law and used every option available on behalf of his client, Jack took a beating, and we had to work hard to make sure his individual legal representation of

Marc Rich did not harm our public affairs firm, which is not a law firm at all.

It was hard for me, personally. Jack is a great partner and a close friend, but I thought Clinton made a huge mistake in granting the pardon. Jack stands by it from a legal perspective, as he did very ably in a nine-hour House hearing and a seven-hour Senate hearing.

Jack took his beating like a man, and I'll always respect him for it. Friends suggested it would be best to dissolve our partnership, but I wouldn't. When you make a commitment to someone you don't cut and run when the going gets tough. You work through it, and you stand by that person in difficult times.

If I had felt that Jack had done something illegal or immoral, I would not have stood by him. I don't agree with his decision to pursue a pardon, but I understand why he did it.

"The worst thing in those situations is that your phone goes dead," said Don Fierce, one of my political mentors, talking about Washington "scandals."

I've always remembered that, and always remembered how much I appreciated it when in the middle of the Enron coverage my friend Charlie Black called to ask if there was anything he could do to be helpful. Ever since then, I've tried to make it a point to call friends who find themselves in tough situations.

I called Armstrong Williams when the media reported that he had written op-eds in favor of the No Child Left Behind Act without noting that his firm was paid by the Department of Education to promote the policy. I called Bernie Kerik when his nomination as secretary of homeland security was scuttled. I called Scooter Libby after he'd been indicted—not for leaking classified information but for not having fully cooperated with a federal investigation—and gave money to his legal defense fund.

On the last day of my RNC chairmanship, before I introduced President Bush, I told him, "Mr. President, I will never embarrass you as your former RNC chairman." He knew I meant that I'd never do anything that would reflect badly on him or his administration.

It's a commitment I consider every time a potential client offering handsome compensation walks through my door.

PART II

THE BATTLE FOR JUDICIAL RESTRAINT

CHAPTER SEVEN

SUPREME COURT SUMMER (AND FALL AND WINTER)

On Tuesday, July 19, 2005, as the Senate Policy Lunch was about to begin, I got a message on my BlackBerry from Ann Gray, my assistant at the White House, where I had been working for a few weeks as a "special government employee" heading up the effort to confirm whomever President Bush nominated to replace retiring supreme court justice Sandra Day O'Connor.

I had taken a leave of absence from QGA to work full-time managing message, preparing for Senate hearings, working with outside groups, and being a link to senators on the Judiciary Committee.

The message was, "Chief looking 4 u."

In a sign of respect and affection, everyone at the White House called the White House Chief of Staff Andy Card "Chief," and referred to him in conversation as "the Chief."

I stepped outside the Mansfield Room and leaned into a windowsill to call him from my cell.

"Dan has asked the networks for time," he said, meaning that Dan Bartlett had requested that the networks preempt their programming that evening to take a live announcement from the president of his nominee.

"Can I tell the senators?"

"You should. It'll be reported shortly."

Indeed. By the time I walked back into the lunch, there was already a buzz as senators had gotten their own messages from staff on their BlackBerries. Senate Majority Leader Bill Frist came in and leaned down to where I was sitting to ask if the reports were accurate.

"Do we have a nominee?"

"We do."

"Can I announce that here?"

"Yes sir."

"Okay. Here we go!"

The Senate Policy Lunch is the one time during the course of a legislative week when all members of the Senate Republican Conference come together. It's an informal lunch in a very formal room—the Mansfield Room, named for the legendary Mike Mansfield, one of the strongest majority leaders in the history of the chamber.

There's a buffet along the side wall, and senators serve themselves and then take a seat at one of the nine round tables around the room. There's chit-chat and informal checking of vote counts on bills and amendments until the chairman of the Republican Policy Committee (at that time Senator Jon Kyl of Arizona) calls the meeting to order and turns to one of his colleagues to offer a blessing of the food.

The RNC chairman attends the Senate Policy Lunch on a regular basis, so my attendance in my capacity as head of the president's confirmation effort marked a return to the lunch for me. I always enjoyed it. Every senator is a major political figure in his or her state, but the policy lunch feels a little like a high school cafeteria.

The elected leaders, the "cool kids," sit at the center table at the front of the room before a huge marble fireplace. The "old bulls" sit by the door near the back, with powerful senators Ted Stevens and Pete Domenici. Younger members like John Ensign, Richard Burr, and John Sununu tend to sit over at the corner table, kind of out of the way. Senior staffers have a designated table in the back corner of the room.

I'm a House guy, but in the course of attending the Senate Policy Lunch over a two-year period as RNC chairman, I really came to know and like the Senate Republicans.

There's a natural rivalry and not a little bit of resentment toward the Senate from House members. Dick Armey summed it up when Florida's Connie Mack decided to first run for the Senate back in 1988. Mack told his friend Armey that he should think about running for the Senate, too.

"You can do so much more as a senator than you can as a House member," he said.

"Awww, Connie, I'm not a big enough asshole to be a senator," Armey joked. "But you—you've got potential!"

As Frist was confirming reports of an evening nomination announcement, my BlackBerry and cell phone were buzzing with messages from reporters chasing down rumors of who the president would name.

As I was leaving the lunch, CNN's John King called me on my cell, and this time I answered it.

"I'm hearing that Michael Luttig has just loaded his family into their car in their Sunday best and are leaving Richmond for Washington. Do you know if that's true?"

Michael Luttig was a highly regarded judge on the Fourth Circuit Court of Appeals. King was fishing, trying to get me to confirm him as the nominee or rule him out. I couldn't do either, and told him so.

"So are you waving me off Luttig?"

"John, I can't wave you off or on anyone."

The media were in a full-fledged frenzy by the time I got back to the White House. I have never been subject to such pressure before. Every reporter I knew was calling or emailing me chasing down rumors.

It's understandable. Washington had gone eleven years without a Supreme Court nomination, President Clinton's 1994 nomination of Justice Stephen Breyer having been the last. A Supreme

Court confirmation is the rare intersection of the executive, legislative, and judicial branches of our federal government.

And it is rare. For context, consider that in our nation's history there have been more than 10,500 members of the U.S. House and a little fewer than 1,900 U.S. senators, but only 110 Supreme Court justices. John Glover Roberts's later elevation to chief justice put him in even more rarified air, as we have had 43 presidents, but only 17 chief justices.

I went straight to Andy Card's office when I got back from the policy lunch at around two-thirty, but he was down in the Oval Office. His assistant Christal West told me I should go to Deputy Chief of Staff Joe Hagin's office, which is a few yards down the hall from Andy's.

When I opened the door, I saw Judge John Roberts seated at the head of a small conference table, Dan Bartlett to his right, White House Counsel Harriet Miers across from him, and her deputy, Bill Kelly, to his left. He stood up as Harriet introduced me to him. I shook his hand and congratulated him on his nomination, then sat in the chair between him and Kelly to join the discussion.

It was interesting to meet in person someone I already knew so much about. I had seen his picture and read a four-inch binder full of his writings and background, and had drafted a Senate floor speech in support of his nomination, but now we were face-to-face for the first time. It seemed to me he knew what my role was even before Harriet made the formal introduction. Unlike some other potential nominees, Roberts was a Washingtonian, and I had a sense he may have read reports that I'd be running the confirmation effort at the White House.

When Harriet and Bill finished walking through important procedural issues concerning his nomination, I began asking biographical questions that I knew would be of interest to the media and the public, and that would also make it harder for the extreme liberal groups to demonize our nominee.

"Did you play any sports in high school or college?"

"How'd you meet your wife? Any children?"

"Do you play any musical instruments?"

Captain of his high school football team—good! Met Jane at a group beach house—normal! Two adopted children—wonderful! Trombone in high school—not drums, but okay.

After fifteen minutes or so, we left Roberts alone to work on his remarks for the announcement. As I was leaving Joe's office I met the judge's wife, Jane. I knew from the background that she was Jane Sullivan Roberts, and I was happy to see that she was an outgoing, attractive Irish lass!

Somewhere along the way in the course of the day the media had come to the conclusion that the president was going to nominate Edith Clement, chief judge of the federal court in the Eastern District of Louisiana. Clement was definitely on the short list, but Roberts had apparently clicked with the president in their interview. Bush ended up bucking the conventional wisdom that he should pick a woman to replace Sandra Day O'Connor as a result.

I popped into Bartlett's office.

"Can you believe this?" I said of the cable news coverage of Clement.

"Don't you think it's getting to be a problem?" he asked. "We may get some backlash when it's not a woman now."

He was, as usual, right. I told him that even Cathy, a staunch conservative and strong supporter of the president, was hoping the nominee would be a woman. Dan noted that the First Lady had expressed the same sentiment in an interview the week before.

"She was giving voice to what a lot of women think," I said.

"I think we've got to knock it down," he said.

"All right. I'll start. It will narrow the field for them, but we can't let this hang out there."

"Well, it's not fair to her," Dan said.

I hadn't even thought about that. Poor Edith Clement. By this time, she knew the news accounts weren't accurate (the also-rans were notified after Roberts had been offered and accepted the nomination), but she wasn't at liberty to confirm or deny them.

By midafternoon we began actively discouraging the Clement speculation, but many in the media cynically assumed we were just trying to throw them off the right track. Finally, someone close to Clement to whom she confided that she was not the nominee told a reporter, and by dinnertime the Clement coverage began to subside.

The fact that the Roberts nomination held until the White House confirmed it to the Associated Press (only after notifying the Senate's "big four"—Majority Leader Frist, Minority Leader Harry Reid, Judiciary Committee Chairman Arlen Specter, and Ranking Member Patrick Leahy) was a source of fascination and amazement to official Washington.

Jim VandeHei of the *Washington Post* asked me on Thursday how it was the name never leaked out. He was working on a process story and seemed to think it was fear that had motivated the secrecy.

I explained to him that it wasn't fear, but respect.

"George W. Bush campaigned all over the country for a second term. It was his name on the ballot, and he's the president of the United States and he gets to nominate someone to the Supreme Court, and he gets to tell the country who he's nominated. It would be an incredible act of self-indulgence and disrespect to deny him that prerogative."

Steve Schmidt and White House Communications Director Nicole Wallace told him pretty much exactly the same thing.

The story never got written, or if it did it never ran.

The night of the nomination, Andy wandered into my office at around seven-thirty.

"Let's go watch the announcement," he said. Candi Wolff, assistant to the president for legislative affairs, and Jamie Brown, one of her "specials" (a special assistant to the president) who was spearheading the legislative affairs shop's part of the confirmation, joined us on the way.

It was Jamie's idea to invite Arlen Specter to the announcement, and he was in the East Room of the White House when we got there.

As RNC chairman, I had helped Specter beat back a primary challenge from Congressman Pat Toomey. Philosophically, I was much more in synch with Toomey, but Specter was the incumbent and the RNC has a policy of supporting all incumbents. In addition to that, from a purely party perspective, Specter was much more likely to hold the seat in Republican hands, and a strong showing for him in his stronghold in the suburban "collar counties" that form a ring around Philadelphia could help the president carry the state's twenty-three Electoral College votes.

I grew up in the Philadelphia media market, and Arlen Specter was a familiar name in the Gillespie home at 50 Clubhouse Road in Browns Mills, New Jersey. He was a dominant force from the time he was a district attorney in Philly, and while he frustrated conservative Republicans like me over the years, there was no denying he was one smart guy.

And tough.

After being named head of the confirmation effort, one of my first steps was to pay the chairman a visit. We met in his Hart Building office, and he had just been through chemotherapy the day before and was drinking some kind of medicinal milkshake and battling an uncontrollably runny nose. Despite all that, he was focused on his job.

One of the tasks you implement in running a confirmation effort is talking to senators and pundits who are going to be on Sunday morning news programs like *Meet the Press*.

One Saturday in August, I talked to Specter on my cell phone while I sat on the beach on Long Beach Island, New Jersey, where he also has a house. I shared with him the White House perspective on how the nomination was going and things I thought important to note.

Specter is not one who will take "talking points." He treasures his role as a chairman of an important committee in a separate and independent branch of government, but he'll hear you out. We had a pleasant talk, and at the end I felt the urge to tell him something personal.

"Chairman, do you mind if I take a moment of personal privilege, as you say in the Senate?"

"Sure, Ed. Go ahead."

"I just want to tell you, I really admire your doing your job so effectively while you deal with the chemotherapy."

"Thank you, Ed."

"I hope you'll take this the way I intend it, sir, but you're one tough SOB!"

Specter laughed.

"I take it as a compliment."

For party regulars and White House staff, Arlen Specter is exasperatingly independent, but in my dealings he has never been anything but honest and forthright and incredibly astute about his colleagues. He clings to an old-school view of the Senate that compels him as a chairman to respect the rights of his committee's minority, and I think it serves him and the institution well. Sometimes the majority has to exercise raw power to get things done, but it's not always the only way.

I was glad he and his wife, Joan, were there in the East Room for the announcement.

The announcement turned out not to go exactly as we wrote it out on the chalkboard, thanks to the antics of young Jack Roberts. Jack was positioned at his mother's side, with his sister Josie on her other side. Jane was holding one of their hands in each of hers as they stood stage left of the presidential podium in the State Dining Room.

As the president began making his remarks, Jack slowly but surely started visibly losing his attention span, first looking around the room, then staring at the ceiling, then noticing the wooden legs of an ornate table behind him carved as eagles.

He reached back to touch the eagle table leg as his mother strained to hold him in place. Finally, he broke free, dropped to his knees, and crawled over to the table to examine the wooden eagle.

The cameras remained fixed on the president and Judge Roberts, and the president and Judge Roberts remained fixed on the cameras. Jack began crawling away from the table, out toward the middle of the cavernous room, toward the space between the television and still cameras and the presidential podium. Jane Roberts reached down and grabbed hold of him, bringing him momentarily to heel, but he soon broke free again, violently jerking his arm away from her.

At which point he wandered toward the bright lights on the floor pointed upward toward the president of the United States and, presumably, the next associate justice of the Supreme Court of the United States.

He leaned down into the bright lights, staring into them closer and closer. He looked back over his shoulder and saw the shadow he was casting.

Then he began to dance. A really funny dance, with the abandon of a four-year-old.

Mrs. Bush was seated directly across from him, and when he looked over at her she warmly gestured for him to come to her, wriggling her index finger toward herself and smiling at him.

He paused to consider the First Lady's offer, then pursed his lips and vigorously shook his head no.

"We're gonna have to grab him," Dan said to me under his breath.

"If we grab him, he might scream," I said. "Right now, he's not on camera. If he screams, they'll have to cut to him."

Eventually, in the midst of Judge Roberts's remarks, Jane was able to snag him by his navy blue jacket and walk him off to the side where Blake Gottesman, the president's "body man," scooped him up and took him to the Red Room to wait for his mother and father.

Dan Bartlett sighed. "Thank God," he said.

I learned later that Jack is a big fan of Spiderman, and he wasn't actually dancing. He was shooting spiderwebs out of his wrists and dodging bad guys in his little mind. While the television cameras never moved to him on the broadcast of the president's announcement and Judge Roberts's acceptance, they had filmed him, however. The next day, the footage raced around the web and "Jumpin' Jack Flash," as we came to call him in the White House, became a household figure.

One who very much humanized his father.

After the announcement, there was a little reception in the "cross hall" that connects the East Room with the State Dining Room, a wide, long white marble corridor punctuated by twenty-foot-high Doric columns every ten feet.

John and Jane Roberts were mortified by Jack's antics, but everyone got a laugh out of it. Mrs. Bush was very reassuring, relating to Jane as a mother of twins, not as First Lady of the United States.

Karl Rove gave Jack a big high five, and I remember thinking Jack had earned it. It may sound cynical, but I knew the little guy had just made it all but impossible for Democrats to cast Judge John G. Roberts as "another Robert Bork."

On Wednesday morning, Roberts had breakfast with the president. I caught up with him in Harriet's office immediately afterward, around eight-thirty.

"How'd you sleep last night, Judge?" I asked.

"Actually, I slept great," he said. "And the best thing is, when I woke up this morning it was all still real."

I knew right then I was going to like working on his behalf.

There is little buffer anymore between the extreme liberal groups and Democrats in the Senate.

What became apparent in the confirmation process of Judge Roberts is that there is little buffer anymore between the extreme liberal groups like MoveOn.org and the National Abortion Rights Action League and Democrats in the Senate.

For example, in the consultation process, Harry Reid actually had suggested that the president should consider Roberts, but after the outside groups objected he came out against him on the Senate floor.

It is simply outrageous that half the Democratic Caucus in the Senate voted against Roberts's confirmation. Ruth Bader Ginsberg had been general counsel to the American Civil Liberties Union (ACLU), and as such had advocated some pretty extreme positions for her clients, yet only three Senate Republicans voted against her confirmation because, by all historical standards of experience, intellect, integrity, and temperament, she was qualified to sit on the Supreme Court.

From the very beginning, Steve Schmidt took to calling this "the Ginsberg Standard," and to holding Senate Democrats to it. When President Clinton nominated Ginsberg, Republican Leader Bob Dole rightly noted that he would never have nominated her, but he had not been elected president.

As the Senate returned from its long August recess, the Roberts confirmation seemed to be in pretty strong shape. In fact, I had concluded that many Democrats were quickly deciding that their best bet was to support Roberts and therefore appear more objective when they inevitably ended up fighting the next nomination, since there was great speculation that Chief Justice Rehnquist would soon step down or that his health would fail him.

I shared my analysis of the Democrats' strategy with Roberts.

"It's like Billy Goat Gruff," he said.

"What?"

"My kids love it when I read them Billy Goat Gruff," he explained. "The billy goat is crossing the bridge when the ogre stops him and threatens to eat him. But the billy goat says, 'You don't want to eat me. My big brother is coming along behind me, and he's a much bigger meal.' I don't know who's coming along behind me, but he'll be a much bigger meal than me."

"Yeah, I guess that's it," I laughed. "They're pursuing the Billy Goat Gruff strategy."

"Well, I'm sorry for the next guy, but I gotta say, I'm happy for me."

It may seem silly, but something tells me John Roberts's direct knowledge of Billy Goat Gruff will serve him well as chief justice of the United States. (The chief justice, by the way, is not the chief justice of the Supreme Court, he is the chief justice of the United States, responsible for the federal judiciary in its entirety, not just the nine who serve on the Supreme Court.)

Despite what seemed to me to be a halfhearted opposition effort by Senate Democrats, the Roberts confirmation effort was not a walk in the park. The media were expecting a contentious nomination, and they were going to cover one whether it materialized or not. The *Washington Post* and the *New York Times* took it upon themselves to scour old documents and try to find old acquaintances who might raise "troubling questions."

One morning on the daily conference call, I said "The *Washington Post* and the *New York Times* have decided that if Senate Democrats aren't going to fight this nomination, they will!"

The worst example came one day when Lea McBride, Vice President Cheney's press secretary, said that she had just had a disturbing phone call with a lawyer who had recently been head of the adoption lawyers bar.

The lawyer said that Glen Justice of the *New York Times* contacted him seeking guidance on how one went about obtaining adoption records.

I then talked to the lawyer directly, and he told me that he found the conversation disconcerting because even after he explained to the reporter that such records are sealed, he kept pressing to explore ways they might be unsealed or obtained anyway.

No one had ever suggested that the Judge and Jane Roberts had done anything inappropriate relative to his children's adoption. There were no charges of "line jumping" or use of influence. This was a pure fishing expedition, and my worst fears were that the real goal was for the *Times* to track down the birth mothers and do some kind of "feature story" on them, revolving around how they felt seeing the children they gave up years ago now on television as the son and daughter of a possible Supreme Court justice.

In the entire time I worked with him, Judge John Roberts let all the criticism and nasty quotations about him roll off his back, but the prospect of a major paper invading the privacy of his children's adoption records understandably bothered him.

"They're not going to get away with it, Judge," I told him over the phone.

"I appreciate you saying that, Ed, but how can you be so sure?"

"Judge, I can't promise you you'll be confirmed. I can't promise you the hearings will be fair. But I promise you this: We will protect your family. I don't want you to worry about this anymore."

It's not a promise I made lightly, and I was honor bound to keep it.

We sat on it for a while, trying to figure out how to stop the *Times* from pursuing such a despicable story.

Steve Schmidt, who had taken to calling Roberts "America's Judge," suggested that we smoke the *Times* out by making it public. He suggested leaking it to Matt Drudge, who often posts media-related stories on his website.

"Make them deny it," he said.

"Slam their fingers in the cookie jar," I said, nodding yes.

After the "alert" went up on Drudge, the *New York Times* did exactly as Steve predicted, issuing a denial that it was pursuing such a story. But it had been, and I knew it because I'd talked to the lawyer myself.

I called Brit Hume and told him the *Times* wasn't being honest in denying that they were seeking to obtain the adoption records.

"Well, what if Roberts used influence to shorten the waiting time, cutting in front of someone ahead of him?" Hume asked.

"Well, first of all, there's been no accusation of that. And second, that's not what the *Times* was doing. They were trying to obtain sealed court documents."

"How do you know?"

"I talked to a lawyer who was contacted by them."

"Would he talk to me? I can't report it unless I can talk to him directly."

"Let me see. Does he have to make his name public?"

"No. I just have to talk to him directly before I report anything."

I called the lawyer, and he agreed to talk to Brit over the phone if Fox would not identify him by name. Hume reported it on his show that night, and there was a huge public backlash against the *New York Times* over its effort.

With no "scandal," Roberts's confirmation came down to the Senate Judiciary Committee hearings, which we had prepared for like there was no tomorrow.

Rachel Brand, the associate attorney general who heads the Office of Legal Policy, was responsible for heading up prep sessions, or "moots," at the Justice Department. We would run through five half-hour blocks of questioning at a time, broken up by issue area (e.g., First Amendment, Commerce Clause, substantive due process), and then go over any substantive questions Roberts might have or any suggestions we might have about dealing with members of the committee.

Rachel and her deputy Kristi Macklin are not only brilliant lawyers, but great people, and Rachel made a point of buying cookies for the sessions (out of her own pocket on a government salary that is about one-quarter what she would command in the private sector).

After one particularly grueling session, we broke after the moot and Rachel lauded Roberts's performance.

"That was great!" She added with a smile, "You can have a cookie."

"Why do I feel like a seal that's just been tossed a fish?" Roberts said with his dry, midwestern humor.

Less than two weeks before the hearings were to begin, Chief Justice Rehnquist passed away, creating yet another vacancy on the Court, and the prospect of not two but three confirmation hearings. If President Bush nominated one of the sitting justices to chief justice—the two possibilities being Antonin Scalia and Clarence Thomas—they would have to be confirmed by the Senate for the new position, and then whomever was nominated to fill the vacancy would also have to be confirmed.

Bush negated that scenario, however, by nominating Roberts almost immediately as chief justice, which did not come as a surprise to those of us who had come to know Roberts in the confirmation process.

In fact, only a few weeks earlier Fred Thompson and I had dinner with Ron Silver of television's *West Wing*, and *National Review* Washington bureau chief Kate O'Beirne, and Thompson predicted that should Justice Rehnquist pass away, Roberts would be the next chief justice.

Thompson was Roberts's "sherpa," the person tapped by the White House to escort Roberts to courtesy visits in the Senate, where Thompson had served from 1994 to 2002, and give him advice on how to deal with the somewhat arcane body. (In Nepal, "sherpas" are the villagers who help mountain climbers navigate their way up Mt. Everest.)

Not only was Thompson knowledgeable about the ways of the Senate, but his former colleagues—on both sides of the aisle—loved him, not just because of his television star status, but because he is a genuinely good guy.

After each day's round of courtesy visits, Roberts and Thompson would debrief the SCOTUS team in the Ward Room of the White House, a small, oak-walled room in the basement of the West Wing just off the White House Mess. Jamie Brown, special assistant to the president for legislative affairs who had point on the confirmation, would read through her notes from the meeting to give the rest of us a sense of how things were going.

The evening after a day that included a meeting with Senator Robert Byrd (D-WV), the venerable dean of the Senate, Jamie gave the good news that Byrd concluded their meeting by saying, "You're going to be the next Supreme Court justice."

"Not this one, but the next one," Thompson deadpanned as Roberts and the rest of us laughed.

Roberts validated the president's faith in him, shining in the hearings and proving without a doubt that he was fully suited to fill the robes of the mentor he had clerked for decades earlier. (Roberts was a pallbearer at Chief Justice Rehnquist's funeral.) His performance was a tour de force, beginning with his opening statement, in which he recalled the endless cornfields of his boyhood Indiana and made his now-famous baseball analogy about the role of a judge ("No one ever went to a baseball game to see the umpire").

Roberts's opening statement was so impressive, the Senate Judiciary Committee members were like Rene Zellweger's character

in the movie *Jerry Maguire.* "You had me at hello!" As he deftly answered and deflected questions over the course of the next three
days, his confirmation became a forgone conclusion.

His most notable exchanges were with Senator Chuck
Schumer (D-NY), who was not only a junior member of the Senate
Judiciary Committee but chairman of the National Democratic
Senatorial Committee, the Senate Democrats' campaign organization. Thus, he had added incentive to clash with the president's Supreme Court nominee (few things gin up liberal campaign donors
more than a fight over the Supreme Court).

One in particular captured both the personal and political dy-
namics of the hearing room. On the third day of the hearing, at the
end of his second round of questioning, Schumer continued to
press Roberts to say how he would vote if confirmed on certain
cases. When Roberts rightly refused and Schumer whined on and
on, Roberts bested him with both humor and principle, as the transcript shows.

SCHUMER: Let me just say, sir, in all due respect—and I respect
your intelligence and your career and your family—this
process is getting a little more absurd the further we move.

You agree we should be finding out your philosophy and
method of legal reasoning, modesty, stability, but when we
try to find out what modesty and stability mean, what your
philosophy means, we don't get any answers.

It's as if I asked you: What kind of movies do you like?
Tell me two or three good movies. And you say, "I like movies
with good acting. I like movies with good directing. I like
movies with good cinematography."

And I ask you, "No, give me an example of a good
movie." You don't name one. I say, "Give me an example of a
bad movie."

You won't name one. Then I ask you if you like

"Casablanca," and you respond by saying, "Lots of people like 'Casablanca.' "

(LAUGHTER)

You tell me it's widely settled that "Casablanca" is one of the great movies.

SPECTER: Senator Schumer, now that your time is over, are you asking him a question?

SCHUMER: Yes.

(LAUGHTER)

I am saying, sir—I am making a plea here. I hope we're going to continue this for a while, that within the confines of what you think is appropriate and proper, you try to be a little more forthcoming with us in terms of trying to figure out what kind of justice you will become.

SPECTER: We will now take a 15-minute break, reconvene at 4:25.

ROBERTS: Mr. Chairman, could I address some of them . . .

SPECTER: Oh, absolutely. Absolutely.

I didn't hear any question. Judge Roberts . . .

ROBERTS: Well, there were several along the way. I'll be very succinct.

SPECTER: You are privileged to comment.

This is coming out of his next round, if there is one.

(LAUGHTER)

ROBERTS: First, "Dr. Zhivago" and "North by Northwest."

(LAUGHTER)

SCHUMER: Now, how about on the more important subject of what . . .

SPECTER: Let him finish his answer. You're out of time.

(LAUGHTER)

SCHUMER: Not out of movies.

ROBERTS: The only point I would like to make, because you raised the question how is this different than justices who dissent and criticize, and how is this different than professors—and I think there are significant differences.

The justice who files a dissent is issuing an opinion based upon his participation in the judicial process. He confronted the case with an open mind. He heard the arguments. He fully and fairly considered the briefs. He consulted with his colleagues, went through the process of issuing an opinion.

And in my experience, every one of those stages can cause you to change your view.

The view you ask then of me, "Well, what do you think, is it correct or not?" or "How would you come out?" That's not a result of that process. And that's why I shouldn't respond to those types of questions.

Now, the professor, how is that different? That professor is not sitting here as a nominee before the court. And the great danger, of course, that I believe every one of the justices has been vigilant to safeguard against is turning this into a bargaining process.

It is not a process under which senators get to say, "I want you to rule this way, this way and this way. And if you tell me you'll rule this way, this way and this way, I'll vote for you."

That's not a bargaining process.

Judges are not politicians. They cannot promise to do certain things in exchange for votes.

As they say on ESPN, "BOOYAH!"

First of all, Roberts demonstrated firmness by not allowing Schumer's diatribe to go unanswered, exerting his right as a witness in appealing to the committee chairman even though the committee was scheduled to adjourn for a break at the end of Schumer's time.

Second, he brought the house down in deadpanning his favorite-movies answer to Schumer's rhetorical screed.

Third, he not only defended himself, but more important, stood up for the independence of the judicial branch of government. What Schumer, and other Democrats in the Senate, were subtly trying to do in both the Roberts and Alito hearings was to subordinate the judiciary to the legislature. "If you commit to me here and now that in the future you will rule the way I like, I'll vote to confirm you."

Roberts's civics lesson was helpful to the public and the media covering the hearings. He put artfully into words the same principle that both Ginsberg and Breyer had abided by in their confirmation hearings.

And his finish was an absolute haymaker. "Judges are not politicians. They cannot promise to do certain things in exchange for votes."

Chief Justice Roberts will be a figure of historic impact on the Supreme Court, and I pray he has a long and healthy tenure there. He'd never forsake his robe for politics, but if he did, he'd be tough to beat.

I didn't think we should even have a fourth day of hearings, but Chairman Specter wanted to accommodate the Democrats on his committee who were pushing for one more short round, hoping to find some chink in Sir John's armor. They were able to negotiate ninety minutes on Thursday morning, after more than eighteen hours of questioning had already been completed.

Chief Justice Roberts is a man of eminent patience, and he largely relished the give-and-take with the members of the committee. He had thought Wednesday would be his last day and wasn't crazy about coming back the next morning, but we all understood the need to accommodate the committee.

When he came in the next morning, "America's Judge" was not in the same positive mindset he'd been in Monday through Wednesday. As we were about to leave the vice president's Senate office for the committee room one last time, I asked for the two of us to have a moment alone.

"Judge, you know and I know that this last round is unnecessary, and it's a pain," I said. "But I just want to make one point to you."

I stretched both my arms out wide, palms facing up.

As I said "ninety minutes," I slightly lowered my left arm and raised my right.

Then I said, "Lifetime appointment," and I heavily lowered my right arm and raised my left.

I went back and forth, like a human scale.

"Ninety minutes" (lightly left).

"Lifetime appointment!" (heavy to the right).

"Ninety minutes" (lightly left).

"Lifetime appointment!" (heavily right).

Roberts chuckled. "All right, I get it!" he said, waving at me to stop.

The morning of the day before the floor vote, Roberts called me with some good news.

"I just got off the phone with Senator Leahy," he said.

"What did he have to say?"

"He said he's going to vote for me, and he's going to the floor to announce his decision shortly."

"Well, Judge, I'm happy for you, but that really screws up my office pool!"

Roberts laughed. "That's all you really care about, isn't it?"

"Hey, I'm out nine bucks."

The day before the Roberts vote on the Senate floor, I made one request of everyone on the confirmation team: I would like to be the first person to call him Mr. Chief Justice.

As we watched the votes come in on the big-screen television set in the West Wing's Roosevelt Room (where the senior staff meets every morning), I was keeping a tally on a small Senate Judiciary Committee notepad I'd picked up in the course of the hearings.

We couldn't get C-SPAN II on the set, so we watched Fox's live broadcast, which also had a running tally graphic on a split screen. I had noticed, however, that its tally was running slightly behind, and when I had fifty-one they were still showing forty-eight.

"That's fifty-one," I said, almost to myself. I turned to Roberts, who was seated on the sofa across a small coffee table from me, and said, "You're confirmed."

The room erupted in applause, and the new chief justice rose to acknowledge the staff's excitement and affection. As he sat back down, I reached across the table and he leaned forward to shake my extended hand.

"Congratulations, Mr. Chief Justice," I said.

As he thanked me, I'm not sure it registered with him that I was the first to call him that, but it is to me one of the most special moments of my life.

Roberts was confirmed by a vote of 78–22.

The president entered the Roosevelt Room and congratulated the new chief justice, saying, "Looks like you got the votes after all!"

Then he invited Roberts to the Oval Office, and to my surprise asked Fred Thompson and me to join them. I sat by the desk of our forty-third president as he signed the commission of our Supreme Court's seventeenth chief justice.

We engaged in some pleasant chit-chat, and then the president asked Thompson and me for some thoughts on the next nomination. Specifically, he wanted our sense of whether it was imperative he choose a woman.

Thompson said he didn't think so, that the most important thing was to choose the best-qualified person regardless of sex.

"What do you think, Eddie?"

"Mr. President, I think if there's a qualified woman it would be good. Cathy's a conservative woman, headed up W Stands for Women, as you know, and I know she'll be disappointed if it's not a woman."

"That's pretty telling," he said. "My gut's telling me I should find a woman."

A couple of hours later, as we were leaving the chief justice's swearing-in ceremony in the East Room, Fred Thompson turned to me and said, "Well, Gillespie, you're on your own now."

And after a dramatic pause like you see on *Law and Order,* he smirked and said, "Don't screw it up!"

Thompson had managed to avoid duty on the next nomination, bowing out because of time constraints. I hadn't been so lucky, but it wasn't for lack of trying. I had informed Harriet, Karl, and Andy that I needed to return to my colleagues and clients at QGA after the Roberts confirmation. But two days before the Senate vote on Roberts, the president had called the confirmation team into the Oval Office to thank everyone for a job well done. The photographer asked the twelve of us to form a semicircle behind President Bush's desk. I was on the president's immediate right, and Fred Thompson was on his immediate left, with the rest of the team arrayed around us.

After the photo, President Bush stood and faced the group.

"You all did a great job," he said. "And we're going to need you for the next one. I'm thinking about who I'm gonna pick, but whoever it is, this next one's going to be tougher. I hope I can count on this team to stay together."

The president was looking directly at me as he said that last sentence.

"Can I count on you all?"

"Yes, sir," people said. I simply nodded my head yes, trying to avoid a verbal commitment.

"Good. Well, let's get back to work."

I was trailing everyone else out of the Oval Office when Karl Rove jokingly grabbed me from behind and put me in a bear hug, physically stopping me from leaving as the president had verbally done.

When he let me go, I felt a hand grasp my arm and turned to see the president.

Now it was one on one, and the president looked me directly in the eye as he continued to hold on to my arm right above the elbow.

"You can do the next one, can'tchya, Eddie?"

Only my brothers and sisters, my friends from my years in the Armey office, and the president of the United States still call me "Eddie."

"Yes, sir," I said.

I had managed to say no to Harriet, Karl, and Andy, but I was tackled on the one-yard line by the big man himself.

In Ireland, there's a Gaelic word for people who are great storytellers and have an ability to sense what's coming in the future—Seanchai (pronounced "Shan-a-key"). My father is a Seanchai. Before the Iraq War, he shared with me his reservations. "I hope to God he (Bush) doesn't do it, son. If we go in there, we'll be in there a long, long time." Before the nineties stock bubble burst, he told me that stocks were selling for more than they were worth, despite what Wall Street was saying at the time.

Family lore has it that he correctly predicted the sex of all twelve of his grandchildren by dangling a pencil from a needle and thread over his expectant daughters' and daughters-in-law's midsections. If the pencil swung back and forth like a pendulum, it would be a boy. If it went round in a circle, it would be a girl.

Jack Gillespie has an uncanny ability to size people up in an instant. His reservations about one of my girlfriends was enough to cause me to look in a different direction for a wife, and his hearty endorsement of Cathy was all it took for me to ask her to marry me (a piece of sage advice he would gloat over forever).

When I was a cocky young political operative, I often dismissed his insights. After all, he didn't have the benefit of a college education as I did (thanks to him, of course).

Then one day, some time after Carrie was born, it dawned on me that far more often than not he was dead on the money.

So I was disconcerted when after the Roberts nomination had concluded in a successful confirmation, Dad said to me, "I hope you're done with that stuff now, Eddie."

"Well, Dad, the president has asked me to stay on to help with the next one."

"Well I hope like hell you told him no."

"Dad, I don't know how to tell the president of the United States no!"

"Easy. You just say, 'Sorry, Mr. President. I can't do it!' "

"I can't do that, Dad."

"I'm worried, Son." When my father calls one of us "Son," it always carries a sense of gravity. "This next one's going to be bad."

"Why do you say that?" I asked, incredulously.

"I don't know, but it's gonna be bad."

Given his track record, this gave me a very unsettled feeling.

The confirmation team immediately began the process of again reviewing binders full of background on various appellate judges who were potential nominees, but in a few days I began to suspect that the next nominee might not be found in any of those binders.

When I first picked up a rumor that Senate Democratic Leader Harry Reid had suggested the president nominate White House Counsel Harriet Miers, my immediate thought was that it might allow the president to confirm without a partisan fight a Supreme Court Justice who shared his view of the proper role of the judiciary in our Federal government.

As the possibility that Harriet might be on the list for consideration became a source of speculation, however, I began hearing rumblings of concern about it among my fellow conservatives, who had not had the benefit I did of having seen her in the Roberts preparation process.

On Friday, September 30, I stopped by Karl's office. I knew the decision point was nearing on the nominee, and was under the impression that Harriet was still very much in the mix.

"I have a bad gut feeling on this one," I said, referring to the next Supreme Court nomination.

"Why?"

"I'm worried we're not going to get an ideological fight if it's Harriet."

"We will."

"Why?"

"She's a conservative."

On Sunday I was playing golf with friends when my White House BlackBerry buzzed telling me of a four-thirty call with Andy, Karl, and Dan. While my foursome mates played their shots, I wandered along the cart path, cell phone to my ear, talking through a plan for the next day. Even then we talked in terms of "the nominee," not Harriet by name, but the pronoun for the nominee was tellingly "she."

That night, as Cathy and I chatted before falling asleep, I confided that I thought Harriet Miers might be the next nominee.

"That'll never fly," she said, matter-of-factly.

"Why not," I asked.

"Nobody knows her. They're going to say he picked his lawyer."

That reaction from someone who knew and admired Harriet made it hard for me to fall asleep that night.

Many in the White House suspected that our conservative base would be disappointed by a nomination of Harriet Miers, but nobody anticipated the reaction with which her announcement was met. The backlash came fast and furious, and rather than waning it only intensified in the forty-eight hours after the Monday morning announcement.

Rachel Brand of DOJ and I went up to the Hill Tuesday to brief the staff of the Senate Judiciary Committee Republicans and were dismayed by the lack of enthusiasm for Harriet—and lack of enthusiasm is putting it mildly.

By Wednesday morning when I went to the weekly meeting of conservative activists held by Grover Norquist, the antitax crusader and grassroots organizer, my friends were up in arms.

I made the president's case for Harriet—trailblazer, real-world lawyer, someone who shares the president's philosophy of judicial restraint.

When I began I was still under the illusion that I could get everyone in the room "on message," as I'd done on so many issues over the years. Within five seconds of finishing my pitch, however, it was apparent that was not to be the case this time.

David Keene of the American Conservative Union, a Bush ally and longtime friend of mine, gave an impassioned critique of the nomination, concluding by saying, "This is his nominee, not ours."

I took question after question. *Wall Street Journal* editorial writer John Fund asked why Harriet had supported an $800 million tax increase as a member of the Dallas City Council, casting the deciding vote in a 6–5 split. I didn't even know about it.

There was much concern about Harriet's contribution to Al Gore's 1988 presidential primary campaign, and her donation to the DNC that year. I had learned of those the day before, and had come to learn that Miers was still a Democrat in 1988, as were many conservative Texans. The process of realignment that Phil Gramm started in 1984 had not yet been completed. And Gore was actually running as the "conservative Democrat" in the '88 primary, with Dukakis being the establishment liberal.

Dennis Stephens, a fellow former Armey staffer, summed up the feelings of the fifty or so people there by saying, "This president has broken our trust. It's like an egg. Once it's broken, you can't unbreak it. And he'll never get that trust back."

A young Hill staffer standing near the back of the room asked how I responded to charges that Harriet lacked the experience for the job. I noted her lengthy history as a practicing lawyer, and her White House experience as counsel, deputy chief of staff for policy, and staff secretary, pointing out that that job is critical, controlling the flow of information to the president in the decision-making process.

An op-ed that morning criticizing the nomination had made it sound as if staff secretary was the little lady who fetched the president's coffee in the morning, and that thought prompted me to make a point that would poorly serve Harriet, the president, and me.

"By the way, it's also worth noting that there is a whiff of sexism and elitism in some of the criticism of Harriet."

The crowd erupted in hisses and catcalls.

"There is," I insisted, surprised by the reaction.

Richard Lessner, who'd been an editorial writer for the *Manchester* (NH) *Union Leader* for years before becoming a full-time consultant, pointedly asked me, "Are you saying people in this room are sexist and elitist?"

I realized now why the room had reacted as it had.

"No, I'm not," I said.

And I meant it. I understood the concerns of conservatives who worried that Harriet might prove to be another David Souter or Anthony Kennedy. I, too, had had my heart broken by justices who'd been appointed by conservative presidents only to prove reliably liberal votes on the Supreme Court.

My complaint about sexism was directed toward those who'd made cheap comments about Harriet's eyeliner ("Tammy Faye Baker–like") or derided her service as staff secretary to the president. Later, liberal columnist Tina Brown would refer to her as the president's "work wife."

And I did detect a whiff of elitism from some of the pundits who'd questioned Miers's intellectual qualifications when they'd never spent five minutes with the woman. How else did they reach such a conclusion, other than by considering that she'd gone to Southern Methodist University instead of Harvard or Yale?

But media accounts of the closed-door meeting cemented a perception that I, acting on behalf of the White House, had attacked conservatives as sexist and elitist for criticizing Harriet's nomination. We were not only at odds with our base, we were in open confrontation.

The problem was compounded by the fact that by Wednesday morning, Democrats had smartly decided to go dark on the matter. For the first time since Bush had taken office, they exercised discipline. They were even smart enough to add fuel to the conservative fire by saying mutedly positive things about her.

Harry Reid, whom we'd expected to face upheaval for his support of Miers in his weekly lunch that Wednesday (usually the Senate Democrats and Republicans meet on Tuesdays, but the Jewish holidays had pushed the weekly meetings to Wednesday that first week of October), got deference from his colleagues. Democrats were united and Republicans were divided over the Miers nomination, with "institutional" Republicans adrift from the ideological core of the party.

The nexus between ideologues (in the best sense of the word) and those in elected positions is a tenuous one. I had historically straddled the divide, promoting conservative policies inside the party but paying attention to the political realities required to win elections.

Elections are won by holding on to those who share your core philosophy—your political "base"—and attracting voters in the middle. Much of the reporting and "analysis" of the 2004 campaign assumed that Bush was running a "base" election, but this ignored the fact that neither party can win a majority of votes in this country with only its base. Getting elected nationally requires motivating your base and getting the lion's share of swing voters on top of that. Appealing to swing voters while alienating your core voters will result in defeat, as will appealing to base voters while alienating swing voters. Striking the right balance is the key to victory in today's closely divided country.

You can't split the difference until you first define it.

"Ideologue" is treated as a pejorative by the Washington establishment—the media, the bureaucrats, the lobbyists, and the political consultants—but ideology is what drives the policy debate. The simple fact is that if it weren't for the extremes on the left and the right, there would be no middle for the establishment to celebrate. You can't split the difference until you first define it.

When I first went to work for Dick Armey, those of us in the conservative policy vanguard disdained the compromisers in the Reagan White House, and later the even worse ones in the first Bush White House. The pragmatists, or "prags" as we derisively called them, were constantly undercutting free-market policies and selling out to the Democrats in Congress. We'd rather fight and lose and demonstrate to the public the differences between the two philosophies of governing than cut a deal that blurred those differences.

The pinnacle of this conflict came in 1990, when former president Bush broke his "no new taxes" pledge in a budget agreement with the Democrats.

With the nomination of Harriet Miers, many of my friends felt that this president Bush had committed a breach of the same magnitude. Where I had been one of the lead staffers in opposing former president Bush's budget deal, helping Armey pass a "no new tax" pledge resolution through the House Republican Conference, I was now one of the leading voices pushing the Miers confirmation in the face of intense resistance from people I'd worked shoulder to shoulder with for decades.

It was depressing, and Cathy was worried about me. I greatly respect and admire Harriet Miers, and it's impossible not to like her. But the truth of the matter is I, too, was looking forward to a vigorous debate over judicial philosophy that her nomination negated.

After Chief Justice Rehnquist passed away, I had shared my thoughts in a memo to Andy, Dan, and Karl.

> The Roberts nomination was largely a process fight with intermittent discussion of philosophy. The next one will be an ideological fight with intermittent spats over process. The opposition's approach will not be quiet suffocation based on documents like they deployed with [former appellate court nominee Miguel] Estrada, but a loud shotgun blast charging extremism.
> WE WOULD MAKE A CRITICAL AND PERHAPS FATAL MISTAKE TO WAGE A PROCESS FIGHT WHILE THEY WAGE AN IDEOLOGICAL ONE.
> A good, heated debate over striking "under God" from the pledge, the merits of governments taking property from individual A to give to individual B, the validity of basing court decisions on foreign law and, of course, abortion on demand is not something we should shy away from.

While I understood some of the concerns of my ideological brethren, I had committed to the president of the United States that I would help guide his nominee's confirmation, and I had done so before he'd even made a decision about who it would be.

In politics, there are times when you have to accept trade-offs, and while I would have preferred that the president nominate one of the leading conservative lights of the judiciary, he hadn't. It was his pick, and I am his guy.

The respect and affection I'd developed for Harriet Miers during the Roberts confirmation process made it easier for me. The argument for Harriet was more than the "trust me" that her critics contended—but the fact is I did and do trust President Bush. I have no doubt he saw in Harriet Miers a person who shared his philosophy of judicial restraint, someone who would apply the laws as written rather than make new laws based on personal point of view.

It was my job to set aside any personal reservations and make good on the personal commitment I had made to the president of the United States. I knew that members of the confirmation team also had reservations, but as their leader I could never let mine show.

The constant pounding from our friends and the pundits was hard on us, but any sign of weariness from me would cause morale to plummet. When you're in a position of leadership, you have to mask any semblance of doubt. I'm sure the president himself had to wonder from time to time if his decision was a mistake, but I never saw his resolve waiver and I'm betting that if it ever did, only Laura Bush knows it.

I think in nominating Harriet, the president was trying to get someone he knew shared his judicial philosophy without a knockdown, drag-out fight in the Senate. But in so doing, he disappointed his core supporters.

The volunteers who had swept through neighborhoods in October and November and manned the phone banks and stuffed the envelopes and stood by George W. Bush through the worst of times are not people who care about capital gains tax cuts or even so much about the war in Iraq.

They worry about the coarsening of our culture, and liberal judges who seek to impose their philosophy on the rest of us without allowing citizens the opportunity to express themselves in the process. *Roe* v. *Wade* and the Massachusetts Supreme Court's sanctioning of same-sex marriage embody this type of judicial activism.

One of the reasons abortion has become such a raw issue in the electorate is that such a personal, sensitive matter was taken from the hands of voters where it was being worked out state by state and taken into the hands of unelected judges. For those of us who believe deeply in the sanctity of life there is a sense that if we were given the chance to make our case in the political arena it would prevail, certainly in areas of broad, common-ground agreement like parental notification and partial birth abortion.

It's the feeling of being denied that opportunity that fuels much of the intensity in the prolife community.

The same is true when it comes to gay marriage. Ballot initiatives and state legislatures are addressing this issue all across the country, as is Congress. Having a reasoned public debate over the negative implications of such a significant change in a fundamental institution like marriage will result in the kind of accommodation and respect that a court ruling can never achieve.

In the long term, I suspect supporters of gay marriage may gain ground in the public arena, while supporters of abortion on demand without limits will lose ground. But to the extent courts encroach on the proper venue for policy-making, any ability to affect direction will be denied the citizens of this country.

The nomination to replace Justice Sandra Day O'Connor was a focal point for the hopes of those who share this frustration, but in Harriet Miers they did not see a nominee who assured them their concerns would be met, and there was open rebellion. Where the president was looking to avoid a fight, they were relishing one.

In fairness, it wasn't just the fight conservatives were looking for, but a measure of certainty. Of course, the greater the measure of certainty, the greater the fight.

Conservatives have good reason to be nervous about Supreme Court appointments, given their history. Among others, Justices Anthony Kennedy and David Souter had been appointed by conservative presidents, only to side consistently with the liberal bloc on the Court, greatly disappointing the people who'd elected the presidents who'd appointed them.

Some of Harriet's earlier writings and speeches while at the Dallas and Texas bar associations didn't allay conservative concerns.

Harriet's nomination represented a break from the recent norm of elevating federal appellate court judges to the Supreme Court. We made what we thought was a compelling case that her real-world experience as a litigator would be an asset on the Court.

More than half the cases considered by the Supreme Court in the term before Chief Justice Rehnquist passed away were not constitutional conflicts, but lawsuits that rose to the highest court in the land. With the passing of Chief Justice Rehnquist, there was now no one on the court who had come there as a practicing lawyer.

In the course of our nation's history, more than a third of associate justices on the Supreme Court had not served in the judiciary before their nominations. Interestingly, six of the nine Supreme Court justices who issued the unanimous ruling in the landmark *Brown* v. *Board of Education* decision had not served on the bench before going on the Supreme Court. Justice Antonin Scalia noted in an interview after the Miers nomination that a practicing lawyer's perspective would be good for the Court.

But the time to press that case was not in the wake of Hurricane Katrina, when President Bush was under attack from his adversaries for "cronyism" because Michael Brown had proven to be an ineffective director of the Federal Emergency Management Agency.

Whereas we were able to slip the punches thrown our way

during the Roberts confirmation fight, every punch thrown our way during the Miers fight seemed to land right on the chin.

For example, the *Washington Post* reported on October 7 that during her courtesy visit with Senator Patrick Leahy of Vermont, the Judiciary Committee's ranking Democrat, "according to several people with knowledge of the exchange," Leahy asked Miers to name her favorite Supreme Court justices. "Miers responded with 'Warren'—which led Leahy to ask her whether she meant former chief justice Earl Warren, a liberal icon, or former chief justice Warren Burger, a conservative who voted for *Roe* v. *Wade*. Miers said she meant Warren Burger, the sources said."

Problem was, the exchange never took place, as Leahy himself acknowledged two days later on ABC's *This Week*.

Still, the damage had been done. An anonymous Democratic source had managed to put a nasty hit on our nominee in the *Post*, which never checked with the White House to see if it was accurate, and it got widespread attention. Incredibly, even after Pat Leahy refuted it on the air, the *Post* reported the story as fact again! I guess it was just too good not to be true.

Three weeks into the fight, Harriet's nomination lay somewhere in no-man's-land. Despite the constant criticism from the right and a steady stream of negative media coverage, no Republican senator had come out against her (nor any Democrat, for that matter). The nomination was not met out in the states with the same virulent response as it had been inside the beltway, and while senators were clearly being swayed by the pundits, none had announced opposition to her confirmation.

The prevailing mindset was to watch the hearings. If Harriet was strong, she'd be confirmed. If she stumbled, she would likely fail.

If she emerged from the committee with a positive or neutral recommendation (that is, if Kansas's Sam Brownback sided with Democrats or if Brownback and Oklahoma's Tom Coburn both voted present), we faced the real possibility of a filibuster.

When a questionnaire she had filled out while on the Dallas
City Council in the eighties for Texans United for Life in which she
had indicated a prolife point of view was released, it became very
possible that Barbara Boxer and others could try to block her from
an up-or-down vote.

The more likely scenario, however, was that if fifty-one or
more Republicans were publicly in support of Harriet at the time of
the vote, Democrats would kick in ten to twenty more on the theory that putting her on was better than having her lose and then
having to face the nomination of a conservative appellate court
judge like Michael Luttig or Samuel Alito or Priscilla Owen. In es-
sence, they'd give the president credit for seeking consensus.

If, however, she had fifty or fewer Republican votes on the
floor, Democrats would probably withhold any support, hoping a
failed confirmation would be a harsh blow to George Bush's presidency with three years still to go.

Before we ever got to that point, however, Harriet concluded
that her role as White House counsel was fast coming into conflict
with her role as nominee. Since one of her central qualifications was
her experience dealing with executive branch decisions as counsel,
senators wanted to see what legal positions she had taken in that
capacity. Disclosing such positions, however, would threaten the
president's—any president's—ability to garner candid advice from
his closest staff.

She walked into the Oval Office at eight o'clock on Wednesday night, October 27, and told the president she could not in good
conscience complete the confirmation process for fear of under-
mining the privilege of presidential communication. The president
accepted her decision and went back to the nomination drawing
board. The next morning I did a round of interviews from the
White House lawn and proudly stood by a good woman.

A few days later, I headed into the White House on Sunday evening, driving through the gate onto West Executive Drive right around five-thirty. I headed straight up to Harriet's office and found her there with a beautiful two-year-old blond girl in a green dress.

"This is Madigan, Steve's daughter," Harriet said. "Isn't she pretty?"

"Beautiful," I said as Steve Schmidt came into the room. "Schmitty, you obviously married up!"

The three of us joined Maddy at Harriet's thick oak conference table, and were shortly joined by Judge Samuel Alito of the Third Circuit Court of Appeals. I had spoken with him Friday on the phone, but this was the first time we'd met in person.

We talked about the next day's events. Alito's nomination would be announced by the President at 8:00 AM, same time as Harriet's had been. But instead of the Oval Office, it would be in what's called the "Cross Hall," the long corridor between the East Room and the State Dining Room punctuated by twenty-foot marble columns.

I was going through my usual silly details—children? hobbies? favorite teachers?—when I noticed that Alito was wearing eyeglasses, which was not the case in his official photo.

"Do you always wear glasses?" I asked.

"No. I wear them and contacts interchangeably."

"Will you wear them tomorrow morning when the president announces your nomination?"

Alito looked at me as if I were an incompetent lawyer appearing before his bench.

"I hadn't really thought about it."

"What do you think you'll do at the hearings? You think you'll wear glasses then?"

"Probably," he said.

It may seem silly, but I didn't want to get distracted anywhere along the way by a typical media armchair psychology exercise.

"Why did he wear contacts at the announcement but glasses at the hearings? Was it vanity? Blah blah blah."

"Well, if you're going to wear glasses for the four days of hearings, it's probably best to wear them when you're introduced to the country tomorrow morning."

"Okay," he said, probably thinking he'd never get back the three minutes of his life we'd just wasted.

Having settled that, Harriet Miers added another piece of advice.

"And don't wear eyeliner!"

Judge Alito, Schmidt, and I laughed out loud at Harriet's self-deprecating humor. It's a good example of why she is so well liked in addition to being well respected inside the White House. The thing I've regretted most about her withdrawal is that there was never an opportunity for the public to see the real Harriet Miers.

They did get to see the real Samuel Alito, however, and they liked what they saw—one of the most brilliant jurists of his generation, a quiet, decent man who reveres the law, and the son of an Italian immigrant who loves his country.

The morning after our meeting in Harriet's office, the president introduced Judge Alito to the nation. Shortly afterward, Judge Alito, his wife, Martha, his son, Phillip, his daughter, Laura, and I piled into a White House van to head up to Capitol Hill for the customary greeting by the Senate leadership.

The van pulled to the corner entrance of the Russell Senate Office Building at First Street and Delaware Avenue. We sat for a moment to let the cameras get in position for Senate Majority Leader Bill Frist to welcome him to the Senate.

I was riding shotgun, with the judge immediately behind me and Martha in the bucket seat to his left, behind the driver. Phillip, a sophomore at the University of Virginia, and Laura, a high school senior, sat in the back. In that moment we waited, I turned to face the judge.

"Do you remember when Chief Justice Roberts said in his

hearings that a judge nominated for confirmation to the Supreme Court is a not like a candidate running for political office?"

Alito nodded yes.

"Well, it's pretty damned close," I said.

He smiled and nodded again as his door was opened from the outside. He grasped his wife's hand and stepped out with her behind him, and they ascended the stairs of the Russell Building with their children behind them, cameras clicking and reporters shouting questions. I watched from behind the tinted window of the van, thinking, "There he goes, into the maelstrom."

The confirmation team did not click on a personal level with Alito as readily as we had with Roberts. Where Roberts is quick with a smile, very gregarious and witty, Alito is reserved, and his jaw gets fixed in a way that can look dismissive.

Over time, I came to realize that he wasn't being dismissive but pensive. And he wasn't aloof, but almost painfully shy. Roberts had a knack for handling the repetitive "courtesy visits" in the Senate, the hour-long one on ones where you pay deference to individual senators who then do a stand-up press availability with the nominee afterward. Where Roberts seemed to relish the back and forth with the Democrats on the committee, Alito seemed to find it laborious.

After one meeting with Specter, the Judiciary Committee chairman asked Alito to autograph a baseball for him, noting their shared affinity for the Philadelphia Phillies.

"That may be the most important thing you'll do in this entire process," I said to Alito afterward as we walked through the wide marble hallway of the Hart Senate Office Building.

"Why?"

"What do you think a baseball signed by an appellate court judge is worth?" I said with a smile.

Because there were ten full weeks between his nomination and his hearings, we probably had too many moots with him, and I worried that we had run the risk of his tiring of the subject matter.

Those fears were quickly allayed, however, once the hearings began.

Chairman Specter called on Alito to give his opening statement. The judge paused, reached for a bottle of water on his witness table, slowly opened it, and very deliberately poured it into a plastic cup, raised it to his lips, and took a long sip, then began his statement.

It seemed as if an eternity passed from the time Specter called on him to the time he actually began speaking, and the silence felt awkward to me. It had the effect, however, of Alito's taking control, and it smacked of confidence. I thought maybe it was something he'd learned in a debate club somewhere, or in some judge's seminar, to assume such authority.

But then I realized what was almost certainly the real explanation.

He was thirsty.

His opening statement was beautiful—more personal than he probably would have preferred, but he had come to understand what people wanted to hear, and he forced himself to talk openly about growing up as the son of an immigrant and going to an elite university only twelve miles from his house but worlds away from the life he knew.

It exceeded all our expectations, and I left the hearing room to hit the media outside it as Alito and the others left for the vice president's office in the Dirksen Building where we bivouacked for the hearings.

I joined the group about fifteen minutes later, and everyone was in great spirits. I told the judge his statement was wonderful, and was getting positive reviews. He smiled.

Then I held up my fist the way baseball players do to one another when they cross home plate. He looked at it, not sure what to do.

"Knuckle me!" I said.

My fifteen-year-old son and I saw a show one time where a

goofy guy trying unsuccessfully to be cool did and said the same thing, and it cracked us up, and when he does something good now I hold up my fist to him and say, "Knuckle me!"

Finally Alito smiled and banged his fist against mine. I was being purposefully goofy, just trying to keep it light.

On the first day of the hearings Democrats on the committee slammed time and time again into the superior intellect who sat before them and failed to lay a glove on him. Alito stoically answered the questions directly and expertly.

Ted Kennedy tried in vain to make an issue of Alito's participation in a case involving Vanguard Funds, in which Alito held shares, but it had already been thoroughly vetted by the media and there was no conflict of interest, and Alito had gone so far as to urge a rehearing of the case to ensure that the plaintiff involved had every confidence in the judicial process.

On the second day, Kennedy shifted gears and sought to make an issue of Alito's having noted on a 1985 application for a political appointment in the Reagan administration his membership in Concerned Alumni of Princeton (CAP), a conservative group that was concerned about the adoption of racial quotas in the school's admissions and a hostility to ROTC on campus.

We had prepared for such a line of questioning in the moots, and Alito told us the only reason he could think of for his joining the group was that he resented the way ROTC had been treated by the Princeton community. Alito was in the ROTC while an undergraduate when it was booted off campus. He didn't remember much if anything about the group, and was surprised in the moots by a quotation Steve Schmidt read him from one of its publications.

But Kennedy cited a much more inflammatory quotation and had it blown up on a big board for the cameras:

"People nowadays just don't seem to know their place. Everywhere one turns blacks and Hispanics are demanding jobs simply because they're black and Hispanic, the physically handicapped are trying to gain equal representation in professional sports, and homosexuals are demanding that government vouchsafe them the right to bear children."

It was a quotation we had not turned up in our own research, and it turned out later to be taken from a 1983 Prospect newsletter piece called "In Defense of Elitism" that was written as satire. It was meant to be funny (whether it was or not), but Kennedy was treating it as representative of the author's actual views.

Alito immediately and rightly repudiated it, but Kennedy pressed on, demanding that the committee be given the opportunity to rummage through a box of files kept by William Rusher, a former publisher of *National Review* magazine and one of the founders of Concerned Alumni of Princeton.

When the hearing took a break for lunch, I talked to Mike O'Neill, Specter's chief counsel on the committee and a very smart staffer who is much more conservative than his boss. We had worked closely on strategy for the Roberts hearings and were constantly in touch during the Alito hearings as well.

"What are you guys going to do about the CAP documents?" I asked.

"I think the chairman's inclined to just get them and review them," he said.

"Why even legitimize the notion that they matter?" I asked.

"Have you seen them?" he asked.

"No. If we did, I could understand the committee wanting to see them, but we considered them irrelevant and think you should, too."

"You should talk to the chairman, then," Mike said.

I placed a call, and about a half-hour later Chairman Specter called me back on my cell. The committee would reconvene in about half an hour, and I was anxious to hear how he intended to handle Kennedy.

"Well, I'm inclined to just send staff over there to go through the boxes," he said.

"Chairman, do you think anything that's in those boxes is relevant to Judge Alito's confirmability?"

"No, do you?"

"No, sir."

"Do you think there's anything in there?"

"No, I don't, but I worry about treating the request as legitimate at all."

"Well, I'm inclined to just let him go through them. I have a call in to Rusher. I think they'll look silly."

By this time, I'd become conditioned to thinking Specter was probably right. His institutional inclination is to simply defuse things, rather than give the minority a procedural excuse to oppose a bill or nomination.

When the hearing reconvened the next morning, Specter opened by noting that the committee staff, including Senator Kennedy's, had gone through boxes of files from Concerned Alumni of Princeton, and there were no letters or articles written by him, no canceled checks from him, not a sign anywhere of his participation in the organization.

Ted Kennedy looked like Geraldo Rivera after opening Al Capone's vault.

Senator Lindsey Graham (R-SC) had been a hero in the Roberts hearings, and as the third day of the Alito hearings was winding down he donned his hero's cape again. Lindsey Graham holds a unique piece of ground in the United States Senate, and is one of the more fascinating political figures I've ever come across. He is largely conservative, but his independent streak makes him unpredictable. He is a reformer. And he is a genuinely good and decent human being who works hard to resist the easy allure of harsh partisanship in an increasingly polarized Senate.

He frustrated a number of his colleagues and me (when I was working with Majority Leader Bill Frist on breaking the logjam over judicial nominations in the spring of 2005) when he joined thirteen of his colleagues in the so-called Gang of Fourteen to bro-

ker a deal that fended off implementation of the constitutional, or
"nuclear" option of allowing judicial nominees to be confirmed by
the Senate with a simple majority rather than the sixty votes required to break a filibuster.

But it reflects his desire to foster a less partisan and polarizing
environment in the Senate and to get back to a time when people
could set aside partisan differences to work things out in a spirit of
comity.

Graham was truly disgusted by the actions of some of his
Democratic colleagues in the Senate and their effort to tarnish
Alito's sterling reputation with veiled inferences that he might har-
bor feelings of racial prejudice. He decided to put their innuendo
right out there on the table, as the hearing transcript shows:

GRAHAM: If you don't mind, the suspicious nature that I have
is that you may be saying that because you want to get
on the Supreme Court; that you're disavowing this now
because it doesn't look good.

And really what I would look at to believe you're
not—and I'm going to be very honest with you—is:
How have you lived your life? Are you really a closet
bigot?

ALITO: I'm not any kind of a bigot, I'm not.

GRAHAM: No, sir, you're not! And you know why I believe that?
Not because you just said it—but that's a good enough
reason, because you seem to be a decent, honorable man.

At this point, the lips of Martha Alito, hearing someone say what
surely she had been thinking for the past two days, began to quiver.
Eventually, the tears came. As she was seated over her husband's
right shoulder and he was facing Graham to his left, she was squarely
on camera the whole time.

I was unaware of it all until my BlackBerry vibrated with a

message from Rachel Brand, which said, "I assume you all noticed that Mrs. Alito just walked out crying."

I had not noticed, but I got up and left the hearing room and walked down the hall to the VP's Dirksen Office.

Martha Alito was in the private office, her feet up on the window behind the desk, being consoled by a family member, who whispered to me, "She's okay." I left them alone and returned to the hearing room.

At the next break I went to work the reporters in the hallway again, and they were abuzz over the episode.

"Why was she so upset?"

"Look, I've known Judge Alito for about three months, and it's been hard for me to sit in that hearing room and listen to them question his integrity and smear his character. I can only imagine what it's been like for his wife, and when Senator Graham rightly called the Democrats' hand on it, I'm sure it resonated with her."

By the time I got back to the VP's office, Martha was standing next to the judge and seemed fine.

I gave her a hug. "You're a good person and they're bad people," I said. "And that's good for us." She smiled.

It was one of those moments that captured the attention of the American public, and they understood right away that the way Alito was being treated by some (not all) of the Judiciary Committee Democrats was why so many good people don't want to serve in important public positions.

Funny thing is, Martha Ann Alito is no frail, timid woman who would cry at the slightest affront. She and the justice are the classic "opposites attract" couple, as she is every bit as ebullient and irreverent as he is reserved and reverential. As I stood next to her in the Roosevelt Room of the White House watching the votes come in for his confirmation, she left no doubt in my mind that she knew exactly which senators were voting against her husband and what they had said about him on the floor of the Senate.

And if any of the senators who questioned Sam Alito's character (as opposed to his judicial philosophy) ever runs into his wife in a dark alley some day, Martha Ann Alito won't be the one who walks out crying!

The Democrats' near-uniform opposition to Alito's confirmation was disgraceful. By every ordinary standard—experience, temperament, integrity, and intellect—Samuel Alito is one of the most qualified jurists ever to be put on the Supreme Court. Years from now when a Democratic president puts forward a qualified liberal jurist, I hope the media remember who changed the standards when Republicans—who voted with few exceptions for Justices Ruth Bader Ginsburg and Stephen Breyer, a former American Civil Liberties Union counsel and a chief counsel to Ted Kennedy, respectively—oppose the nomination.

For members of the confirmation team, our faith in him and John Roberts has already begun to bear out, as the Roberts Court seems to be one with fewer dissents and concurring opinions and one with joint opinions that reflect the vast majority, if not always all, of the members of the Court. In addition to being a brilliant jurist, the chief has a way with people, and the country will benefit for generations from a Court that issues rulings that are clearly written and enjoy the broad support of its justices.

And Justice Alito has proven to be a thoughtful, careful jurist who applies the law as written by legislatures or our Constitution, rather than seeking to make new law from the bench. Their combined impact will shape the Court for generations.

PART III

NOW AND LATER

CHAPTER EIGHT

MAINTAINING A REPUBLICAN MAJORITY

Political fortunes ebb and flow, but the overwhelming force in American politics is toward a sustained center-right majority. The late political scientist Samuel Lubell described the dynamic between the two major parties in terms of the Sun and the Moon. At any given moment, one of the parties is the Sun Party, at the center of the political universe burning bright with ideas and energy, while the Moon party reflects its light.

For decades, beginning with Franklin Roosevelt, the Democratic Party was the Sun Party. From Roosevelt's New Deal through Lyndon Johnson and the Great Society, its vision of greater power in the hands of a centralized federal government was the dominant one. Even Richard Nixon and Republicans in Congress in the early 1970s accepted that philosophy.

In 1980, Ronald Wilson Reagan firmly established the Republican Party as the Sun, with the political planets revolving around his vision of a more limited federal government and a strong national defense. Bill Clinton's two terms in the White House were marked not only by his statement that "the era of big government is over," but by the Republicans' taking over the U.S. House of Representatives for the first time in forty years in the middle of his first term.

But now Republicans, with a two-term presidency and more than a decade in control of the House, must guard against burning out. To do so, we must reinvigorate our policy agenda and expand our party.

Campaigns are fought over three general issues: national/homeland security, the economy and health care, and cultural values. Here are a few quick thoughts on how Republicans should approach each to help keep our majority.

NATIONAL SECURITY

After the terrorist attacks of September 11, 2001, President Bush put forward a vigorous approach to national and homeland security that is likely to shape the GOP for at least a generation. It is centered on the policy of preemption.

President Bush's most important principle is that after September 11, the United States will act preemptively to protect its citizens. This principle was central to the war in Iraq, and because of failures in intelligence relative to Iraq's possession of weapons of mass destruction it is now subject to immense second-guessing and criticism.

British prime minister Tony Blair made the best case against such second-guessing in his brilliant July 17, 2003, speech to a Joint Session of Congress. He said, "If we are wrong, we will have destroyed a threat that, at its least, is responsible for inhuman carnage and suffering. That is something I am confident history will forgive. But if our critics are wrong, if we are right, as I believe with every fiber of instinct and conviction I have that we are, then we will have hesitated in the face of this menace when we should have given leadership. That is something history will not forgive."

As a party we should stand by the Bush doctrine of preemption. In a time when the greatest threat to our country is chemical or biological weapons in the hands of Islamic extremists who want to bring an end to the Western way of life, an unwillingness to act preemptively could result in a tragedy that could dwarf the destruction of the Twin Towers.

America prevailed in the Cold War because Republicans prevailed in the presidential elections of 1980, 1984, and 1988 and embraced Reagan's willingness to confront the Soviet Union ("Mr. Gorbachev, tear down this wall!").

We will prevail in the War on Terror by embracing President Bush's willingness to fight the terrorists where they live and plot, knowing that if the fight is not waged in places like Kabul and Baghdad it will be waged in places like Kansas and Boston. A majority of Americans intuitively understand this, despite frustration over the pace of progress in Iraq.

In his powerful book *The Case for Democracy: The Power of Freedom to Overcome Tyranny and Terror,* Natan Sharansky does a better job than anyone I have seen of articulating the rationale for President Bush's commitment to fostering freedom and democracy in the Middle East. Fulfillment of that vision will take years, but it will result in a safer United States of America.

HEALTH CARE

Health care is likely to be the dominant domestic policy issue of the next decade. Our existing system is a platypus, a strange animal that's part government-run, part government-subsidized, part employer-provided, and part individual. It's anachronistic and unsustainable in our modern economy, and it's time to just plain have it out in our political process.

I believe Americans will confront the inherently incompatible aspects of the health care economy in the 2008 presidential campaign. Whomever the Democrats nominate will propose a government-run system that will make Hillary-care '93 look like something Milton Friedman came up with. The Republican nominee will put forward a plan that shifts the emphasis to the private sector and puts the consumer more directly in control of health care expenses.

More than 16 percent of our nation's GNP is now spent on

health care services (nearly $2 trillion in 2004), versus less than 5 percent in 1950. Spending on health care is outstripping annual income growth by an average of 2.5 percentage points a year. Since 1990, health insurance premiums have increased by as much as 60 percent in constant dollars. America's health care problem is not a problem of spending too little.

Between half and three-quarters of this massive expenditure is made by people other than patients themselves. The separation of patients from health care spending decisions is largely a result of wage controls enacted in World War II, which compelled employers to offer health coverage as a way of luring employees in lieu of higher wages. Consequently, out of today's population of 296 million people, 220 million receive their health coverage through their employer or a government-funded program.

The remainder is made up of two groups—27 million Americans who pay directly for their health care coverage and the nearly 50 million who, for a variety of reasons, go without coverage entirely. Getting coverage to those 50 million will entail changing how those with coverage get theirs.

The share of workers who receive health insurance from their employers has fallen from nearly 70 percent in the late 1970s to less than 50 percent now, down from 55 percent just five years ago. The steepest decline has occurred among small firms and those companies employing low-skilled workers.

There are distinctions between American health care and care in other countries that we must maintain. We have the most advanced hospitals in the world, and they do the most innovative research. We have the finest, most highly trained health care professionals in the world. We lead the world with a system of private medicine that encourages innovation and change. In a survey of doctors published in the December 6, 2005, issue of *Health Affairs,* it was stated that eight of the ten most important medical breakthroughs of the past thirty years originated in America.

Following the five principles outlined below would ensure

that efficiency, affordability, and availability would prevail in the health care sector in the same ways they are taken for granted in other sectors of our economy—such as food, clothing, laptop computers, and automobiles.

1. Consumers Should Pay the First Dollar

One of the greatest challenges in reforming our health care system is to restore the primacy of the user or consumer as a player in the process. Imagine a world in which third parties decide where you live, what kind of car you drive, or even where you buy groceries. We wouldn't tolerate it, and it wouldn't work. Yet this is precisely what we do with health care.

As John Goodman and Gerald Musgrave note in their thought-provoking book, *Patient Power*, "In today's bureaucratically dominated health care system, the patient's major role is to sign the forms that authorize one large, impersonal organization to release funds to another. Government, through Medicare and Medicaid, buys close to half the health care provided in America today. Most of the other half is paid for by insurance companies, through policies purchased by third parties, because the tax laws encourage people to rely on first-dollar health coverage from their employers."

Consumers today spend less than a quarter of every dollar spent directly on their own health, a percentage that's declining as overall costs are rising. Additionally, federal and state governments have passed so many rules that they've taken practically all the choices and decisions away from consumers. Overuse is the rational response of consumers who do not have to pay the entire cost of their medical care and have little real control over their coverage.

A dramatic change in this dynamic is necessary. Individual users and their families should have more say about which services they want. Arguably, health care coverage is qualitatively much more important than the type of car you drive, but Americans spend millions of hours annually mulling and haggling over a car purchase and only a fraction of that time making health insurance decisions. Why? Because there's no competition at the consumer level.

One way to bring patients back into the picture is for them to pay the first dollar. Instead of employer-based policies, consumers would purchase services directly from insurers. Employers could instead agree to make matching or even supplemental payments similar to the ones they make today, except that they'd no longer actually choose the companies providing coverage. With consumers in charge, policies could be tailored to make them attractive to consumers and their families rather than to the employer. The automobile industry spends billions on marketing and rebates in order to gain market share. If consumers become the primary purchasers of health insurance, similar incentives would likely develop.

Additionally, the insurance policies themselves need to change to reflect this principle. Instead of patients' paying five or ten dollars per doctor's visit, insurers should require greater initial cost sharing for the consumer, decreasing over time. In other words, patients would pay 25 to 50 percent of the cost of their medical visits until they reach a certain threshold (say, between one thousand dollars and twenty-five hundred dollars in a given year). Such an approach would fundamentally alter the incentives for health care use.

This shift would lead to greater competition in and self-selection of health care coverage and health care use. This happens today in the field of elective health care services such as Lasik eye surgery and cosmetic dental treatment, where consumers do pay the first dollar. In each instance, cost to consumers has dropped dramatically while technology and innovation flourish.

2. Coverage Should Be Portable

In today's increasingly fluid and mobile workforce, fewer workers obtain health care coverage from one employer for their entire careers. Few eighteen-year-olds entering the workforce today expect to retire from the company they've just gone to work for. Yet in the current system, every time a worker leaves or loses a job, he or she also forfeits health care coverage.

This has predictable consequences. Employers have less incentive to invest in the health of their workforce through preventive care programs if they believe workers will not be with them when the benefits pay off. Employees are forced to accept breaks in coverage. Families are often forced out of insurance coverage they like because their new employers do not provide the same policy as their old employers.

The lack of health insurance portability is a major problem of today's health care system. The Health Insurance Portability and Accountability Act of 1996 (HIPAA) was intended to expand health insurance coverage by weakening the bond between insurance coverage and specific employers. Unfortunately, HIPAA has had only limited success. It has made it somewhat easier for currently insured workers to retain their access to group health insurance coverage when they change jobs, but it does so only if they are subsequently employed by other (typically large corporate) firms that also offer group health coverage. Additionally, it set up restrictions on the types of policies that could be portable.

True portability would sever the tie between employment and health care altogether. People don't stop getting sick when they leave IBM to work for Microsoft or become self-employed. Access to health coverage shouldn't depend on whether one is employed, or who one is employed by.

Portability means policies go wherever you do. Rather than mandate a nationwide policy regulated by the federal government, a change could be made so that policies for insurance companies are not deductible for individuals or business unless the insurers agree that the policies are portable and can be purchased in all fifty states. As long as an insurer is legally operating under the rules of a given state, it should be allowed to offer insurance in all fifty states. Forcing insurers to compete in all fifty states would lower prices and improve services. Today's patchwork of insurers and policies limited to states or regions prevents much competition. Simply changing deductibility based on portability would result in more affordable coverage being made available quickly without having to wait for state commissions or legislatures to approve changes.

In an April 2004 study by Ehealthinsurance.com, an internet provider of insurance quotes, researchers analyzed more than sixty thousand policies sold in forty-two states and the District of Columbia. They found that individual premium costs ranged from a high of $4,044 per year in New Jersey to a low of $1,188 in Iowa and Wyoming. Why shouldn't families in New Jersey be able to buy policies from firms in Iowa?

A national market for health insurance would lead to a nationwide marketing effort for health insurance like the one we see in the auto or property and casualty insurance markets. We would see discounts, rebates, and even packages designed to make insurance products more attractive to families.

In a national market, individuals and families would have the opportunity to purchase health plans sponsored by organizations that share their values on sensitive matters relating to the provision of health care services, including ethical health plans, faith-based health plans, and plans sponsored by religious organizations and institutions. And finally, removing the fragmentation of insurance markets would lower administrative costs and lessen the impact of adverse selection.

3. Tax Treatment Should Be Equitable

Today's tax code provides unlimited tax relief for the purchase of health insurance as long as it comes through employers. However, when employers do not offer health care coverage as part of their compensation packages, their employees have little tax incentive to purchase health insurance. Americans purchasing individual health insurance outside the workplace must pay for coverage with after-tax dollars, which could add as much as 40 percent on top of the cost of the premium—on top of other costs incurred in the administration, marketing, and regulation of individual health plans.

Imagine what the car-buying experience would be like if 75 percent of all purchasers were businesses and government. Corporations taking deductions could provide luxury SUVs to their employees, while stretched small businesses would probably be able to afford only small economy cars that barely fit the needs of American families. The selection, the service, the dealers—everything about the car-buying experience would be different.

Those few individuals buying cars with their after-tax dollars in this scenario would see few similarities to today's auto market. They would find severe limits on the types of cars available to them, few to no financing options (since corporations and governments don't need loans), and shockingly high prices. Pricing, marketing, and products would be tailored to the major purchasers—not families and individuals.

Today, the automobile market is segmented to represent the needs of the typical purchasers—individuals and families. While businesses and corporations buy vehicles, they don't do so on a scale great enough to tilt the market away from families and individuals. Our health care system operates in almost exactly the opposite manner —families and individuals influence the market only marginally, if at all. Most of the players in the market are responding to corporate and government purchasers. This distortion hinders the efficient distribution of health coverage.

In order to level the playing field in the health insurance market, we must extend to health insurance purchased outside the workplace the same tax relief employers enjoy. Also, Americans who purchase Heath Savings Accounts (HSA) qualified insurance policies on their own should have the same tax advantages as people who obtain insurance through their employer.

Out-of-pocket health expenditures by individuals and families should also be given support in the tax code. The tax code currently subsidizes health care purchased through insurance but generally does not subsidize health care paid for out of pocket. This encourages excessive reliance on third-party insurance for even predictable, noncatastrophic care, which in turn reduces consumer sensitivity to the cost of health care.

All Americans should be allowed to cover all their out-of-pocket expenses through HSAs. Employers and employees alike should be allowed to make annual contributions to their HSAs up to the maximum amount. And their insurance policies should allow people to pay out of pocket for their health care expenses, not just their deductible.

4. End the Lawsuit Lottery

Our current broken medical liability system serves the interest of trial lawyers at the expense of doctors and families. Doctors who have never been the subject of a lawsuit are being forced to limit or move their practices because of rising liability premiums. One in five hospitals have cut back on critical services as a result of frivolous lawsuits, reducing the availability of emergency services in many communities. OB/GYNs have left their communities to escape rising liability premiums, and in some areas of the country expectant mothers must drive sixty miles for prenatal care.

Malpractice costs include lawyers' fees, damage awards, and settlements in cases in which doctors know they are innocent but settle to avoid long and costly legal proceedings. These costs are passed on to patients, and it is a particularly undue burden on lower-income families. The Congressional Budget Office estimated that malpractice costs account for about 2 percent of health care spending, or about $28 billion per year. In 2002, malpractice costs equaled $225 per household in America—nearly half of what the average household spends on prescription drugs.

The CBO study does not even count the cost of defensive medicine. Doctors afraid of being sued order expensive tests and procedures that they would otherwise consider unnecessary so they have a defense if targeted by trial lawyers. One study puts the cost of such defensive medicine expenses at an additional $60 billion to $108 billion a year. Together, liability and defensive medicine costs combine to snatch between five hundred and one thousand dollars from American households annually.

Medical liability reforms would secure an injured patient's ability to get quicker compensation for economic losses, while reducing junk lawsuits and excessive jury awards that end up jeopardizing access to care.

5. All Adults Participate

Surveys suggest that 25 to 50 percent of the uninsured are voluntarily so, choosing to forgo the purchase of health insurance because they believe the costs are too high or they are healthy and don't need it. However, these individuals are opting out of the system only until they become ill, at which point the cost of their care falls on the rest of society through subsidized care from the public sector or cost-shifting practices in the private sector.

In other words, they ultimately end up receiving health benefits without having paid into the system. This "free rider" phenomenon is expensive and further stresses an already overwhelmed health care system. Also, since these free riders tend to be younger, healthier individuals, the insurance market without them in it is disproportionately elderly and ill, which also results in higher premiums.

Given the guarantee of treatment, there is no "moral hazard" associated with forgoing health care coverage. Using the auto market analogy again, imagine if people could choose to go without a car, knowing when they needed one they'd be given the use of a car for free or at a substantial discount. Who would want to make car payments? This is actually a rational choice in our present health care system. Is it any wonder that the number of people opting to go without insurance has outpaced population growth over the last decade?

A more rational approach is to ensure that every emancipated adult capable of providing for his or her health care do so. One way to accomplish this is to use the tax code to gain compliance. Annual filers would have to attest that they have some form of health coverage or else the "standard deduction" on their income tax would be cut in half. Another approach would be the creation of tax-free Health Savings Accounts that would be refunded after a certain period for any use. If after seven years, an individual didn't use his HSA funds for health care, the money would be treated like an income tax refund. The inducement of tax-free savings for those who are healthy would provide an incentive for more people to obtain insurance coverage.

According to the Kaiser Commission on Medicaid and the Uninsured, over 40 percent of uninsured adults have no regular source of health care. Delaying or not receiving treatment can lead to more serious illnesses and afflictions that could be avoided by regular care. It is no surprise, then, that the uninsured are more likely to be hospitalized for conditions that could have been avoided.

Bringing the "voluntarily" uninsured back into the insurance pool would have a huge benefit. Public assistance health programs would be less stressed. New consumers would be more discerning and bring increased competitive pressures into the health insurance market, and the enhanced mix of healthy and unhealthy would lead to greater variety in the types of policies offered.

Implementation of the five principles outlined above would revolutionize health care in America. They mirror the free market system that exists in so many other areas that work successfully in our economy.

America is rightly recognized as a special place in the world. Our country offers more prosperity and opportunity for more people than any other by balancing public and private interests in a way consistent with personal autonomy and economic freedom. In the arts and in industry, the benefits of limited government and free markets are obvious for all to see. Unfortunately, this is not the way our health care system works. Until it does, many Americans will remain disappointed and frustrated with the services it provides.

CONTROLLING FEDERAL SPENDING

In April 2006, the United States Treasury took in more tax revenue than every other month in our nation's history except one. It was the second highest monthly total ever.

We don't have a deficit because Americans aren't paying enough taxes, we have a deficit because our government is spending too much money.

We should reign in Federal spending not only so spending equals revenue, however. We should reign in Federal spending because when the Federal government grows beyond its proper size and scope we diminish individual responsibility, stifle innovation, and sap economic growth.

For Republicans, too much Federal spending is not a matter of math, it is a matter or principle.

And that principle is subsidiarity.

The principle of subsidiarity says if something *can* be done at the individual level, it *should* be.

If it *can* be done at the community level, it *should* be.

If it *can* be done at the municipality level, it *should* be.

If it *can* be done at the state level, it *should* be.

If it can't be done at any of these levels, only then should it be done at the Federal level.

In addition to these government functions, I would add that if something can best be done in the private sector, it *should* be.

The Republican Party is united when we are cutting spending

to balance the budget, as we were doing in the 1990s. Our unity breaks down when members of congress focus on "bringing home the bacon."

Earmarking is a singular pursuit in a parochial interest. Budget cutting is a collective exercise in the national interest. The sooner we as a party again make a priority of cutting spending, the better off we'll be.

Regardless, we'll never outspend the Democrats. Can Republicans do better than Republicans are doing now at controlling spending? Absolutely. Can Democrats do better than Republicans are doing now at controlling spending? Absolutely not.

CULTURAL VALUES

The issues that constitute "values" are often treated as a red-headed stepchild of American politics, not by the voters but by the media elite. But issues like abortion, school prayer, gay marriage, welfare reform, and gun control are every bit as legitimate as economic and national security issues. Indeed, such values are often more determinative of the outcome of an election than national security and economic issues.

As important as the issues themselves is the way in which candidates and the two parties approach them. In the late 1990s, the Republican Party suffered from a perception that cultural conservatives in our party were condemnatory of people who embraced more liberal ideas, but today the Democratic Party and the social liberals who form a wide swath of its base are the ones demonstrating an unwillingness to accept those with different points of view. This perception rightly hurts Democrats with the voting public.

I believe the Second Amendment right to bear arms should be no more revered than the First Amendment right to freedom of speech or the Fourth Amendment right to due process, but it should not be any less revered, either. That doesn't make me a "gun nut," by the way. I don't even own a gun. It makes me someone who treasures our Constitution.

I am happy to accept gay people for who they are and love them, to respect the rights of those who choose not to belong to any organized religion, and to understand that some people enjoy shock value in their entertainment.

I have become tired, however, of being told that unless I am willing to support government sanction of same-sex marriage then I am guilty of bigotry, tired of having my religious convictions scorned instead of respected, tired of my children being confronted with shocking images every time they turn on the television or go on the internet.

The Republican Party platform is clear: We believe "marriage" is the legal union of one man and one woman. Americans want to see changes in our tax code, changes in our schools, and changes in our health care system, but there is no public clamor to change the definition of marriage as being between one man and one woman. In fact, polls consistently show that two out of every three Americans oppose recognizing same-sex marriage.

We cannot allow tolerance to be redefined as having to agree with one another on every issue. The eighty-six senators who voted in 1996 to allow states to decide for themselves whether they will recognize gay marriage rather than having that decision imposed upon them by another state's activist supreme court are not "gay bashers," as John Kerry called them when he was one of fourteen to vote against the Defense of Marriage Act.

Wanting to promote a culture of life does not make me a member of the Taliban, as former Vermont governor and current Democratic National Committee chairman Howard Dean has said. And not wanting my children to grow up too fast makes me a caring father, not a "troglodyte," as liberals have called those of us who worry about the coarsening of our culture.

The New Intolerance

Tolerance should mean accepting and respecting those who think differently, not requiring everyone to think the same, but as far as the left is concerned, we can no longer in this country agree to disagree. They seek to redefine tolerance from accepting our differences of opinion to accepting their opinion. This is the new intolerance.

The old intolerance was marked by prejudice, religious bigotry, and fear of positive change. The new intolerance is marked by elitism, antireligious bigotry, and disdain for long-held values that have served our nation well. The old intolerance too often bordered on tyranny of the majority. The new intolerance too often borders on intimidation by the minority.

From enclaves dotting the land from Manhattan to Beverly Hills, a liberal elite seeks to impose their views on the rest of us through their vast personal fortunes, their dominance of television and movie studios, and their control over editorial pages, faculty lounges, and public employee unions.

Actress Bo Derek, still stunningly beautiful decades after making the movie *10,* is one of the few stars in Hollywood to openly support a conservative for president. She once told me that many actors and producers would whisper to her that they, too, supported President Bush. They were simply afraid to be public about it for fear of hurting their careers. In the 1950s when Republican senator Joseph McCarthy of Wisconsin was attacking the entertainment industry as a bastion of communist sympathizers his efforts were derided as "blacklisting," but in today's entertainment industry the practice is not only accepted but condoned when it comes to conservatives.

President Bush proved willing to stand firm against the constant onslaught of political hate speech directed at him in 2004 and answer the intolerance with calls for those of us who agree with his policies to approach the debate with civility and goodwill regardless of the bitter and angry rhetoric of our opponents. He understands that not everyone shares his commitment to his faith, but is unapologetic about his own beliefs.

There is a fine line between letting people live their lives as they choose and respecting their privacy, and forcing others to embrace their choices through government sanction.

A personal experience with a close friend one August evening in 2005 typifies the new intolerance for me. My wife, Cathy, and I sat with a lifelong friend who was a network news producer and his wife on the deck of our beach house on Long Beach Island, New Jersey, talking about raising children. Our friends had just had a beautiful baby daughter, and Cathy and I shared some thoughts on child rearing (experts that we are!).

At one point, Cathy mentioned Dr. James Dobson's book *Bringing Up Boys* and recommended it to our friends even though they had a daughter.

By his reaction, you would have thought she'd recommended *Mein Kampf.*

"I'm not going to read anything by James Dobson," he said.

"Why not?" I asked. "It's a good book."

I don't ascribe to everything in Dr. Dobson's book, but he makes many important points about the inherent differences between girls and boys, and raises legitimate concerns about the popular culture's diminishment of the importance of fatherhood and fathers in our society.

"He's an extremist," my friend said in response to my question.

"Have you ever read anything he's written?" Cathy asked.

"No!"

"Then how do you know he's an extremist?" she said.

"Because I know about him."

"You know about him from there," I said, tapping the network news logo adorning his polo shirt.

"Tell you what, I'll make you a deal," I said. "You read *Bringing Up Boys* by James Dobson, and I'll read any book you want me to read."

"That's ridiculous."

"Any book at all. You name it. And you read Dobson."

My friend responded the way that just about any other big-city liberal would to such an offer.

He passed.

I would have read an Al Franken book, even though I know from personal experience how obnoxious he is. I would have read any of the screeds against President Bush, from David Corn to Michael Moore to E. J. Dionne.

The difference is, I see and hear that stuff all the time as part of the minimum daily requirement of my Mainstream Media diet. I have to go outside the MSM to get information from someone like Dr. James Dobson, but I get Michael Moore without even trying.

IMMIGRATION POLICY AND
THE HISPANIC VOTE

Immigration policy is the most divisive issue in the Republican Party today. It is important to me philosophically, for as a conservative I believe it is a defining issue.

It is important to me politically, for as a former Republican Party chairman, I see this issue as posing the greatest threat to our majority status if handled wrongly.

And it is important to me personally, for as a first-generation American I appreciate the opportunities that have been provided to my father—and by extension to me and my three children—by the greatest country ever to grace the face of the Earth.

Let me address it from each perspective.

Conservatives should support commonsense policies that foster legal immigration because freedom and economic growth are cornerstones of our philosophy. Clarence Thomas once said people in Washington should ask the big-picture questions, starting with this one: "What is there about this country that will lead people to crawl through sewers, get on inner-tubes and float across miles of water, to sneak out in the middle of the night, to cram in under trucks and buses, and other things, risk their lives going across mountains. What is it about this country that people will do all those things to come in, and what is it about the Soviet Union or Cuba or the Eastern Bloc countries that would force people to do those same things to get out?"

Ronald Reagan, the father of the modern Republican Party, said in his 1990 Westminster Memorial Speech, "You can go to live in France, but you can't become a Frenchman. You can go to live in Germany or Italy, but you can't become a German, an Italian. But he said anyone, from any corner of the world, can come to live in the United States and become an American."

As the words "he said" indicate, Reagan was actually quoting someone else, attributing the line simply to a "letter from a man."

There is an important element to that quotation in that "letter from a man" that's worth noting: assimilation.

I believe the concerns over immigration shared by so many Americans today reflect less an anti-immigration sentiment than a pro-assimilation one.

Diversity makes us stronger as a nation, but the presumption in the notion of a "melting pot" is that the different races and ethnicities blend together. Multiculturalism is as responsible for what is seen as anti-immigration sentiment as is the flood of illegal immigrants coming across our southern border.

For more than a century, immigrants to this country settled in Chinatowns, Little Italys, and Little Saigons, but the new citizens there interacted in the broader community. Glimpses of my father's brogue poke through his speech now and then, especially after a few Jamesons, but his mother insisted that he and his brothers and sisters shed their brogue because Americans don't talk that way.

Today, we have population pockets in our country where an

individual can live a lifetime without ever speaking English. This lack of integration and assimilation breeds resentment and mistrust, and it's not the model that made America great.

As conservatives, we must also stand for the rule of law. A rational immigration policy that allows workers to enter and exit this country for temporary employment will minimize the incentive to enter the country illegally and stay for fear of not being able to return if they leave.

Peggy Noonan eloquently wrote in the *Wall Street Journal:*

> What does it mean that your first act on entering a country—your first act on that soil—is the breaking of that country's laws? What does it suggest to you when that country does nothing about your lawbreaking because it cannot, or chooses not to? What does that tell you? Will that make you a better future citizen, or worse? More respecting of the rule of law in your new home, or less?

A new policy would increase compliance with U.S. laws, but not reward with citizenship those who are here by virtue of breaking our laws.

While resentment toward those who come into the United States illegally is legitimate, much of the resentment toward immigrant labor is based on the misperception that it is a drain on our economy and resources. However, researchers at the Academy of Sciences for the U.S. Commission on Immigration Reform have demonstrated that:

- Immigrants add about $10 billion annually in net economic output due to the increased supply of labor and resulting lower prices.
- A typical newcomer pays in eighty thousand dollars more in taxes than he or she takes out over the course of a lifetime.

The researchers said revenue from the future earnings of immigrants far outweighs the fiscal impact of benefits they receive, since immigrants receive proportionately fewer benefits from programs such as Social Security and Medicare, but proportionately more from programs such as Supplemental Security Income, AFDC, and food stamps.

From low-wage workers who harvest crops in the noon sun to high-end workers who lend their technology and engineering expertise to U.S. companies, immigrant labor provides critically important human resources. Eliminating their participation will not result in more Americans' filling those jobs, but in Florida orange groves being sold to developers and in the planting of new groves south of our border, and in U.S. technology companies moving employment centers from Boston, northern Virginia, and Silicon Valley to Bangladesh and Shanghai.

Conservatives who believe in freedom, economic growth, the rule of law, and preserving our culture should support immigration policies that secure our borders but are also pro freedom, pro-growth, and pro-assimilation.

America needs a new temporary worker program that will match willing foreign workers with willing American employers, when no Americans can be found to fill the jobs. This program would offer legal status, as temporary workers, to the millions of undocumented men and women now employed in the United States, and to those in foreign countries who seek to participate in the program and have been offered employment here.

This new system should be clear and efficient, so employers are able to find workers quickly and simply.

Participants who do not remain employed, who do not follow the rules of the program, or who break the law will not be eligible for continued participation and will be required to return home.

Employers would also have key responsibilities. Employers who extend job offers must first make every reasonable effort to find an American worker for the job at hand. Employers must not hire undocumented aliens or temporary workers whose legal status has expired.

They must report to the government the temporary workers they hire, and who leave their employ, so that we can keep track of people in the program, and better enforce immigration laws. There must be strong workplace enforcement with tough penalties for any employer violating these laws.

This new temporary worker program will bring more than economic benefits to America. Our homeland will be more secure when we can better account for those who enter our country, instead of the current situation in which millions of people are unknown to us.

Law enforcement will face fewer problems with undocumented workers and will be better able to focus on the true threats to our nation from criminals and terrorists. And when temporary workers can travel legally and freely, there will be more efficient management of our borders and more effective enforcement against those who pose a danger to our country.

Polling done in 2005 by the Tarrance Group shows that while 84 percent of voters agree with the statement that "the immigration system is broken and needs to be fixed," voters also strongly support—by 75 percent—a comprehensive approach that:

1. Increases border security,
2. Toughens enforcement of current laws,
3. Registers current illegal immigrants, and
4. Allows illegal immigrants to earn legal status—though not citizenship—by working, learning English, paying taxes, and living crime-free.

Passing policies like these will help Republicans make gains in the electorate, but past experience shows that policies that seek to penalize immigration harm my party.

The California Republican Party struggles today because of what Hispanics saw as an assault on them more than a decade ago by then-governor Pete Wilson.

In my home state of Virginia, Republican gubernatorial candidate Jerry Kilgore ran last-minute anti-immigration ads that didn't move his numbers with swing voters and probably cost him important votes in the El Salvadoran, Guatemalan, and Nicaraguan enclaves of northern Virginia.

Had President Bush not increased his margins with African-American and Hispanic voters in 2004, John Kerry would be president today. Anti-immigration rhetoric is a political siren's song, and Republicans must resist its lure by lashing ourselves to our party's twin masts of freedom and growth, or our majority will crash on its shoals.

At the same time, we should not blur the lines between being *anti-immigration* and being *anti-illegal immigration.* Wanting to strengthen our borders and enforce existing laws does not make one "anti-immigrant."

People who come legally to this country with nothing but the clothes on their back and work in the most menial ways to get a new start should feel at home in our party. As a rule, they are hardworking, freedom-loving, and patriotic Americans.

This is not something I learned from a book. It's something I learned from my father, who came on a boat to this country from Donegal, Ireland, in 1933 as a nine-year-old with nothing but the clothes on his back.

He was processed through Ellis Island. He worked as a janitor, Nazi bullets ripped through both his legs in the course of his earning a Purple Heart, a Bronze Star, a Bronze Star with Oak Leaf Cluster, and a Silver Star for his adopted country. He started his own business, and made his children the first generation of Gillespies ever to attend college.

I am proud to be the son of an immigrant. Like many first-generation Americans, I think it has made me treasure the benefits of U.S. citizenship even more.

I began by quoting Justice Thomas and President Reagan on the topic, but another distinguished scholar may capture my sentiments even better.

I'm referring, of course, to Bill Murray as Private John Winger in *Stripes,* when he movingly noted:

"We're all very different people. We're not Watusi, we're not Spartans. We're Americans.

"And you know what that means? That means our forefathers were kicked out of every decent country in the world!

"We are the wretched refuse.

"We're the underdog.

"We're mutts!"

RECLAIMING THE
AFRICAN-AMERICAN VOTE

Properly handling the debate over immigration reform will ensure Republicans continue to make gains with Hispanic voters, but the party's greatest opportunity for gains in the electorate may lie in the African-American vote.

For more than thirty years, Democrats have taken the black vote for granted and Republicans have not contested it vigorously enough. But my party has a proud history with black voters, beginning with the fact that it was founded by Abraham Lincoln, the Great Emancipator.

Frederick Douglass, Booker T. Washington, Sojourner Truth, and Harriet Tubman were supporters of the Republican Party. The first African-Americans ever elected to the United States Senate and House of Representatives were Republicans.

In 2004, we celebrated the fiftieth anniversary of *Brown* v. *Board of Education.* It's worth remembering that those were Democratic governors standing in schoolhouse doors, and it was a Republican president who called in the National Guard to enforce the promise of equal access to our public schools.

A higher percentage of Republicans in the U.S. House and Senate voted for the Civil Rights Act of 1964 than did Democrats, but Lyndon Johnson, a Democratic president, signed it. He built on the gains made by Franklin Roosevelt, Harry S. Truman, and John F. Kennedy, who made the historic call to the Reverend Martin Luther King in his jail cell.

Democratic appeal and Republican erosion with African-Americans only accelerated over the late seventies, eighties, and nineties, with the Republican presidential nominee averaging 10.25 percent of the black vote over the past four presidential elections.

As the party of Lincoln grew in strength in the states of the Old Confederacy, African-Americans were drifting away (perhaps not coincidentally) from their historic home. I believe that in the cycle of politics, the Republican Party and African-American voters have come to a point in time where it is in their common interest to renew their historic bonds.

One out of seven African-Americans who self-identified as Democrats in 2000 changed their political affiliation in 2002, according to the National Opinion Poll conducted by the Washington, D.C.–based Joint Center for Political and Economic Studies. The 2002 poll found that 63 percent of African-American adults identified themselves as Democrats, down from 74 percent in 2000. In 2000, only 4 percent of African-Americans identified themselves as Republicans, but 10 percent did in 2002. That's a seventeen-percentage-point swing in one election cycle.

In 2004, there were two African-American lieutenant governors in America. Both were Republican. The state with the most African-American statewide elected officials was Texas, and all three were Republican.

Republican candidates in statewide races across the country have been getting increasing percentages of black voters. In South Carolina, reformer Lindsey Graham reached out to black voters in his successful bid to replace Strom Thurmond. In North Carolina,

Elizabeth Dole got about 16 percent of the black vote in her bid to replace Jesse Helms, running an ad on black radio touting her pride in sitting beside Coretta Scott King while her husband, Bob Dole, served as floor manager for the legislation establishing the Martin Luther King federal holiday.

President Bush has appointed more minority members to important positions than any president in recent history, including Bill Clinton. Secretary of State Condoleezza Rice and Colin Powell before her, former education secretary Rod Paige, Secretary of Housing and Urban Development Alfonso Jackson, Labor Secretary Elaine Chao, Commerce Secretary Carlos Gutierrez, and many others hold the positions they hold because of the content of their character and the quality of their work, but they prove that people of color can rise to the most important positions in our federal government.

President Bush deserves credit not just for the people he has appointed, but for the policies he has pursued. On issues central to the well-being of African-American families—public education, health care, capital formation, job creation, national security, and community values, President Bush's policies are working.

The President's commitment to the idea of greater cooperation between government and church-based charities should be applauded. Churches have always been alternatives to welfare and other social problems, and they have always been more empowering. When my father got off that boat at Ellis Island, it was the Church that helped his family put food in their bellies, clothes on their backs, and a roof over their heads. They also benefited from what was then called "public assistance." Government programs are necessary, but in order to confront poverty and family disintegration, and resist attacks on mainstream values, President Bush has sought many ways to tap the moral leaders in America's communities.

Not only are religious leaders the ones who can make a great difference in people's lives, but too often they are the only ones who want to, the only ones who assume the leadership in their communities to make that difference.

President Bush's progrowth agenda is extremely favorable for small-business men and women. This is especially significant for African-Americans, when you consider that the number of small business launched by minorities is growing fast—up 17 percent annually in 2003, according to *Fortune* magazine.

But economic policies alone will not increase our percentage of the African-American vote. In my discussions with leaders in the black community who are open to hearing from Republican candidates, one of the things that became clear to me is that we will not get the votes of the bulk of upper-middle-class African-American voters in the suburbs until we demonstrate our commitment to poor African-Americans in the inner cities.

A black lawyer married to a black doctor in Prince George's County, Maryland (the wealthiest concentration of African-American voters in the country), may stand to benefit from a reduction in the capital gains rate, but most wealthy African-Americans are not going to abandon their allegiance to the Democratic Party over that difference between the two parties.

I grew up in a very racially diverse community. In my high school graduating class of more than four hundred students, 45 percent were African-American, Hispanic, or Asian-American. Our senior class president was Filipino. The principal was African-American. Interracial dating was common even in 1977. Partly because of this background, it came naturally for me to embark upon one of the proudest aspects of my RNC chairmanship, outreach to African-American voters.

Throughout 2004, I traveled to cities in battleground states like Philadelphia, Milwaukee, and Cleveland, going to black churches, Urban League meetings, and inner-city precincts to help the party of Lincoln reconnect with African-American voters.

I was joined in the effort by Maryland's lieutenant governor Michael Steele, the first African-American ever elected statewide in the Free State, former Miss America Erica Harold (the second African-American Miss America), Texas Railroad Commissioner Michael Williams, and others. Most visible, perhaps, was boxing promoter Don King.

I met King when he came to my office in 2003 to encourage me to aggressively court the black vote. King is not a Republican. He calls himself a "Republicrat," someone who votes for candidates whom he believes are best for the America he loves regardless of their party.

He wasn't urging me to do this because he thought it would be good for the Republican Party (though he knew it would), but because he knew it would be good for African-Americans if both parties competed for their votes. Ever the capitalist, King knows that competition in the political arena would be good for black voters.

Don King's public persona is that of the fast-talking huckster, and he would be the first to tell you he is no saint. In person he is an incredibly thoughtful, kind, and generous man of deep faith, and no one could argue that he is one of the best marketers in our country's history. His dedication to U.S. troops is heartwarming, and we had a lot of fun traveling the country together in support of President Bush.

Once, we took Amtrak from Philadelphia to New York, and as we waited in Philly's Thirtieth Street Station everyone was coming up wanting to get their pictures taken with Don—sixty-year-old white women and twenty-five-year-old black males and everyone in between.

Everybody loves Don King, and the reason is, Don King loves everybody.

He took me back to his old neighborhood outside Cleveland where I spoke at a black church in the middle of a run-down section of town. Liberal activists were picketing out front, handing out leaflets accusing the Republicans of all kinds of awful things and making it hard for people to enter the church.

When I spoke to the hundred or so people who had persevered to make their way into the pews, I was candid.

"I know a lot of people told you it's a waste of your time to come here tonight to hear the chairman of the Republican Party, so thank you for coming. Truth is, a lot of people told me it's a waste of my time to come here to talk to all of you tonight.

"I don't believe it, and you shouldn't either."

I went on to share my thoughts about the importance of African-Americans' having the benefit of a two-party system, and highlighted how the president's policies were benefiting African-Americans. As I got going, I was treated to a few "Amens" here and there, and afterward people came up to me genuinely appreciative of the discussion.

In Ohio, the state that proved decisive in his victory, President Bush got 16 percent of the African-American vote against John Kerry, versus 9 percent in 2000 versus Al Gore. I don't attribute all of that to Don King.

But I do attribute a bunch of it to him.

Before the '04 election, when it seemed that Senator John Kerry might win, some of King's friends in the black liberal establishment told him they had planned a special ceremony in which they were going to bury a coffin with his name on it to note that he was "dead" to them for having supported President Bush.

But, as is his knack, King had picked the winner, and his liberal friends were denied the opportunity.

Ken Mehlman, my successor as RNC chairman, built on our outreach efforts, driving the effort down into the grassroots level. Success at breaking into the African-American vote will take a sustained effort like the one Ken and I have made. If we continue working at it, however, there is a natural coalition of active military and veterans, entrepreneurs and religious conservatives in the African-American electorate that could result in Republican candidates doubling or even tripling our 10 percent average over the next decade.

This is not a change that will be incremental, by the way. We won't go from 10 percent to 11.5 percent to 14 percent to 17 percent over three cycles. Whatever moves the Republican Party from 10 to 20 percent with the black electorate will likely move it from 10 to 30. I am a proponent of the dam-break theory. Once a critical mass of African-American voters begins voting for Republican candidates, a lot more will follow.

CHAPTER NINE

MIDTERMS AND BEYOND

Historically, the second midterm election in a two-term presidency is a bad one for the party in the White House, and 2006 is the midterm election of President Bush's second term. In the twentieth century, the incumbent president's party has averaged a loss of twenty-eight seats in the U.S. House of Representatives and four Senate seats.

This historic pattern is known as the "six-year itch," and the GOP must rally if we are to buck the trend and gain seats, as we were able to do in the first midterm of the Bush presidency, or at least mitigate losses so we don't cede control of the House or Senate to the Democrats.

After twelve years of control of the House and two presidential victories, there is a risk of Republican complacency, but the stakes in the '06 election are too high for such complacency. The differences between the two parties on issues involving national security, economic growth, and cultural values remain sharp, and the choices could not be more clear.

The national Democrats seem intent on winning House and Senate majorities in 2006 by pursuing a strategy centered on attacking what they call a "Republican culture of corruption," and seem to base this on what they see as a similar strategy in 1994 when Republicans took control of the House.

They will point to the House bank scandal and the post office as parallel circumstances. The problem for national Democrats is that this is revisionist history. The fact is that 1992's House bank scandal, in which members of Congress were regularly overdrawing their House bank accounts in a way that would have resulted in ordinary Americans' "bouncing" checks, hurt members on both sides, most notably the colorful Democrat Charlie Wilson of Texas (made famous in the book and soon-to-be movie *Charlie Wilson's War*) and Republican Vin Weber of Minnesota, one of the brightest young House members, who'd already been elected to leadership as conference secretary. Both chose not to run for re-election, with Wilson telling reporters, "Sometimes it's better to take the bullet than wait for the bullet" (one of my favorite political lines of all time). And that was in the 1992 cycle, not 1994.

The only member to lose his seat over the post office scandal, in which members were cashing in government-provided postage stamps for personal cash, was former Ways and Means chairman Dan Rostenkowski.

Such institutional scandals can contribute to an anti-incumbent environment that is logically more damaging to the party in power, but generally does not result in defeat of incumbents not directly involved.

Indeed, when Republicans made scandal the centerpiece of our midterm strategy in 1998, focusing on Clinton's impeachment instead of a positive policy agenda, Democrats bucked the historic pattern and *gained* seats in a second midterm.

Of course, Clinton's second midterm had come four years earlier, in 1994, when Republicans picked up fifty-two seats in the first midterm—not as the result of the House bank or post office scandals, but for policy reasons.

Rather than being the "new Democrat" who had been advertised in the 1992 election, Bill Clinton turned out to be a very liberal president in his first year in office, beginning with an effort to repeal the ban against gays in the military (where was that mentioned in campaign ads?!), raising taxes in record fashion, and trying to pass a government-run health care system cooked up by his wife and a cloistered bunch of liberal academics.

On top of that, the Democratic majority ran aground with a crime package in the summer of '94 that was repugnant to voters, fractured their conference over gun control, and had enough ridiculous provisions (remember "midnight basketball," where we were going to curtail crime by providing federal funds to late-night basketball games at the YMCA on the theory that if muggers only had a place to go to hoop it up they wouldn't demand people's wallets at gunpoint?) to cut a dozen different campaign ads.

It was in this environment that House Republicans introduced the Contract with America, providing Americans with a reason not only to vote against Democrats, but to vote for Republicans.

You can't win elections without both rationales, and that's the Democrats' dilemma. They want to run a purely anti-Bush, anti-Republican campaign in the midterm without offering specific proposals of their own.

And the reason is that they know deep down that their worldview has been rejected, and they are on the wrong side of history. If they put forward their actual policies, codifying their rhetorical call for an immediate withdrawal from Iraq and raising taxes, they'll face certain defeat.

Consequently, Democrats are in the unenviable position of being damned if they do and damned if they don't. If they offer a specific policy agenda they can actually agree on, voters will reject it, but they can't get across the finish line without a specific policy agenda. Therefore, Democrats are likely to pick up seats in both chambers of Congress in 2006, but not enough to gain control of either chamber.

Republicans, however, can help elect Democrats in November, not by voting for them but by not voting. This is usually what happens in a second midterm, and may especially be true in 2006, since Bush was able to buck historic patterns in 2002 and gain seats in the House and Senate, the first time the party of the president had made such gains in a midterm in sixty-eight years.

There are structural reasons why 2006 won't be the Democrats' 1994. Every round of redistricting seems to winnow the number of truly contestable seats, and the number of House members who might actually face a race every two years is down to about forty, a little under 10 percent.

Congressional district boundaries are now drawn with the precision of a plastic surgeon remaking someone's face. With the help of computer databases and incumbent-friendly state legislatures, members of Congress get districts drawn to their liking.

Representative Tom Davis of Virginia, who chaired the National Republican Congressional Committee, says, "Voters used to pick their member of Congress, now members of Congress pick their voters."

'08 PREVIEW

In 2008, for the first time in fifty-six years, there will be no incumbent president or vice president seeking one of the major party's presidential nominations. In other words, both processes are wide open.

That's not to say there aren't early frontrunners, and on the Democratic side a de facto nominee in Senator Hillary Rodham Clinton. If she can fend off former Virginia governor Mark Warner, who will make a case that the Democrats should nominate someone with a proven ability to win in a "red" state and others, she'll be the nominee and have all the money she'll need to compete in every state.

It's hard to see either John Kerry or John Edwards beating her. Indiana senator Evan Bayh lacks charisma, and Senator Joseph Biden embarrassed himself in the recent Supreme Court confirmation hearings—donning a Princeton hat at one point in the Alito hearings to make a point (though I'm not sure what it was). In 2004, when Biden announced he wasn't running, Karl Rove and I were having dinner in New Orleans and we were relieved by the announcement, but at this rate, if there's another vacancy on the Supreme Court before 2008, he'll be lucky to get re-elected to the Senate.

A dark horse may be Wisconsin Senator Russ Feingold, who voted against the Iraq War resolution but in favor of funding our troops in Iraq. He may have the ability to attract mainstream liberals and antiwar Democrats.

Some of my Republican friends express glee at the prospect of Hillary Clinton as the Democratic nominee, but we underestimate her at our own risk. She is every bit as political as her husband (though nowhere near the natural politician), every bit as smart, and a whole lot meaner.

RNC Chairman Ken Mehlman points out that Democrats relished the idea of running against Ronald Reagan in 1980, thinking he was too conservative for the country.

On the Republican side, there are more than a dozen potential nominees, including at least four governors, at least five senators, and three "rock stars"—individuals known by only their first names in the same way Elvis, Madonna, and Cher are known.

The senators are Arizona's John McCain, Tennessee's Bill Frist, Virginia's George Allen, Kansas's Sam Brownback, and Nebraska's Chuck Hagel.

The governors include Mitt Romney of Massachusetts, Mike Huckabee of Arkansas, Tim Pawlenty of Minnesota, and George Pataki of New York. (If Jeb Bush were Jeb Smith, there would be five governors on this list.)

The rock stars are Newt, Rudy, and Condi—former House Speaker Newt Gingrich, former New York City mayor Rudy Giuliani, and Secretary of State Condoleezza Rice.

Senators

JOHN MCCAIN: The current environment could not be better for John McCain of Arizona, who has to be considered the frontrunner for the GOP nomination in 2008. Rank-and-file Republicans are fed up with too much federal spending, sick of pork-barrel projects and "earmarks," concerned about the corrupting influence of money and special interests, and consider national security a top priority. These are all sweet spots for McCain.

His stout support for President Bush in 2004 helped endear him to core Republicans who vote in caucuses and primaries, and he remains strong with the Independents who have a major impact in New Hampshire's open primary.

In addition to that, the Republican Party has a much stronger tendency than the Democrats to confer our nomination on the person "next in line." Richard Nixon, Ronald Reagan, former president Bush, Robert J. Dole, and even George W. Bush all benefited from this tendency.

BILL FRIST: Tennessee's Bill Frist is one of the most decent men ever to grace the national political stage, and is in the mold of a citizen legislator. Always a doctor first, Frist has been tied down with the unforgiving responsibilities of the Senate majority leader, a role from which he'll be freed when he leaves the Senate in 2007.

Impressively intelligent and thoughtful, Frist will have a chance to improve his public speaking when he spends more time in Iowa farmhouses and New Hampshire cafeterias and stops speaking in the Senate chamber.

GEORGE ALLEN: Perhaps the most "Reaganesque" candidate in the field is this very successful former governor of and current senator from Virginia. George Allen has a folksy style, a keen political intuition, and an intellect that can be underestimated because of his aforementioned folksy style. He has the ability to cover all three legs of the Republican stool as a cultural conservative, an advocate of free market policies, and a supporter of a strong national defense.

At six feet four even without his ever-present cowboy boots, he is an imposing figure. He has an important niche in the field at the moment, which is that of the optimist. Republicans tend to gravitate to optimists like Reagan and Bush—and Allen. His stock is rising among the political oddsmakers, and he has made his way into the top tier quickly.

(I am a Virginian and currently serve as treasurer of Allen's leadership PAC.)

SAM BROWNBACK: Senator Brownback of Kansas is usually pigeonholed by the pundits as a single-issue candidate, that issue being abortion. It's a too-limited view. Brownback has strong foreign policy credentials as well, and a demonstrated commitment to human rights.

He was impressive in the Roberts and Alito hearings, and comes across as a very thoughtful, compassionate man. There is no substitute for sincerity and conviction in politics, and I think he is going to exceed the political class's expectations, especially in his neighboring Iowa, where Christian conservatives play a critical role in the caucuses.

CHUCK HAGEL: There is always room for a maverick in the field, and Nebraska's Chuck Hagel wears the moniker with relish. Like McCain, Hagel is a decorated Vietnam War veteran with definitive views about national security. While there's always room for a maverick, there's not usually room for two. It may be hard for Chuck Hagel to run as John McCain when John McCain is running as John McCain.

Governors

MITT ROMNEY: While in Boston for the Democratic Convention, I spent a day with Governor Mitt Romney. We did an event with GOP candidates for the state legislature, which was notable for the fact that Romney had recruited a Republican candidate for every Assembly seat in the state, which we had not been able to boast as a party for decades and was a testament to his strength as a party leader.

We did a press conference in which he very eloquently took the wood to John Kerry—pretty gutsy for a sitting governor from the same state. That evening, he invited me to join him at Fenway in seats on the third-base line that he's had for more than twenty years, and I sat with him and his son, who was running one of the state legislature campaigns.

Sox fans were coming up to him throughout the game telling him what a good job he was doing. At the seventh-inning stretch everyone sang "Take Me Out to the Ballgame," and he has a really nice voice. At this point I was almost starting to get angry, thinking, "Does this guy do anything badly?"

Any Republican who can win the governorship of Massachusetts, where registered Republicans account for a mere 13 percent of the electorate, is a proven campaigner. His plan for health care coverage in his state is innovative and stakes him out on a position that will be of great importance in the '08 campaign.

GEORGE PATAKI: Just as I spent time with Governor Romney in Massachusetts for the Democratic Convention, I spent time in New York with Governor Pataki for our own convention. Like Allen, Pataki possesses an imposing physical stature and, like Romney, he has proven himself able to get elected in a big, heavily Democratic state.

Whereas Romney chose not to seek re-election after his first term, Pataki ran and won three times in New York. In order to do so, however, he had to adopt a number of positions that may not be attractive to Republican primary voters and could more than offset the respect he rightly earned for his leadership after September 11.

MIKE HUCKABEE: As mentioned, health care is likely to be a defining issue for voters in the '08 general election, and Governor Huckabee is one of the few politicians in the Republican Party who is at ease with the complexities of health care policy (Barbour, Gingrich, and Romney being others).

His own battle with diabetes and being overweight are experiences many voters can relate to. He's successfully led a swing state, and did very well with African-American voters in Arkansas.

TIM PAWLENTY: Minnesota's Tim Pawlenty does not show up often in '08 stories, but I'm including him here because I think it's more than just in the back of his mind. (If "in the back of his mind" were the sole criterion, I'd have to list every GOP governor but Schwarzenegger, who's barred from running by the Constitution because he was born in Austria.)

Pawlenty is a young (forty-four in 2006) governor of a big swing state in the Heartland, and our party favors governors for nominees (whereas Democrats are much more open to senators). He's a reformer, a Catholic (Catholics have disproportionate impact as swing voters with higher than average voting populations in key states like Pennsylvania, Florida, Ohio, and Wisconsin, among others), and energetic.

Rock Stars

NEWT GINGRICH: Five years ago people would have scoffed at Gingrich's inclusion on a list of presidential aspirants, and some still might, but it's not an absurdity today and is less likely to be so by 2007.

Gingrich's entrance in the race would have a significant impact on it, as he would throw off ideas that others would be forced to respond to. He, like Huckabee, actually enjoys a good discussion of health care economics.

He has become more disciplined since his days in the House, but possibly not disciplined enough for a presidential campaign. Regardless of whether he can win the nomination, whoever does will have spent a lot of time talking about what Newt wanted to talk about.

RUDY GIULIANI: In my time in politics, there are only two politicians I have seen who have an effect on voters that seems to compel them to physically touch a candidate: Elizabeth Dole and Rudy Giuliani. It's a sign of natural charisma and unnatural accessibility for national figures.

Giuliani is unique in a number of ways, but the most important is that he is the only mayor with national security credentials as a result of his truly remarkable leadership after 9/11.

More important, that leadership revealed a man comfortable in his own skin, which is also important to voters. His support of abortion and gay marriage will make it difficult for him to capture the GOP nomination, however.

CONDOLEEZZA RICE: Secretary of State Condoleezza Rice's nomination as Republican candidate for president in 2008 would completely tip over the political table in the United States, and it would take months to understand its impact. It would probably take the seven months between nomination and Election Day, actually, as its true effect would only then be known.

An already historic figure with charisma to spare, Rice would dominate the foreign affairs aspect of the debate.

And, of course, she is an African-American woman. I've always believed the first African-American president will be a Republican, just as Britain's first woman prime minister was a conservative. You have to cut against type. It's why Hillary Clinton has been very careful to burnish her credentials as tough on national security issues.

Because so many African-American politicians are liberal, it would be harder for a black Democrat to convince voters that he or she wasn't outside the mainstream than it would be for a black Republican.

In my estimation, the toughest thing to be in politics is an African-American Republican. They are often subject to vicious attack from the left because they threaten the stranglehold the Democratic Party has on the black vote. Liberals love diversity, but they hate diversity in their diversity.

If the Iraq War remains unpopular through 2008, however, it could be held against Secretary Rice. Whether she pursues the nomination or not, there is no doubt she will be atop our nominee's short list of potential running mates.

Conclusion

Regardless of who wins either party's nomination, or even who goes on to win the White House in 2008, the American political system will remain the envy of the world. Those of us who are fortunate enough to play a role in it should work hard to build it up, and defend it from cynics whose often uninformed criticism only tends to suppress voter participation and undermine faith in our government.

Legitimate criticism is essential, and there is always more we can do to improve the integrity of our electoral process, but we should resist the easy temptation to paint everyone in politics as somehow inherently dishonest or unethical.

As I hope this book demonstrates from personal experiences, the vast majority of people who sling on the armor and weigh into the battle of ideas do so for honorable reasons, and more people should want to engage in our political process.

ACKNOWLEDGMENTS

I want to thank the many people who helped in the completion of this book, starting with those who helped me remember specific aspects of certain campaigns, especially Ken Mehlman, Karl Rove, Dan Bartlett, and Nicole Wallace of Bush-Cheney 2000 and 2004 and Mark Stephens and Brian Nick of Dole 2002.

My father, brothers, and sisters were all helpful in reviewing early drafts, so thanks to Jack Gillespie and Dennis, John, and Tracy Gillespie, and to Sharyn Taets and Joanne Gibbs, and also Rick Powell, Sherry Rimoczy, and Katie Neal at Quinn Gillespie and Associates.

Of course, I could not have written a book to begin with if not for the writing genes I inherited from my late mother, Constance E. "Conny" Gillespie.

My friend Horace Cooper, an adjunct professor at George Mason University, helped me with many of the health care and immigration policy ideas found in Chapter 8, and helped make sure the book is factually accurate. Lou Castro provided the technical support that made completion of this book possible.

I appreciate the efforts of Bob Barnett, Louise Burke, David Rosenthal, Carolyn Reidy, Mary Matalin, and Kevin Smith for making this book a reality, and I'm thankful to my political adversary and personal friend Donna Brazile for her advice in the process.

Last but not least, I must acknowledge the sacrifice of my children, John Patrick, Carrie, and Mollie Brigid, who tolerated my additional absence after the 2004 campaign while I wrote most of this book, and their wonderful mother, Cathy Gillespie, without whom I might still be parking cars in the Senate parking lot.

INDEX

45897825R00168

Made in the USA
Lexington, KY
14 October 2015